**About the author**

Tim Dyson is professor of population studies at the London School of Economics. He was educated in England and Canada, and has held visiting positions at the Australian National University in Canberra, the International Institute of Population Sciences in Mumbai, and the American University of Beirut. His research interests include world food and agricultural prospects, the causes and consequences of famines, the demographic basis of urban growth and urbanization, climate change and global warming, the demography and epidemiology of HIV/AIDS, and the past, present and future population of the Indian subcontinent. He is a past president of the British Society for Population Studies and was elected a Fellow of the British Academy in 2001.

# Population and development
## the demographic transition

Tim Dyson

*Population and development: The demographic transition* was first published in 2010 by Zed Books Ltd, 7 Cynthia Street, London N1 9JF, UK and Room 400, 175 Fifth Avenue, New York, NY 10010, USA

www.zedbooks.co.uk

Set in OurType Arnhem and Futura Bold by Ewan Smith, London
Index: ed.emery@thefreeuniversity.net
Cover designed by Rogue Four Design
Printed and bound in Great Britain by CPI Antony Rowe, Chippenham and Eastbourne

Distributed in the USA exclusively by Palgrave Macmillan, a division of St Martin's Press, LLC, 175 Fifth Avenue, New York, NY 10010, USA



A catalogue record for this book is available from the British Library
Library of Congress Cataloging in Publication Data available

ISBN 978 1 84277 959 0 hb
ISBN 978 1 84277 960 6 pb
ISBN 978 1 84813 912 1 eb

# Contents

# Figures and tables

## Figures

## Tables

# Preface

This is a book about the central role of the demographic transition in the creation of the modern world. It argues that you cannot understand the modern process of 'development' unless you put the demographic transition centre-stage. The great declines in human mortality and fertility that define the transition, plus the major changes in population size and structure that result from these declines, all have immense implications for the past, present and future of the world.

Because the demographic transition has often been accompanied by economic growth, it has often been assumed that it is largely a consequence of economic growth. Most certainly, however, that is not the view that is taken here. Instead, the transition is seen as something which occurs largely independently of prevailing economic circumstances. The transition's implications for the economy are probably greater than the economy's implications for the transition. And, more generally, the transition has played at least as important a role in the overall process of development as has the phenomenon of modern economic growth.

For several reasons, the demographic transition provides an excellent framework for studying development. For example, it is a truly global phenomenon – one that has already affected all of humanity to varying degrees. For most countries, the trends in death and birth rates which define the transition can be gauged relatively accurately, and located fairly precisely in time. Crucially, as societies go through the transition they invariably experience several major demographic processes in roughly the following order: mortality decline, population growth, fertility decline, urbanization, population ageing. Furthermore, these overlapping processes are causally related to each other – a fact which explains why they always occur in more or less the same sequence. Thus, mortality decline causes population growth; and fertility decline causes population ageing. It will also be argued that mortality decline is both the underlying cause of fertility decline and the main process behind urbanization.

All of these demographic processes have huge consequences for development. Indeed, they have helped to shape what the concept of development means. A key aim of the book is to examine the interrelated effects of these processes across many aspects of life – for example, in relation to matters of social psychology, family life, gender, education, economy, politics and, briefly, the environment.

Of course, other phenomena – such as economic growth and technological change – have also contributed to the modern process of development. Demographic change does not explain everything. It can sometimes be difficult to distinguish the influence of alternative phenomena from that of the transition. The demographic processes examined here are themselves conditioned by other factors. And synergistic interactions – processes of cumulative causation – are often involved as well. Moreover, the context in which the transition occurs is always important in influencing how it unfolds.

The origins of the demographic transition lie in the rise of science and the emergence of increasingly secular attitudes in Europe and its offshoot populations during the eighteenth and nineteenth centuries. And the fact that European populations were really the first to experience the phenomenon explains why it is important to consider their historical experience here.

Although other phenomena have played major roles in the modern process of development, this book is focused squarely on the demographic transition – *its* constituent processes and their principal societal effects. The argument is that once mortality decline is under way, then all of the other demographic processes are virtually certain to occur, eventually. Moreover, other things equal, the same probably applies to the principal societal effects.

The fact that the demographic transition has played a fundamental role in the creation of the modern world has been neglected to a remarkable degree. Many of the pieces which I use here to construct the central argument already lie scattered around. Yet rarely, if ever, have they been brought together in a single place.

Just why this big story has been so neglected cannot be addressed in much detail here. Part of the explanation, however, lies in the scant knowledge of basic demography that is imparted to people at university – consider, for example, how many social scientists believe that mortality decline is the principal cause of population ageing. Another part of the explanation may lie in the increasingly specialized nature of academic research. Demographers, for example, tend to focus on the individual components of the transition – often fertility. When they do stand back and contemplate the phenomenon as a whole – almost always in relatively short academic papers – they usually devote little or no space to urbanization, let alone anything much beyond.

Another reason why the story has been neglected is that the major demographic processes examined in these pages occur fairly slowly – at least if they are gauged in terms of the length of an average working lifetime. This means that social scientists frequently miss the operation of these processes, and the ways in which they affect other things. The result is that explanations of change in the nature of society are often framed in terms of more visible and immediate considerations.

Yet the demographic changes considered here are actually enormous, and they are also fairly rapid if viewed in historical terms. A recurring theme of this book is that these demographic processes affect other aspects of development in *remote* rather than in proximate ways – and this helps to explain why their influence is often overlooked. And whereas the rationale provided by social scientists to explain certain major changes in society has often been economic, the argument here is that the underlying cause of these changes has often been at least as much demographic.

Furthermore, to appreciate the full range of effects that arise from the transition it is necessary to approach the matter from the direction of the transition itself, rather than from the direction of any particular discipline.

The book would not have been written without a two-year Research Fellowship awarded by the UK Economic and Social Research Council (ESRC Award RES-063-27-0159). I am extremely grateful to the ESRC, and its anonymous reviewers, for the time and the intellectual freedom that this fellowship has provided. As noted, the book is concerned with the telling of a big story. Therefore, it is appropriate to acknowledge the influence of many friends and colleagues who, over the years and in different ways, have had a major impact on my thinking. Jack Caldwell, Robert Cassen, Chris Langford, Mike Murphy, Máire Ní Bhrolcháin, Chris Wilson and Tony Wrigley deserve special mention. My views have also been influenced by John Cleland, Ernestina Coast, David Coleman, Monica Das Gupta, Jane Falkingham, Griff Feeney, Andrew Fischer, Sean Fox, Michel Garenne, Eilidh Garrett, Sharon Ghuman, Arjan Gjonka, Simon Gregson, Seamus Grimes, Terry Hull, Arup Maharatna, Karen Mason, Sam Preston, Neil Price, Radhika Ramasubban, Peter Razzell, David Reher, Zeba Sathar, Ken Shadlen, Richard Smith, K. Srinivasan, Simon Szreter, Arland Thornton, Ian Timaeus, Leela Visaria, Ben Wilson, Bob Woods, Peng Xizhe and Basia Zaba, among others. Naturally, in all of these cases the usual disclaimer applies. I am extremely grateful to Mina Moshkeri for drawing the diagrams. While this is not a textbook, its origins lie in a course on Population and Development which I teach at the London School of Economics. And, in this connection, I must record that I have learnt a great deal from teaching the course and interacting with the students.

Some words are required on organization. Chapter 1 briefly introduces the subject. Chapter 2 provides a sketch of the main argument regarding the role of the demographic transition in the creation of the modern world. Chapter 3 reviews past growth of the global population, and the unprecedented demographic diversity that exists in the world today – both of which are unintelligible without knowledge of the transition. This chapter also introduces some basic considerations of population dynamics. Chapter 4 examines the transition itself – the empirical facts, and attendant theoretical considerations. A key argument here is that mortality decline is the remote cause of fertility decline. Chapter 5 discusses urbanization, including urban growth. It considers how these processes arise from the transition. The argument is hardly new, but it is surprisingly little known. By the end of Chapter 5 the major processes of the transition have each been addressed. Therefore the book turns to some of the effects of these changes, although necessarily only in outline form. This is done with respect to the past experience of developed countries. And it is done with respect to variation in development as it exists in the world today. Chapter 6 considers what can broadly be regarded as the social consequences of the transition. And Chapter 7 does the same for the economy and the distribution of political power. Finally, Chapter 8 draws things together, and concludes with some brief remarks on the future. An Appendix contains comments on data and approach.

The demographic transition promises many good things that can be experienced by societies that are still fairly poor in narrow economic (i.e. material) terms. Therefore, in general, the story that is told in these pages is a positive one.

The story also has its downside, however – in particular, the considerable increase in population scale that the demographic transition often entails. Population growth – *past*, as well as present – plays a significant role in relation to global warming and the threat of climate change. And, even if that extremely important subject is put on one side, it remains the case that the future of many poor countries with rapidly growing populations will be appreciably better if they can reduce their fertility faster, rather than more slowly. There is no real doubt about that. In that connection, there can be few happier changes – both for individuals and the societies in which they live – than those provided by access to, and the free adoption of, modern methods of contraception.

Throughout, the text is fairly informal. The subject is important. So I have tried to make the contents accessible to as many readers as possible. Hopefully others will pursue some of the ideas that are expressed here.

Tim Dyson

# Glossary

*Birth control.* Behaviour aimed at preventing sexual intercourse resulting in a live birth. It includes sexual abstinence, induced abortion, contraception and sterilization. The term is often used, however, as a synonym for contraception.

*Contraception.* Conscious effort to prevent conception. Contraceptive methods, of varying efficacy, include condoms, intrauterine devices, oral and injectable contraceptives, sterilization and withdrawal.

*Crude birth rate* (CBR). The number of births per 1,000 population in a specified period (usually a year). The rate is described as 'crude' because the total population, rather than a subgroup within it (e.g. women aged 15–49), is used as the denominator. The simple term 'birth rate', however, is sometimes used in the text to refer to the CBR.

*Crude death rate* (CDR). The number of deaths per 1,000 population in a specified period (usually a year). The rate is described as 'crude' because the total population is taken as the denominator. The simple term 'death rate', however, is sometimes used in the text to refer to the CDR.

*Crude rate of natural increase* (CRNI). The crude birth rate minus the crude death rate, i.e. the rate at which a population is increasing (or decreasing) because of an excess (or deficit) of births compared to deaths. The rate is sometimes expressed in percentage terms, rather than per 1,000 population. The term 'rate of natural increase' is sometimes used to refer to the CRNI.

*Dependency ratio.* The ratio of those age groups in a population which are deemed to be economically dependent (e.g. 0–14 and 65+) to those deemed to be economically productive (e.g. 15–64). The overall dependency ratio can be subdivided into the child and the old-age dependency ratios.

*Fertility.* The reproductive performance of an individual, couple or population. Births as an element of population change. A common measure of fertility is the total fertility rate (see below).

*Infant mortality rate* (IMR). The probability of dying between birth and the first birthday, usually expressed per 1,000 live births.

*Less developed regions (and countries).* Taken here to comprise Africa, Asia (except Japan), Latin America and the Caribbean. Sometimes referred to in the text simply as developing regions/countries.

*Life expectancy (or expectation) at birth* (LEB). The average number of years a newly born child could expect to live if it experienced the death rates prevailing at different ages in a population during a specified period. Unlike the crude death rate, life expectancy is unaffected by population age structure.

*More developed regions (and countries).* Taken here to comprise Europe, North America, Australia/New Zealand and Japan. Sometimes referred to in the text as developed regions/countries.

*Mortality.* Deaths as an element of population change. The level of mortality in a population is commonly represented by life expectancy at birth (see above).

*Natural increase.* The excess (or deficit) of births over deaths (see also crude rate of natural increase).

*Population ageing.* The process whereby the average age of a population rises. The process is often studied with reference to changes in the median age – i.e. the central age which divides the population into two equal halves.

*Population growth multiple.* Taken here to mean the ratio of the size of a population at the end of the demographic transition to its size at the start. This can usually only be gauged in rough terms, at best.

*Population growth rate.* The rate at which the size of a population is increasing (or decreasing) owing to natural increase plus net migration. It is usually expressed in percentage terms and, in the absence of migration, it equals the crude rate of natural increase (see above).

*Population momentum.* The tendency of population growth to continue despite the attainment of replacement-level fertility (see below). Population momentum results from a young age structure.

*Replacement-level fertility.* The level at which, on average, a cohort of women will be succeeded by just enough daughters to replace itself. The higher the level of mortality in a population, the higher is the level of replacement fertility. In modern circumstances, however, replacement-level fertility usually corresponds to a total fertility rate of slightly more than two births per woman.

*Total fertility rate* (TFR). The number of live births a woman would have during her reproductive years if she experienced births at the rates prevailing at different ages in a population during a specified period. Unlike the crude birth rate, total fertility is independent of the effects of population age structure.

*Urban growth*. Growth of the urban population. This can happen because of urban natural increase, migration from rural areas, and the reclassification of rural areas as urban areas (which is often done to reflect growth brought about by natural increase and migration).

*Urbanization*. The process whereby the proportion of a population living in urban areas increases. The level of urbanization is simply the percentage of the population living in urban areas at a given time.

*Vital rates*. The term commonly used to refer to crude birth and death rates (see above) – births and deaths being the main 'vital' events.

**For Sue**

PART ONE

# Introduction

# 1 • Introduction

This book addresses the central role of the demographic transition in the creation of the modern world. It considers how the major processes involved in this transition have unfolded during the modern era. And it examines the immense – and often unrecognized – impact that these processes have had on many key aspects of life.

At the start of the twenty-first century, every country in the world is being affected by the demographic transition. Indeed, most countries are still experiencing it to varying degrees. The transition is a phenomenon that will continue to transform human society for many decades to come. So an appreciation of its major causal processes, and their principal societal effects, is important.

The demographic transition is a global phenomenon – one that, at its heart, involves the movement of all human populations from experiencing high death and birth rates to experiencing very much lower death and birth rates. Essentially, these are the processes of *mortality decline* and *fertility decline* respectively. As populations go through the transition, they always increase in size. That is, they experience a period of *population growth* due to natural increase. And they always undergo two fundamental changes in composition: they move from being predominantly rural to being predominantly urban (i.e. the process of *urbanization*); and they move from having young age structures to having old age structures (i.e. the process of *population ageing*). These are the five main processes of the transition.[1]

These demographic processes are causally related to each other. As a result, they always occur in a similar order. In brief: mortality decline is the crucial initiating process – it causes population growth; in turn, population growth leads to stresses and strains in society which eventually bring about fertility decline; urbanization is in large part the result of mortality decline; and fertility decline is the main cause of population ageing.

These five processes usually unfold over very long periods. Indeed, even in its swiftest manifestations the movement of a society from having high death and birth rates to having low death and birth rates can take almost a century to occur. And because they involve changes in population composition, the processes of urbanization and population ageing are usually even slower. Therefore, viewed from the perspective of our own individual lives, the transition's constituent processes happen very slowly. In fact, they may be so gradual that they go virtually unseen. This helps to explain why their wider effects are often missed by social scientists – in favour of more immediate, but often shallower, explanations.

Viewed in historical terms, however, the demographic transition is a phenomenon that has occurred – and is occurring – with remarkable speed. The changes involved are huge, and so are their societal effects. But to appreciate this it is necessary to stand back and examine how the processes unfold over the very long run. It is also important to realize that the transition's processes affect other dimensions of life in remote (i.e. underlying) rather than in proximate ways. This is another reason why the transition's influence in bringing about social, economic and political change is often neglected.

Notice that the logic of the argument put forward here is that provided mortality decline occurs in a population – i.e. provided the death rate falls from high to low levels – then *all* of the transition's other major demographic processes will happen. That is, there will be a period of population growth, the birth rate will fall from high to low levels, urbanization will take place, and the population will become markedly older in its age composition (as the transition draws to a close). Of course, these statements are made *other things equal*. As we shall see, it is possible for 'third factors' to intervene and delay the occurrence of these basic causal relationships. As we will also see, however, experience suggests that the delaying influence of any such factors is usually limited – at least if things are viewed in relation to the very long run.

Naturally, the processes of the demographic transition do not happen in exactly the same way in every population. The phenomenon varies a lot in its details. The overall *context* – historical, geographical, institutional, socio-economic, political, cultural, etc. – is important in this connection. Clearly, we would not expect the experience of, say, Poland, to be identical to that of Chile, Egypt or Vietnam, for example. Therefore the transition's main processes – including their timing and speed – are influenced greatly by the circumstances in which they unfold.

Nevertheless, it should be emphasized that the demographic transition has occurred – and is occurring – in every kind of context. For example, it has happened in populations with widely varying cultures and religions. It has happened in societies with very different political systems. It has happened in rich countries, and it has happened in poor countries. There is no reason to believe that a major rise in per capita income is required for the constituent processes of the transition to unfold. Ultimately, the central demographic chain of cause and effect appears to be both reasonably self-contained and inexorable over the long run. Although most countries are still at some stage of the transition, there is every reason to think that we are dealing with processes that will eventually be completed everywhere. And the same may well be true of the transition's principal societal effects.

Turning to these effects, the influence of the demographic transition on general development processes has often gone unnoticed. Yet the phenomenon provides a unique framework for studying many aspects of development, and in an integrated way. The falls in death rates and birth rates which in many ways define the phenomenon are a key part – indeed, arguably they are *the most important part* – of whatever is meant by the term 'development'. Surely, no aspect of human progress is more precious than the banishment of death rates that are capricious and high – circumstances which mean that people's very hold on life is full of great uncertainty. Moreover, the fall in fertility that is integral to the transition allows women, in particular, to be freed from lives that are otherwise usually dominated by childbearing, childcare and related concerns of the domestic domain.

Insofar as the influence of the demographic transition on general development processes has been considered, it has commonly been in relation to whether population growth has a positive or a negative effect on economic growth. While this is an important issue, it is also a relatively narrow one – in that it focuses on the aggregate economic effects of just one of the transition's major processes (i.e. population growth). The consequences of urbanization and population ageing for development have also received some attention – although the transition's role in causing these processes is often unacknowledged.

This book, however, is written from the position that the effects of the demographic transition on general societal development have been, and are, both broad and profound. Taken together, the transition's processes lead to a complete transformation in the nature of human society. For example, mortality decline means that people can think about the future with much greater confidence. Death becomes a relatively rare and distant event. The circumstances in which people live become increasingly stable, and in these new conditions it makes increasing sense to save and invest. The acquirement of formal education becomes increasingly important. The transition also brings about major changes in family institutions. It operates to make marriage both a more flexible and a weaker institution. Fertility decline allows women to lead lives that are much less constrained by household affairs – lives that gradually become more like those experienced by men.

The concentration of people in towns which arises from the demographic transition produces societies that are unprecedentedly varied, complex and mobile. The division of labour increases, and so does the extent of competitiveness. There are reasons to believe that the emergence of modern democratic institutions is related to urbanization and population ageing. Urbanization itself has been a key engine of economic development. And in many ways, and in many places, the transition's constituent processes have had beneficial economic effects. That said, the influence of rapid population growth (i.e. growth at 2 per cent per year or more) for long periods on the economic welfare of people in poor developing countries appears to be decidedly negative. The book will also touch on the implications of the transition for the environment – and here the most important outcome is probably the increase in the size of the human population that has been caused by the world demographic transition.

It should be clear that matters of context are also important when considering the transition's effects. And, again, other considerations – third factors – can intervene to complicate and delay what happens. Moreover, in accounting for fundamental changes in the nature of society it can be difficult to disentangle the influence of the transition from the influence of other major phenomena – such as modern economic growth. That said, the view taken here is that no other force has had greater consequences for development than has the demographic transition. And, with respect to several key dimensions of societal development, it will be argued that once the transition gets going then certain consequences are sure to follow – other things equal, and in the long run.

Conventional explanations of the transition emphasize the role of socio-economic processes – such as industrialization, economic growth, and more recently the spread of mass education – in bringing the transition about. These socio-economic processes have often accompanied those of the transition sufficiently closely to encourage the idea that they are its cause. Indeed, processes like industrialization and economic growth feature prominently in conventional versions of demographic transition theory.

It is important to emphasize, however, that the core 'theory' contained in this book is *not* of that kind. The explanation of the transition put forward here is overwhelmingly demographic in nature. And, to reiterate, it is largely self-contained. Thus, provided there is mortality decline then all of the remaining demographic processes will occur, eventually. Moreover, none of these processes – including mortality decline – is nowadays very dependent upon the occurrence of much economic growth.

The book has four parts. The first is introductory. The next chapter sketches the central argument regarding the role of the demographic transition in the creation of the modern world. And it is followed by a chapter that outlines the current state of the transition in the world. The second part of the book focuses on the major processes and causal dynamics of the transition. It shows that while the details of the phenomenon vary greatly, essentially we are dealing with something that is uniform. The book's third part addresses the transition's principal societal effects. For simplicity, these are dealt with under three broad heads – the social, the economic and the political. The book's final part addresses some of the points that may be raised in relation to the argument, and it concludes with some remarks on the future.

One of demography's strengths is that, for large populations and time horizons of just a few decades, it allows some relatively firm forecasts to be made. Thus the world's population – which has already grown hugely as a result of the demographic transition – will grow quite a lot more in the coming decades. It will also become increasingly urban and increasingly old in its composition. To repeat, the transition is something that will continue to shape human society for a long time to come.

In general, and other things equal, the argument promises some good things as humanity proceeds through the demographic transition. But the phenomenon has its problematic side too – particularly as regards the unprecedented scale of population growth resulting from the transition. Moreover, in the future, especially with climate change, other things may not always be equal. With this as background, we turn to an outline of the argument.

# 2 · The demographic transition – origins, processes, effects

This chapter is concerned with the major causal processes of the demographic transition and their principal societal effects – social, economic and political. These processes and effects are considered in greater detail in later chapters. However, some of them are brought together here in order to provide a taste of the book's central argument.

In many ways, what is proposed here is a partial theory of world development.[1] The argument is that a sizeable fraction of what we now regard as constituting 'development' has its origins in the processes of the demographic transition. This is not to say that all of the transition's consequences are beneficial. Nor is it to deny that other phenomena have made major contributions to world development.

The chapter has three parts. The first considers the demographic transition and its processes. The second addresses the phenomenon's principal societal effects. The third part discusses several qualifications to the central argument, and it concludes with a few remarks about the implications of the transition for the future.

## The transition and its major processes

Figure 2.1 helps to illustrate the argument. It sketches some – though not all – of the relationships that will be examined here. The general direction of flow is from left to right. In broad terms, the figure addresses fundamental changes in the structure and nature of human society. Clearly, it is a highly simplified representation – for example, it is very selective, and it shows no feedback mechanisms. Nevertheless, it is helpful in presenting the case.

*The nature of pre-transitional and post-transitional societies* Figure 2.1 lists certain 'start' and 'end' conditions. These conditions relate to *pre-transitional* and *post-transitional* populations respectively. In many ways, what is revealed by comparing them is the difference between the 'traditional' and the 'modern' worlds.

Until quite recently in human history, all societies were subject to relatively high death rates and relatively high birth rates, i.e. high mortality

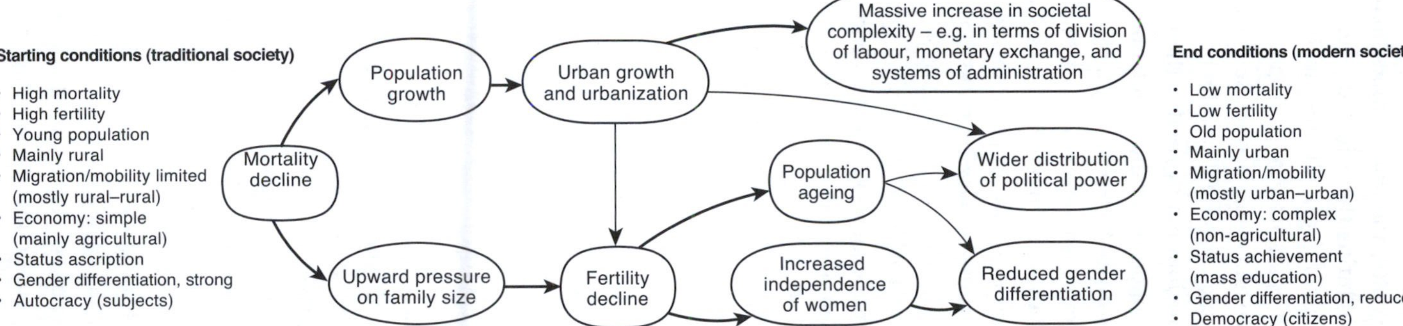


*Notes*: Clearly, the diagram is highly simplified and selective. For example, it makes little reference to the social, economic and educational consequences of the transition. There is no attempt to specify interdependent processes and feedback effects. More important causal relationships are indicated in bold. Later in the book, Figure 5.3 provides elaboration on how mortality decline leads to urban growth and urbanization; and Table 6.1 provides some elaboration regarding the huge increase in societal complexity that results from the expansion of the urban sector. See also Dyson (2001).

**Figure 2.1 The role of the demographic transition in world development—key relationships**

and high fertility.[2] Average life expectancy at birth would usually fall somewhere between 20 and 40 years, and women might have an average of between 4 and 7 births each during the course of their reproductive lives (i.e. between about ages 15 and 50). All pre-transitional societies were *young* – meaning that a comparatively large proportion of the total population consisted of children and young people. Somewhere between 35 and 45 per cent of the population would usually be aged under 15 years. All such societies were predominantly rural in their composition. In other words, only a small proportion of the population – commonly less than 10 per cent – lived in anything resembling a town. As a result, when people moved – for example, to get married or find work – this would generally involve them moving from one rural location to another (i.e. migration was mainly rural to rural). In pre-transitional societies most people were engaged in farming, or work that was closely related to farming. It would be rare for more than 20 per cent of the labour force to be engaged in other forms of employment. In such circumstances, few people received much formal education. Most individuals led lives that were similar to those of their parents – usually involving farm work, domestic work, or perhaps some basic craft. The sort of life an individual had was overwhelmingly an 'accident of birth', i.e. people's status was largely ascribed. In pre-transitional societies gender roles tended to be fairly distinct. And pre-transitional societies were overwhelmingly autocratic in nature. Power lay in the hands of a few. Ultimately, most people were the subjects of some kind of ruler.

Of course, this sketch of pre-transitional society *is* a characterization. Nevertheless, insofar as there was greater complexity to life this was largely confined to the relatively small urban sector.

Turning now to the 'end' conditions listed in Figure 2.1, the circumstances of life and the overall nature of society are very different in a population that has gone through the demographic transition. Taken together, these conditions have only been approximated for a significant period of time in a few countries – think, in particular, of those of western Europe (e.g. Belgium, Denmark, England, France, the Netherlands, Norway, Sweden) and their main historical 'offshoot' populations (Australia, Canada, the United States, New Zealand).[3] In post-transitional societies people can expect to live to a ripe old age. Average life expectancy is typically at least 75 years, and it is rare for someone to die at an age below 50. Post-transitional societies have low birth rates. Women have only a small number of births during the course of their reproductive lives – often just one or two. Post-transitional societies have *old* populations. They commonly contain more people aged over 60 years than people aged under 15. Indeed, it is usual for less than 20 per cent of the population to be aged under 15. Not surprisingly, then, issues raised by the process of population ageing – such as pension provision and care for elderly people – are matters of considerable public concern.

In post-transitional societies most people live in urban areas (i.e. the towns). Indeed, it is usual for at least 70 per cent of the population to be classed as living in the urban sector. Therefore, when people migrate they tend to move from one urban area to another (i.e. migration is mainly urban to urban). In any case, most people who live in rural areas actually have fairly similar socio-economic characteristics to those who live in urban areas. In these societies only a small proportion of the population are employed in agriculture – usually under 5 per cent. Instead, there is a wide range of occupations – mostly in the industrial and service sectors. All young people receive education and training for quite a few years. And formal qualifications are often significant in determining the course of people's lives. In these societies, women are becoming more prominent in key areas of life – e.g. in the fields of education, employment and public affairs – although this is a development that is still under way. Finally, these societies are all established political democracies – albeit imperfect ones. Of course, socio-economic inequalities remain, but at least every adult citizen has the right to vote (see Figure 2.1).

*Two examples of the transition* The five main processes of the demographic transition provide the backbone for Figure 2.1. Therefore, although the phenomenon will be examined in greater detail in Chapters 4 and 5, it is helpful to consider two examples of it here.

Figure 2.2 plots annual vital rates (i.e. relating to deaths and births) for Sweden and Sri Lanka. These countries are unusual in having good data for long periods. The figure also shows the corresponding rates of natural increase. The rate of natural increase is the difference between the birth rate and the death rate, and – in the absence of migration into or out of a country – it is equal to the rate of population growth. Sweden is used here to represent the 'historical' transitions that were experienced in Europe in the past. Sri Lanka is used to represent the 'contemporary' transitions that are occurring in every developing country today.

It is important to emphasize, however, that there was considerable variation between different 'historical' transitions. And looking at contemporary countries in Africa, Asia and Latin America, there is a huge amount of variation in their experience of the transition – not least

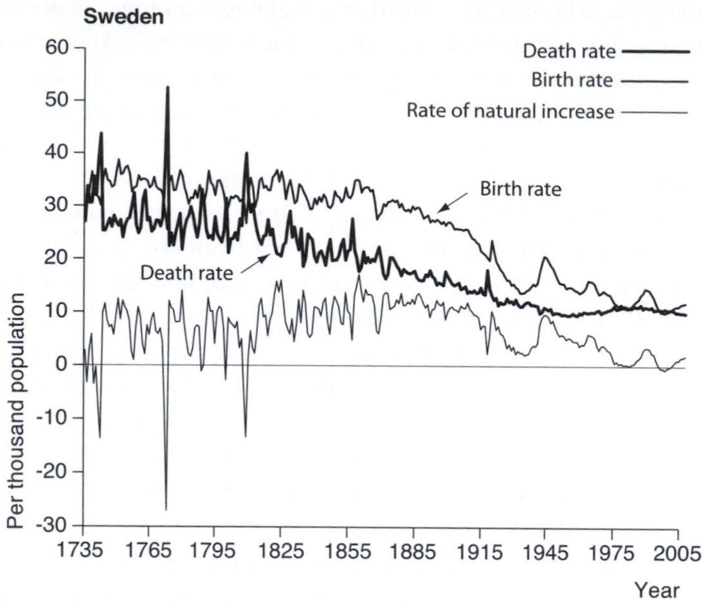


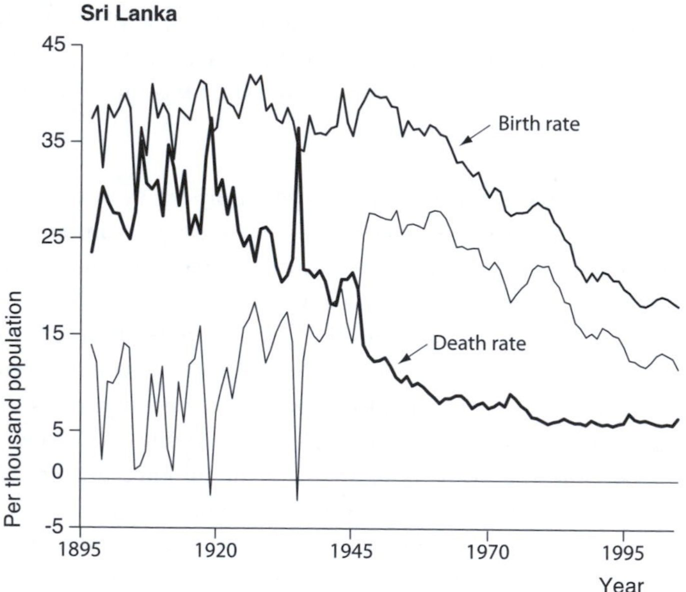


*Principal sources*: Sweden 1735–1984 (Chesnais 1992), 1985–2008 (Statistics Sweden 2009); Sri Lanka 1897–1934 (Mitchell 1982), 1936–2005 (Sri Lanka 2009)

**Figure 2.2 The demographic transition—vital rates in Sweden and Sri Lanka**

because they have entered it at different times. Therefore, the cases of Sweden and Sri Lanka should be regarded as representative only in the very broadest sense. Nevertheless, they both show the *essentials* of the phenomenon; and they also illustrate some of the 'second order' differences between the historical and the contemporary transitions.

For Sweden, annual vital rates are available from as early as 1736. Figure 2.2 shows that fluctuations in the death rate gradually became less common. This was because mortality crises – caused by events like famines, epidemics and wars – decreased in both frequency and scale. As a result, there was some natural increase (i.e. excess of births over deaths) during the eighteenth century. Then, following a mortality crisis due to war with Russia in 1808/09 – when the death rate briefly exceeded the birth rate – the death rate subsequently stayed *below* the birth rate until about 1980. This means that the annual rate of natural increase remained positive for a period of about 170 years. Notice that the rate of natural increase in Sweden tended to rise until some time in the middle of the nineteenth century, and then it slowly declined. Because of the big fluctuations in the death rate during the eighteenth century, it is impossible to identify a precise time when the fall in the death rate really began – although it was almost certainly in the eighteenth century. That said, it is reasonable to say that a *sustained* fall in the death rate dates from about 1810, and that the birth rate fell from around 1865 (see Figure 2.2).

If, for illustration, we take 1800 as roughly representing *pre-transitional* circumstances in Sweden, then life expectancy was about 35 years, and women had an average of about 4.4 births each. These figures actually represent a rather favourable level of life expectancy and an unusually low level of fertility for a pre-transitional society. If we take 1980 as roughly representing *post-transitional* circumstances, then life expectancy had increased to around 76 years and women were having about 1.7 births each on average. During the period of 170 years when there was sustained natural increase, the rate of natural increase rarely rose much above 10 per thousand population per year, i.e. 1 *per cent* per year (see Figure 2.2). In 1800 Sweden's population numbered about 2.3 million. By 1980 it had grown to about 8.3 million – giving a rough population 'growth multiple' of 3.6 (i.e. 3.6 = 8.3/2.3).[4] The structure of the population also changed in fundamental ways. Thus in 1800 only about 10 per cent of people lived in towns, but by 1980 the figure was 83 per cent. And whereas in 1800 a third of the population consisted of children aged under 15 years, by 1980 this figure had fallen to 19 per cent. Furthermore, Sweden's population was still getting older in 1980.[5]

In Sri Lanka the transition began approximately a century later than in Sweden. Moreover, Sri Lanka's transition is still not complete today (see Figure 2.2). The country's death rate fluctuated quite a lot during the early decades of the twentieth century – the last major peak was caused by a malaria epidemic in 1935. However, the death rate had actually begun to fall in a sustained manner from about 1920. The war years, 1939–45, saw some stagnation, but the death rate then fell rapidly in the late 1940s, and it continued to fall, although at a slower pace, for several more decades. As a result, there was a marked rise in the annual rate of natural increase – which peaked at about 27 per thousand (i.e. 2.7 per cent per year) during the 1950s. The beginnings of the fall in the birth rate in Sri Lanka were in the 1950s. By the start of the present century the birth rate had declined a lot – from about 40 births per thousand population in the 1950s to about 19 in 2005. In 2005, however, the birth rate was still much higher than the death rate. Therefore, although the rate of natural increase had fallen – reflecting the fall in the birth rate – it was still quite high, at about 12 per thousand (i.e. 1.2 per cent per year). Moreover, notice that after 1950 the rate of natural increase exceeded the death rate, something which never happened in Sweden (see Figure 2.2).

Of course, the falls in Sri Lanka's vital rates reflect huge declines in mortality and fertility. If, again very roughly, the year 1900 is taken as representing pre-transitional conditions, then life expectancy was around 36 years and women had an average of about 4.9 births each (these figures too are suggestive of rather low levels of mortality and fertility for a pre-transitional society). However, by 2000–05 life expectancy had risen to about 73 years, and women were having only about 2.1 births each. Even so, the United Nations projects that it will not be until about the year 2030 that the birth rate equals the death rate, and natural increase ceases to occur. On that basis Sri Lanka will have experienced fairly sustained natural increase for a period of about 110 years. In 1900 the country contained about 3.5 million people. In 2005 the number had grown to 19.8 million – representing a still-not-complete growth multiple of 5.7. In 1900 about 40 per cent of the population was aged under 15 years, but by 2005 the figure had fallen to around 25 per cent. Whereas in 1900 only about 10 per cent of people lived in urban areas, if the same criteria were used to define places as 'urban' in 2005 then well over half of the country's population would be classed as urban. Moreover, in the first decades of the twenty-first century Sri Lanka's population is still ageing and urbanizing.[6]

The Swedish and Sri Lankan examples both illustrate the essential features of the demographic transition. In short: the death rate declines first, the birth rate declines somewhat later, and this sequence causes a period of natural increase – i.e. population growth – in between. In both cases there was initially a *rise* in the rate of natural increase – as the death rate declined – and then a *fall* in the rate of natural increase – as the birth rate declined (see Figure 2.2). In both countries the period of natural increase extended over a very long time. Both countries also experienced ageing and urbanization. Clearly, Sweden is much more advanced – indeed, it has now completed the transition in virtually every respect. However, even in Sri Lanka, where the phenomenon is still under way, the statistics cited above suggest more a transformation of the basic conditions of the society rather than a mere transition.

The Swedish and Sri Lankan cases also point to some second-order differences between the 'historical' and the 'contemporary' transitions. In brief, the historical transitions were more gradual affairs, and they extended over especially long periods. In the historical transitions birth rates rarely exceeded death rates by very much – so the accompanying rates of natural increase were seldom very high. Recall that in Sweden the rate did not go much above 1 per cent per year. In contrast, more recent transitions have been significantly *faster* in several respects. For example, they have involved much faster falls in death rates, bigger gaps between birth rates and death rates, and therefore faster rates of natural increase. They have also tended to involve more rapid fertility declines – and falls in birth rates – once such declines have begun. Although most contemporary transitions are far from complete, population growth multiples ranging between 5 and 15 are likely to be frequent, and quite a few countries will experience much higher growth multiples.[7]

In some ways, these basic differences between the historical and the contemporary transitions can be seen in terms of differences in the nature of mortality decline – the initiating demographic process. Broadly speaking, in historical transitions mortality decline arose fairly gradually from changes that were largely internal to the societies themselves.[8] However, more recent transitions have involved much more abrupt changes. Thus the basis for mortality decline in Asia, Africa and much of Latin America came originally from sources that were largely external to the societies themselves. The earlier experience of Europe and its 'offshoots' had shown that death rates *could* be reduced from high to low levels. And Europe and its offshoots also provided much of the knowledge (e.g. regarding the basis of disease transmission) and technology (e.g. drugs, immunizations, insecticides, etc.) that were later used to reduce death rates comparatively quickly, and at relatively low cost, in the rest of the world. Thus whereas in Sweden it took 130 years for the death rate to fall from 30 to 10 per thousand, in Sri Lanka this was achieved in around 35 years, i.e. between 1920 and 1955 (see Figure 2.2).

*Origins and spread of the transition* The origins of the demographic transition lie in the countries of north-western Europe in the eighteenth century. This was the time of the Enlightenment – a very special period in terms of world development. The Enlightenment saw a marked acceleration in the influence of secular knowledge and science. Intellectual horizons expanded; religious authority was in retreat; political change was in the air. This period saw both the American and the French Revolutions. And most scholars believe that it also witnessed an Industrial Revolution in England – something which produced a sharp acceleration in the rate of economic growth. This was the phenomenon of 'modern economic growth' which Simon Kuznets (1966) describes as involving a sustained rise in per capita output and major structural economic change – especially the process of industrialization. There is some debate as to when modern economic growth began. Much of western Europe was certainly experiencing it by about 1820, however (Maddison 2007). Subsequently, modern economic growth has had a profound impact on human affairs. Both its origins, and those of the demographic transition, lie in the Enlightenment.

The first major process of the transition – i.e. mortality decline – began to be evidenced in the countries of north-western Europe during the second half of the eighteenth century. Mortality crises became less frequent, and there was then a long and gradual fall in the death rate (as in Sweden). This fall became a little more pronounced during the nineteenth century, and it eventually flattened out in the middle of the twentieth century. The death rate decline reflected a major rise in life expectancy. It is important to appreciate that the improvement in mortality was mainly due to progress made in reducing deaths from *infectious* diseases. In north-western Europe in the eighteenth century this category of disease included afflictions like diarrhoea, measles, smallpox, tuberculosis and whooping cough. The start of the fall in the death rate preceded the start of the fall in the birth rate. Therefore, the countries of north-western Europe experienced a lengthy period during which their populations grew. The main reason why the birth rate eventually fell from high to low levels was because of the spread of various forms of contraception and birth control.

The rest of the world has entered the demographic transition at different times. Offshoot countries – such as the United States – also had very early experience of the transition. However, the *starting* conditions in these countries were different to those in Europe. In particular, the offshoots were sparsely populated and still being settled by migrants from Europe. Therefore, their experience was distinctive in certain respects.[9] Countries in southern and eastern Europe generally followed those of the continent's north-west by several decades.

In Asia, both Japan and Taiwan experienced some mortality decline during the second half of the nineteenth century. Indeed, these populations were so advanced that by the end of the twentieth century they had low vital rates, and had effectively completed the transition. Countries elsewhere in Asia began to experience mortality decline at different times during the first half of the twentieth century. By the start of the *present* century most Asian populations had experienced very substantial falls in their death rates, and sizeable declines in their birth rates as well. However, there are still some remote places (e.g. Afghanistan) where there has been little or no decline in fertility and birth rates.

In Latin America, countries with a relatively high fraction of people of European origin tended to be comparatively early in experiencing the transition (see Beaver 1975). Thus both Chile and Argentina experienced a fall in the death rate from late in the nineteenth century, although it was several decades before their birth rates fell by much. Most countries in Latin America began to experience a fall in their birth rate only from around the 1960s. And, at the start of the present century, no country in the region could be said to have completed the demographic transition – in the sense of having low and roughly equal vital rates.

In Africa, populations along the Mediterranean – such as Egypt, Morocco and Tunisia – were relatively early in experiencing falls in their death rates and, later, their birth rates. Even so, the transition still has a considerable way to go in these societies. Sub-Saharan Africa (including the countries of the Sahel) was the last major world region to enter the demographic transition. Good evidence is lacking. Mortality decline, however, often dates from the middle decades of the twentieth century. And, at the start of the present century, fertility decline had really only just begun in many sub-Saharan countries.

Looking at the developing world as a whole, there was a modest fall in death rates during the first half of the twentieth century. Birth rates, however, remained high – so there was a modest degree of population growth. After 1945, however, there was a substantial and sustained improvement in mortality. Therefore death rates fell a lot. Again, most of the mortality decline was due to reductions in infectious (and parasitic) diseases – such as diarrhoea, cholera, malaria, measles, pneumonia, smallpox, tuberculosis, typhoid and yellow fever, to name a few. However, in general birth rates in the developing world began to fall only from the 1960s and 1970s. Therefore, the second half of the twentieth century was a time of – often rapid – natural increase. The rate of population growth in the developing world probably peaked in the late 1960s. But the demographic transition will not approach its final stages in the developing world as a whole until the second half of this century (i.e. the twenty-first).

In fact, it seems likely that some developing countries – including very populous ones like China and India – will experience population growth multiples as a result of their transitions which are not very different from those experienced by some European countries. Many other developing countries, however, have experienced much faster rates of population growth for extended periods of time, and in some of these cases it is likely that much greater growth multiples will be experienced. The point is underscored in Chapter 3, where the current world population situation is examined. Nevertheless, in both the historical and the contemporary transitions the essential features of the phenomenon prevail. A decline in the death rate sets things off; the birth rate starts to fall somewhat later; and, as a result, there is a period of population growth – first rising, then falling.

*Why fertility declines* The fact that all transitions bear some resemblance to the basic sequence illustrated in Figure 2.2 has led to the realization that what is being observed resembles a socio-demographic system which (i) falls out of a rough initial degree of equilibrium in which both the death rate and the birth rate are high, and then (ii) re-establishes a rough degree of equilibrium in which both the death rate and the birth rate are low (see, for example, Wilson and Airey 1999). During the first part of the transition the rate of natural increase rises because of the fall in the death rate; during the second part it decreases because of the fall in the birth rate. So, in essence, the demographic transition is a lengthy period of *disequilibrium* during which the birth rate adjusts to the fact that the death rate is falling because of the establishment of a new, low mortality regime.

When studying both historical and contemporary transitions, social scientists have considered many possible causes of fertility decline. These have included: industrialization, economic growth, urbanization, the spread of mass education, the influence of so-called 'Western' values, and government interventions designed to reduce fertility (i.e. 'family planning' programmes). There is no doubt that these and other factors can be a significant part of the *context* in which fertility declines occur, and that they can *condition* the timing and the speed of fertility decline. However, substantial fertility decline has happened in populations that have not industrialized, urbanized or experienced much economic growth. Fertility decline has occurred in populations with little or no education, and where the influence of Western values has been minimal. Fertility decline has happened in many places where there has been no policy or programme aimed at bringing it about. Fertility decline has never occurred, however, in the absence of mortality decline. And this constitutes powerful evidence that mortality decline is the underlying (i.e. remote) cause of fertility decline (see, for example, Casterline 2003; Ní Bhrolcháin and Dyson 2007).

The details of how the first process leads to the second – i.e. the details of the mechanism involved – are complex and highly variable. However, it is obvious that alterations in the behaviour of individual men and women are always required. To a limited degree, a decline in the birth rate can be brought about by a reduction in marriage – women, in particular, can marry at a later age or perhaps not get married at all. In the long run, however, fertility decline always reflects the spread of birth control. It involves a change in behaviour so that sexual relations can be enjoyed without running the risk of pregnancy. This, of course, is the purpose of contraception.[10]

In pre-transitional circumstances, most parents were faced with rearing only a small number of children. Birth rates were high, but so were death rates. Therefore, while women gave birth to a fairly large number of children, few if any of these children were living at any one moment, and only a small number of children survived into adulthood. Indeed, a significant proportion of parents would end up being 'childless' in the sense that they would leave no *surviving* children (Bongaarts 1987). With mortality decline, however, the number of children that survive rises. The natural increase of the demographic transition involves a counterpart increase in the number of people living in families. Indeed, the more mortality declines, the larger households tend to become. Eventually, the rise in the number of living children is likely to produce stresses and strains for parents – e.g. in terms of overcrowding, and the amount of childcare that is required.

Moreover, sustained mortality decline is likely to produce other pressures on parents (and potential parents) as well. For instance, in some places the growing number of people who survive into adulthood may lead to land fragmentation – i.e. conditions where households are forced to live on smaller and smaller plots of land. In other places the increase in the number of individuals entering the labour force may lead to a fall in real wages – making it harder for people to get married and start a family. To reiterate, the precise details of how mortality decline eventually produces fertility decline are variable and multifaceted. Eventually, however, a sustained fall in mortality from high to low levels means that people are faced with the choice between either reducing the number of children they have, or experiencing a fall – or slower rate of improvement – in their standard of living (Macunovitch 2000).

Notice that this trade-off will arise eventually irrespective of whether general economic conditions are improving, staying the same, or getting worse. The individuals who are faced with making the choice are likely to explain their adoption of birth control in terms of the circumstances that they confront in their own lives. Thus they are likely to refer to the costs involved in rearing children – e.g. in terms of childcare, educational expenses or various opportunities forgone (e.g. those of women to engage in paid work). They can refer to these costs irrespective of whether economic conditions are improving or deteriorating. But the point is that both the parents, and their children, will be better off if there are fewer children in the household – i.e. if fertility is controlled. The fact that the choice has ultimately been raised by the process of mortality decline is not recognized by the people who make it. They have no idea that in turning to some form of birth control they are effectively *re-establishing* circumstances that prevailed before the demographic transition – when parents generally had only a small number of surviving children. Thus the adoption of birth control by parents can be viewed as an attempt to restore family size, rather than an attempt to decrease it (Reher 2004).

The idea that mortality decline is the remote cause of fertility decline has been around for decades (see, for example, Davis 1963). However, it has often been disregarded in favour of explanations that are quite close to the reasons given by people themselves for turning to birth control – e.g. 'we cannot afford to have any more children'. Such statements and explanations are not without interest. But they miss the fundamental cause of the process. It is particularly easy to make this mistake if one is studying fertility decline in a single country, or if one is considering a comparatively short period of time. When you stand back and examine the experience of many different populations over long periods, however, then it is difficult to avoid the conclusion that mortality decline is the underlying cause of fertility decline.

*Why populations grow old* Population ageing occurs because of fertility decline.[11] The causal relationship is deterministic – the consequence of basic population dynamics (see, for example, Coale 1964).

Pre-transitional populations have young age structures because their levels of fertility are high. The median – i.e. central – age in such a society will typically be somewhere between 18 and 25 years (depending on the level of fertility). In these circumstances, the term 'population *pyramid*' is usually appropriate. Conversely, post-transitional societies have old age structures because their levels of fertility are low. The median age in a post-transitional population is likely to be at least 35 years.

As fertility falls within the demographic transition it has a direct impact on the age composition of the population only at the *base* of the structure. Eventually, therefore, sustained fertility decline leads to a population with a relatively small proportion of young people, and a relatively large proportion of people at older ages. It takes a long time for the process to work itself out completely. However, assuming that the death and birth rates become low and approximately equal towards the end of the demographic transition, then not only will the population stop growing, but eventually the number of people in all age groups except for the oldest will be roughly comparable.[12]

Within the transition, the effect of mortality decline on the age structure of a population is much weaker. This is because mortality decline benefits people at *all* ages to some degree. Therefore, death rates are reduced at all ages, and consequently the impact on the population's proportional age composition is relatively limited. In fact, during the early stages of mortality decline the fall in death rates tends to be particularly pronounced at childhood ages (i.e. ages under 5). Consequently, the resulting saving of many young lives can have a temporary *rejuvenating* effect, i.e. it can make an already young population age structure slightly younger still.[13] But this effect is likely to be relatively short lived – and it will be overridden as soon as the process of fertility decline gets under way.

To illustrate these ideas, Figure 2.3 compares the population age structures holding in Sweden and Sri Lanka at an early stage of their transitions with those holding around the year 2010. Notice that all four structures are shown in percentage (i.e. proportional) terms. Whereas both countries once had fairly young populations – more or less resembling a pyramid – by 2010 they both show the effects of fertility decline. In Sweden the process of ageing is now very advanced – the population is old (median age about 41 years). In Sri Lanka, however, although by 2010 women were having only about two births each, the overall process of ageing clearly still had some way to go (median age 29 years).

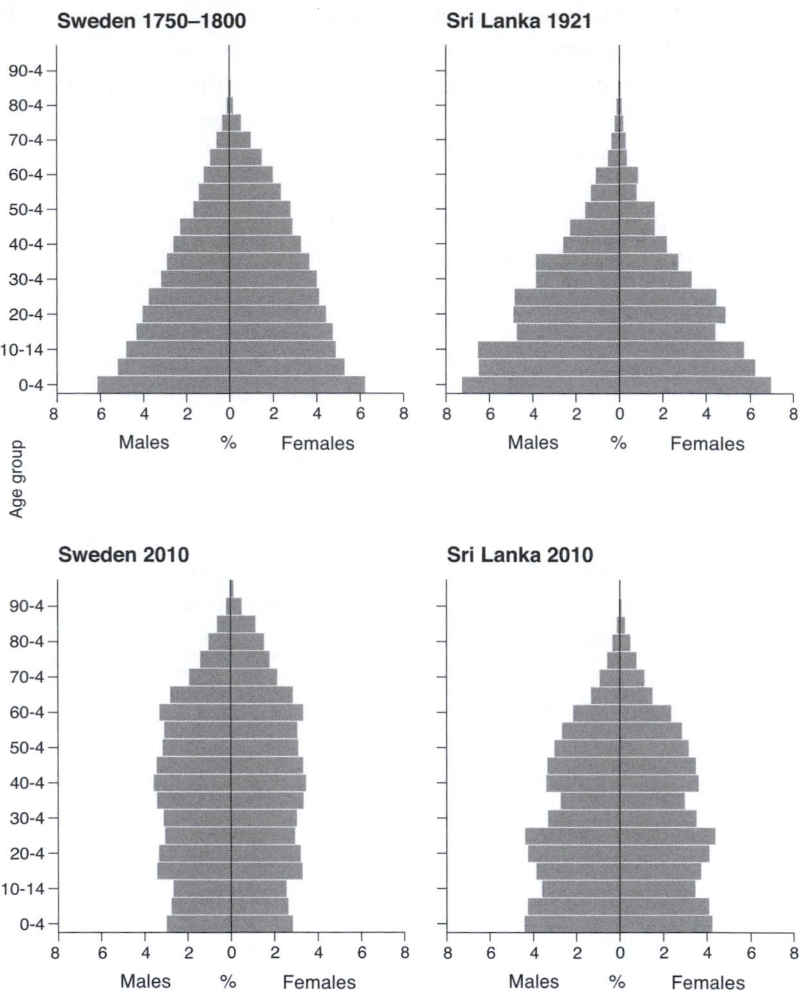


*Sources*: Sweden 1750–1800 (based on data in Thomas 1941), 2010 (United Nations 2009); Sri Lanka 1921 (Ceylon 1923), 2010 (United Nations 2009)

**Figure 2.3 Population ageing—the changing age distributions of Sweden and Sri Lanka**

Chapter 3 will examine how population age structures reflect – and influence – other demographic changes within the transition. Here it will suffice to say that the first countries to experience sustained population ageing were, of course, those that were the first to experience fertility decline. Accordingly, by the start of this century the populations of Europe, North America and Japan had all become old. But populations elsewhere in the world exhibit a wide range of age structures – reflecting the wide variation in the timing and speed of their fertility declines. Nevertheless, while most developing countries still have relatively young age structures, virtually all of them are now getting older – some of them quickly.

*Explaining urbanization and urban growth* Urbanization is both a characteristic and a key engine of societal development (see Figure 2.1). The modern process of urbanization involves the movement of a country's population from being largely rural in its composition to being largely urban. In other words, the proportion of the population living in towns rises from a low to a high level. Clearly, in a country with a growing population, urbanization requires that the urban population grows at a faster rate than the rural population. The main *proximate* reason why this happens is the net migration of people from rural to urban areas. However, a full explanation of the process requires consideration of that other main cause of urban population growth – namely urban natural increase (i.e. the excess of births over deaths occurring in the urban sector). Urbanization and urban growth are closely related, and they are discussed in detail in Chapter 5. Today virtually all developing countries are urbanizing, and this involves very considerable urban growth.

The modern process of urbanization is very new in historical terms. Looking at different world regions, there is a broad correspondence between the timing of the start of the demographic transition and the beginnings of urbanization. Before the Enlightenment levels of urbanization were relatively low everywhere. For example, it has been estimated that in Asia in 1750 only about 5 per cent of people lived in urban areas, and the figure for Europe was perhaps 7 per cent (see Grauman 1977). Sustained urbanization really began in north-western Europe at the end of the eighteenth century, and it affected the United States at roughly the same time. The process then spread to the rest of Europe; and from around the end of the nineteenth century it was under way in Japan. Elsewhere, countries that were relatively early in experiencing the demographic transition – e.g. Chile and Argentina – also tended to be relatively early in experiencing urbanization. Latin America as a whole probably began to urbanize from late in the nineteenth century. There was a small degree of urbanization in Asia, and even sub-Saharan Africa, during the first half of the twentieth century. But with the exception of Latin America – a somewhat anomalous 'developing' region – urbanization is a process which really gains momentum in the developing world from around the middle of the twentieth century. The United Nations estimates that between 1950 and 2010 the proportion of the world's people living in urban areas rose from about 29 to about 50 per cent (United Nations 2008).

To understand what caused this process, it is helpful to consider pre-transitional circumstances – when levels of urbanization were low. The proportion of any major population that could live in the urban sector (i.e. the towns) was constrained in several ways. Thus the towns had to be provisioned by the rural population – most obviously in terms of food, but also in terms of fuel (e.g. for cooking and heating) and other basic supplies (e.g. timber). Of course, the extent to which such constraints applied varied. For example, in some places urban populations could cultivate some of their own food (e.g. in kitchen gardens). Also, urban fuel requirements were greater in cold climates than in warm ones. And, for logistical reasons, it would have been much more difficult to supply one very populous town than a larger number of less populous ones. Nevertheless, in the era before 'modern economic growth' these kinds of constraint limited how 'urban' any country could become. Around 1750 the 'Low Countries' of the Netherlands and Belgium may have been the most urban part of the world. In the Netherlands perhaps one third of the total population lived in urban areas. However, this remarkably high level of urbanization was made possible only by a canal system that could carry provisions to the towns at relatively low cost, and by the ready availability of supplies of peat fuel (see, for example, van der Woude et al. 1990).

There was, however, an even more important restriction on the level of urbanization prior to the transition – a demographic one. Recall that in pre-transitional circumstances death rates were high because of infectious diseases. These diseases tended to thrive in urban areas, i.e. they varied *directly* with population density. So early towns were extremely unhealthy places. High levels of crowding, and exceedingly unsanitary living conditions, were very conducive to the maintenance and spread of infectious diseases. As a result, urban death rates were usually significantly higher than rural death rates. Indeed, urban death rates were usually higher than urban birth rates – meaning that the urban sector was a demographic *sink* (i.e. a net destroyer of people). In this situation, the long-run existence of the towns depended upon people continually migrating out of rural areas. Without such a flow of migrants, the towns would eventually have ceased to exist. In these circumstances, there was effectively a ceiling on how 'urban' any major population could become. The level of the ceiling was determined largely by the level of mortality that prevailed in the urban sector. A figure of one third urban, as in the Netherlands, was probably close to the upper limit for a pre-transitional population (see de Vries 1990).

Therefore, mortality decline is required for the modern process of urbanization to occur. The details of the process vary between different contexts. A stylized summary of the basic causal dynamics can, however, be given. Thus, in pre-transitional circumstances, the urban death rate was exceptionally high. In addition, however, the urban birth rate was often unusually low – partly because there was frequently an imbalance between the numbers of men and women of marriageable age living in the towns. So the urban sector was a sink – i.e. the urban rate of natural increase was negative. The rural rate of natural increase, however, was slightly positive – and ultimately this was the source of the migrants who came from the rural areas and thereby maintained the existence of the towns.

At a relatively early stage in the demographic transition, however, the urban death rate becomes lower than the urban birth rate. At this point the urban rate of natural increase becomes positive for the first time (de Vries 1990). This means that the urban population now has *two* distinct sources of growth. The first is its own (rising) rate of natural increase. The second is the continuing net flow of migrants coming from the rural sector – a flow that is likely to be boosted as mortality decline in rural areas raises the rate of natural increase there. The pace of urbanization is now relatively fast. And the rates of natural increase prevailing in the urban and the rural sectors become fairly similar. However, migration from rural to urban areas means that the urban population grows appreciably faster than the rural population – and, in this sense, migration from rural areas is indeed the immediate cause of urbanization. Naturally, as the level of urbanization rises, so a higher and higher proportion of urban growth is generated by natural increase in the towns.

With the occurrence of fertility decline, the rate of natural increase falls in both the urban and the rural sectors, and the dynamics of the process begin to come to an end. Fertility decline usually happens somewhat earlier in the towns, but death rates are now lower there too – so the rates of natural increase in the urban and the rural sectors remain fairly similar. However, as the rural rate of natural increase becomes low, so the continuation of migration out of rural areas brings about a fall in the number of people living in rural areas. At the end of the transition death and birth rates are low and roughly equal everywhere. But most of the now much bigger population now lives in the towns.

This account of the mechanics of urbanization will be illustrated in Chapter 5 using data for Sweden and Sri Lanka. Notice, however, that

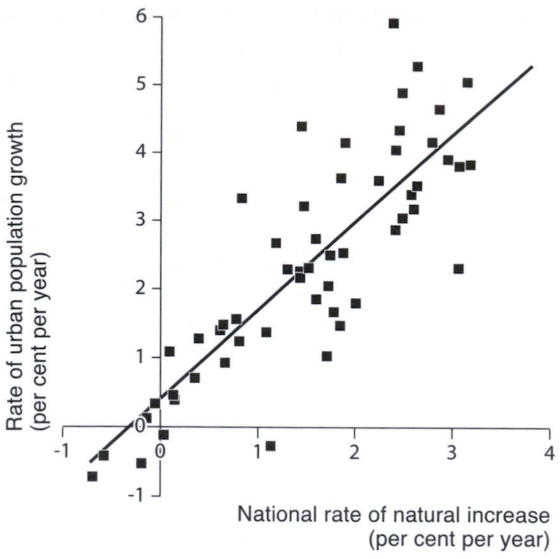


*Sources*: United Nations (2008, 2009)

**Figure 2.4 The rate of natural increase as a determinant of urban growth, fifty-six countries, 1995–2005**

the account is framed largely in demographic terms. Ultimately, a society that is mainly rural in composition can become urban only through changes in mortality, fertility and migration. In this context mortality decline plays a crucial, and often unrecognized, role.

Of course, in reality urban growth and urbanization are influenced by many other things. For example, there could be no large urban centres without developments in transport systems, and increases in agricultural productivity. And another subject which must be addressed is why – both before and throughout the entire process – some people decide to move from rural areas to live in the towns. The immediate reasons for this migration include economic betterment and the more exciting social conditions which tend to prevail in urban areas.

That said, the process of urbanization is commonly explained largely in terms of modern economic growth. This account stresses how the expansion of industry in towns leads to the creation of new jobs – initially in manufacturing, but later in services. Living standards in urban areas improve, and this and the rising opportunities for employment attract people to urban areas. At the same time, improvements in agricultural productivity reduce the possibilities for rural employment, and this also contributes to the movement of people to the towns. This economic explanation for urbanization certainly has force. It reflects the fact that in many places – from Europe in the nineteenth century to China today – the processes of industrialization, economic growth and urbanization have gone hand in hand. There is no doubt that such processes have often had a major influence on the course of urbanization.

However, that does *not* mean to say that urbanization is solely – or even mainly – the product of these economic processes. As is discussed in Chapter 5, there is at least as much reason to consider that urbanization brings about these basic changes in the structure of employment, and that it underpins economic growth. At the very least, two-way interactions are involved. While no society that has experienced modern economic growth has failed to urbanize, there have been populations that have urbanized without experiencing much economic growth. Indeed, one need look no further than contemporary sub-Saharan Africa to find examples. No society that has experienced mortality decline, however, has failed to experience urbanization. This constitutes strong evidence that mortality decline is the most important factor in the overall process.

In concluding this discussion, a few words are in order regarding urban population growth. The appalling living conditions found in many fast-growing towns in Africa, Asia and Latin America today mean that urban growth is often regarded as problematic. It tends to be assumed that such growth is mainly due to migration from rural areas – whereas, in fact, it is often more the result of urban natural increase. However, irrespective of whether urban natural increase or rural-to-urban migration is the main contributor to urban growth, *both* of these proximate causes of urban growth reflect natural increase resulting from the demographic transition (Preston 1979).

In this context, for the period 1995–2005 Figure 2.4 shows the relationship between the national rate of natural increase and the rate of urban growth for the fifty-six countries that were estimated to have populations of 20 million or more in 2010. These countries form the basis for all of the illustrative scatter-plots presented in this book (see the Appendix for further details). It is very clear from Figure 2.4 that countries with higher rates of natural increase tend to experience higher rates of urban growth.[14] Moreover, at any given rate of natural increase, the rate of *urban* growth in a country tends to be appreciably greater – reflecting the fact that the world is urbanizing.

Unsurprisingly, the urban growth that is associated with the contemporary demographic transitions is generally much faster than the urban growth that was associated with the historical transitions. And rapid urban growth raises many challenges for contemporary developing countries. In addition, however, Chapter 5 argues that the rate of urbanization that is being experienced in contemporary developing countries is also somewhat faster than applied in the past.

### The effects of the transition

We now address the transition's principal societal effects – the focus of Chapters 6 and 7. Several preliminary remarks are required.

First, it is important to bear in mind the differences between the historical and the contemporary transitions when considering the phenomenon's effects. Thus, as we have seen, the early transitions were comparatively gradual affairs; they arose from developments that were largely internal to the societies that were experiencing them; and they are now largely complete. In contrast, more recent transitions have involved faster processes; they have been greatly influenced by events in the wider world – especially as regards the capacity to reduce death rates; and contemporary transitions are at many different stages of completion.

It is also important to emphasize that the demographic transition has now affected all countries to some degree – including the poorest ones. Provided warfare is absent, and there is a reasonable degree of social stability, it has proved possible to engineer an appreciable fall in the death rate in almost any setting – and this is crucial, because mortality decline is the transition's initiating process. To a considerable extent, then, the transition is something that can occur independently of economic level. This is true in relation to mortality decline, and it is true in relation to fertility decline. It follows that the phenomenon's principal effects can also unfold in both rich and poor contexts. As Figure 2.1 implies, the transition brings about certain basic changes in society largely irrespective of economic or indeed most other considerations.

Another point to make is that the full societal effects of the demographic transition are probably not yet complete even in those countries that experienced the earliest – i.e. the historical – transitions. Recall that even if we restrict ourselves to demographic processes, then both urbanization and population ageing are lagged on preceding mortality and fertility declines. The consequences of these demographic processes for society, however, are themselves lagged. Therefore, the full societal effects of the transition may be observable only many decades after the phenomenon itself is complete.

In addition, we live in an increasingly integrated world. This means that some of the changes brought about by the historical transitions have influenced other societies somewhat independently of the stage that those societies may have reached within the transition. Simply put: as well as the transition itself, some of its major effects have acquired a life of their own – and have been exported. It has been possible for countries to 'jump ahead' of their own stage in the demographic transition. Relatedly, the idea of 'development' has itself been widened to include concepts like women's empowerment and democratization. But the practical realization of these ideas, in their modern forms, has itself been influenced by the historical transitions.[15] And it was partly because of this that these concepts eventually came to be considered as integral components of development.

Lastly, it should be clear that *all* of the transition's major demographic processes have important societal effects. And several of them can combine in bringing about a given change in the nature of society.

With these comments as background, we now briefly discuss the transition's effects in relation to: the family, issues of social psychology, marriage and gender relations, and the general degree of societal complexity. Having considered these more 'social' consequences, we proceed to examine the transition's implications for economic growth and the distribution of political power in society. The text is necessarily selective. And it is often useful to contrast pre-transitional and post-transitional circumstances in a stylized way. Further detail and qualification are provided in later chapters.

*Effects on family size and structure* Comparing pre-transitional circumstances with those holding after the transition, there may be little difference in average family size.[16] But, as has been noted, during the transition itself there is upward pressure on family size – pressure that has almost certainly been significantly greater in the contemporary transitions. The pressure occurs chiefly because mortality decline raises the number of surviving children. In addition, however, there may be a short-lived rise in the level of fertility per woman (Dyson and Murphy 1985). Notice that while the upward pressure on family size is eventually reversed – as birth control spreads, and fertility decline occurs – the period during which it happens is likely to be one of particular consequence for women, not least because they tend to perform most of the tasks associated with childcare.

Although average family size may be little different before and after the transition, the demographic dynamics of the family are very different. Thus, in pre-transitional conditions high death rates mean that families do not last for very long. The chance that one of the partners to a marriage will die while they are still at a relatively young age is considerable. And the surviving partner in the marriage may not live on for long.[17] In these circumstances, the structure of families (and therefore households) tends to have relatively little time depth. Any surviving grandparents are not likely to remain alive for many years. Moreover, because levels of child mortality are high, the size of a family does not correspond closely to the number of births that the woman has had. In pre-transitional circumstances births and deaths are common events in families.

After the transition, however, the level of child mortality is very low. Indeed, as previously noted, death is rare at both young and middle ages. Accordingly, the number of children in a family does now correspond closely to the number of births that the woman has had. In post-transitional conditions it is very unusual for parents to lose a child. A married couple can expect to live for many years before one of them dies – and the surviving partner may then live on for quite a few more years. It is now common for young children to have grandparents alive. In other words, family structure has much greater time depth. Indeed, vertical kin relationships – i.e. those across the generations – are now much more prominent. Births and deaths are rare events. And, in these circumstances, families – or at least their constituent members – exist for much longer durations of time, although not necessarily as part of the same household (see below).

Given such considerations, the demographic transition has important implications for people's basic attitudes towards life.

*Socio-psychological implications* In pre-transitional circumstances death was common, unpredictable, and it could happen at any age. Thought of one's own mortality could never have been far away. In many ways, life was a matter of day-to-day survival. It made comparatively little sense to plan for the long term. People had virtually no control over either their health or their fertility. Fatalistic attitudes were probably fairly frequent with respect to both deaths and births. Sickness and death were interpreted largely in supernatural terms. And, in these circumstances, people often took what we would regard as a rather unfeeling approach towards life – including the fate of young children. In many pre-transitional societies practices like infanticide, child neglect and child abandonment were sometimes used to influence family size and composition. Indeed, such practices may have been resorted to even more during the phase of the demographic transition when parents were faced with rising numbers of surviving children, i.e. upward pressure on family size.[18]

After the transition, however, people exert much greater *control* over their own lives. Conditions of low mortality eventually have major psychological effects. Death is now an uncommon – even distant – event. It is restricted almost entirely to elderly people. There is now a greater sense of personal agency about in society. If a family member becomes sick then medical assistance will be sought. The practical response to sickness is unlikely to be chiefly religious and supernatural in nature. In these conditions, children tend to be planned and particularly precious. They are the focus of family life. The fact that child mortality is extremely low tends to heighten the emotional intensity that is experienced by parents in the unlikely event that they do lose a child. Indeed, it can be argued that mortality decline tends to augment the value that is attached to human life – perhaps especially in relation to children (see Livi Bacci 2000).

After the transition women have only a few births, but virtually all offspring survive into adulthood – representing a major increase in demographic efficiency. In these much more secure and stable conditions, people can contemplate the long term – indeed, they *must* do so. Partly as a result, considerable importance is now attached to education. It seems reasonable to suggest that neither the rise of mass education in society, nor the savings and investment required for sustained economic growth, would have occurred to anywhere near the extent that they have without the greatly increased levels of confidence brought about by mortality decline.[19]

*Marriage and gender relations* The preceding discussion has been framed partly with reference to a couple getting married in order to have children. However, mortality decline and fertility decline bring about major changes in the nature of marriage and the position of women in society. These effects take decades to unfold, and they are probably not yet complete in any society. But there are reasons to think that they may become established everywhere eventually, to some degree.

The essential argument is that as childbearing and child-rearing have come to occupy a much smaller fraction of women's lives, so the institution of marriage has become weaker. Moreover, the lives of women have become increasingly similar to those led by men. That is, there has been a reduction in gender differentiation as a result of the demographic transition.

Before fertility decline, women have a sizeable number of births during the course of their reproductive years. This means that most of their lives were – and in many places still are – preoccupied with the related facts of pregnancy, breastfeeding and childcare. Indeed, in a pre-transitional society it was commonly the case that a majority of women aged in their twenties or early thirties were either pregnant or lactating at any one time. Moreover, the fact that life expectation was short only served to magnify the role of childbearing and children in women's lives. In these circumstances it was understandable that the existences of most women were bound closely to the domestic (i.e. household) domain.

Contrast this situation with a society that has passed through the transition. In post-transitional circumstances most women, if they do give birth, do so only once or twice. If a couple get married to have and raise children, then they might expect to spend perhaps twenty-five years doing this. But their childcare responsibilities are likely to diminish while they are still only in their forties or fifties. Recall that life expectancy is now probably at least twice the length it once was. The upshot is that the bearing and rearing of children now occupies a much smaller fraction of women's – now much longer – lives. This transformation in demographic conditions raises the issue of the purpose of marriage – which previously functioned as a lifelong arrangement for the having and nurturing of children. It also raises the issue of what women, in particular, will do for most of their lives when there are no children around to look after.

There are strong reasons to believe that these basic demographic changes have led to a reduction in the significance that is attached to marriage in societies that have gone through the transition (see Davis and van den Oever 1982). Marriage – in the sense of a formal lifelong commitment for the having and rearing of children – has become a much weaker institution. Consensual unions have become more common, and are increasingly accorded a legitimacy of their own. More and more children are born outside of formal marriage. Divorce, separation and single parenthood have tended to increase. Nowadays many young women choose to live alone. In general, then, in post-transitional societies people are less likely to marry, and if they do get married they are much more likely to divorce or separate before the death of one of the partners. These developments contribute to the emergence of smaller and, in some respects, simpler household structures (although the formation of new unions, following divorce or separation, also complicates things).

For women, the move to low fertility means that there is now much less to differentiate their lives from the lives of men. The fact that marriage provides women with less economic security has almost certainly contributed to the increased significance that parents attach to educating their daughters. In post-transitional circumstances, women have more time – and greater incentive – to pursue their own education and individual careers. In turn, this may lead to a further weakening of the institution of marriage, and it may also contribute to a movement towards exceptionally low levels of fertility. In short, there may be a cumulative social dynamic in which, for women, having fewer children and living more independently from men are processes that tend to reinforce each other. Moreover, within families and households, authority and responsibilities are increasingly shared between women and men.

While the foregoing sketch draws mainly on experience in Europe and North America, there are clear signs that similar developments are under way in other parts of the world where fertility decline has occurred more recently. For example, in South Korea, Thailand and Malaysia, young women are said to be 'staying away from marriage in droves' (Jones 1997a: 74). And, asked why she is still not married, a young Indonesian woman produces the telling response: 'Why should I marry one baby in order to have another?' (Hull 2002: 8). Furthermore, as will be seen in Chapter 6, these are not the only ways in which gender relations are being altered by fundamental demographic changes.

*Implications for societal complexity* The effects dealt with so far are perhaps best thought of as unfolding at the level of individuals, families and households. Nevertheless, it is clear that these same effects also have implications at higher levels of aggregation – e.g. in terms of the demand for education in society, the propensity to save and invest, and the likelihood that women will enter the labour force. However, the transition also has effects which are best conceived of as operating at higher levels of aggregation – although, in turn, these same effects often have implications at lower levels of aggregation (e.g. for individuals and households). In this context, recall that the demographic transition always involves population growth and urbanization – two processes that come together in urban growth.

Given that the transition is the main engine of urban growth, it follows that it also plays a key role in expanding the division of labour in society, and in increasing societal complexity more generally (see Figure 2.1). Notice that here we are addressing *structural* changes in the nature of society which – at least to some degree – can be conceived of as occurring independently of economic circumstances. In other words, these effects could be expected to occur to some extent even if there were to be no great change in living standards. Again, these structural effects are most apparent and advanced in relation to societies that were the first to experience the transition. However, since urban growth is occurring in almost all countries today, these more aggregate societal effects are virtually universal.

It has long been recognized that an expansion of population scale tends to be accompanied by increases in both the division of labour and the general level of societal complexity (see, for example, Schnore 1965). This is especially evident in relation to urban growth – which essentially represents the concentration of the population increase that results from the demographic transition. Moreover, as the transition proceeds so not only do the towns expand, but they also increase greatly in number.

There are several reasons why urban population growth tends to stimulate a major increase in the division of labour. One is the requirement to supply the growing urban sector with basic provisions (e.g. food, fuel, timber). This necessitates the expansion of transport systems between rural and urban areas, the development of storage facilities in both rural and urban areas, and the growth of systems of distribution (e.g. warehouses, markets, shops) within urban areas.

Another source of increased occupational differentiation derives from the fact that the growing urban population must create a range of products to exchange for the supplies that it gets from the rural sector. Many items can help fulfil this role. The manufacture of agricultural implements designed to help farmers raise their crop and livestock production, however, is worth mentioning. This is because there are strong reasons to believe that, rather than increases in agricultural productivity leading to the growth of towns, it is the growth of towns which leads to rises in agricultural productivity (see Jacobs 1972).

A further source of the enlargement of the division of labour resulting from urban growth comes from the fact that towns raise distinct challenges of their own – challenges that must be addressed, eventually. Here one is thinking of problems in the control of urban fires, the supply of water, and coping with the growing quantities of urban waste. The urban sector is also likely to raise particular requirements in relation to the control of crime and the maintenance of public health, for example.

Yet another source of the increased differentiation that comes with urban growth stems from the fact that the expansion of towns tends to stimulate economic growth through greater specialization, interaction and competition – processes which tend to interact synergistically with each other in the expanding urban areas (see below).

The greatly increased scale and complexity of the urban sector, which results in large part from the transition, brings new challenges in relation to issues of social order and administration. The heightened social interaction characteristic of urban areas raises the prospect of more intense and disruptive forms of conflict – contributing to the growing requirement for systems of policing. In addition, the expansion of services in relation to the control of things like fire, crime and waste is necessarily accompanied by an expansion of systems of urban administration (see Figure 2.1). This is a significant development in itself, but it also contributes to the general growth of societal complexity.

In pre-transitional circumstances the limited degree of differentiation that existed in society with regard to political, legal, educational, artistic, religious and other matters was located mostly in the small urban sector. As the towns expand, however, so it is inevitable that there is increased differentiation with respect to all of these aspects of life. Therefore, within the framework that is provided by the transition, a pre-transitional economy that was dominated by subsistence agriculture in rural areas is progressively superseded by an economy that is characterised by complex exchange – both between rural and urban areas, and increasingly between different parts of the growing urban sector. Growth in the division of labour and societal complexity also means that education and training become more important (see Figure 2.1).

*Consequences for economic performance* There has been considerable research on economic aspects of the demographic transition. Much of this work has focused on the influence of population growth on economic growth – a subject that has been of particular interest because of the high population growth rates prevailing in many poor countries in recent decades. Research has also recognized, however, that other demographic processes – e.g. urbanization and ageing – have significant economic consequences. This is a large and complex field, and the conclusions of researchers can vary according to the populations that are being considered. The following discussion, which is elaborated in Chapter 7, is organized around the transition's main processes. The relationship between population growth and economic growth is addressed last.

Considering mortality decline *by itself*, it seems safe to surmise that it generally has beneficial effects for the economy.[20] After all, the decline in the death rate from high to low levels involves the improvement of a society's health status – and healthier people tend to be more productive, both mentally and physically. The length of people's working lives is also extended greatly by mortality decline – a fact which raises the level of experience found among workers. In addition, as previously noted, mortality decline creates circumstances in which people are encouraged to plan more for the future. Eventually, this is likely to lead to higher levels of savings and investment, and higher economic output as a result. Of course, when life expectancy reaches high levels almost all deaths occur at advanced ages – and this may well bring increased costs from the treatment of various *chronic* diseases, such as cancer, heart disease and dementia (infectious diseases having been greatly reduced). Moreover, this adverse effect will be heightened by population ageing – since elderly people now form a much larger proportion of the total population. That said, mortality decline also raises the number of healthy years of life experienced by older people. There is little reason to think that the costs involved in treating the health problems of elderly people are outweighed by the benefits that derive from their having lived many more years of healthy and active life.[21]

Almost certainly, fertility decline also benefits the economy. Of course, within the transition it is the process which brings about the fall in the rate of population growth. But it has long been recognized that – compared to circumstances where the birth rate remains high – a decline in fertility from high to low levels allows a population to save and invest more – both in terms of human capital (i.e. education and training) and in terms of physical capital (e.g. roads, factories, machinery, etc.). This important realization is of long standing (see, for example, Coale and Hoover 1958). It is sometimes illustrated by contrasting circumstances of 'capital widening' – in which fertility remains high and a given quantity of investment in, say, schooling is spread over a continually rising number of children – and a situation of 'capital deepening' – where fertility falls, and the same quantity of investment is spent on a smaller number of children, leading to higher investment *per child* (see World Bank 1985).

A related benefit of fertility decline is discernible at the household level (see, for example, Desai 1995; Merrick 2001). Research shows that children in smaller families tend to do better in terms of their nutritional, health and educational status, compared to children in larger families (i.e. children with more siblings). For parents, having fewer children means that they can invest more in each individual child – not just materially, but also in terms of time, energy, care and affection. Indeed, one characterization of why people eventually decide to adopt birth control is that they become more concerned with the 'quality' of their children, and less concerned with their quantity. In turn, better-quality children are likely to be more productive economically when they become adults.

This discussion would be incomplete without noting that fertility decline also underpins the movement of women into the labour force, where they contribute to the formal economy. This represents a significant economic benefit, although the speed and extent to which it happens will be influenced by prevailing circumstances (e.g. culture and institutions). It should also be recalled that in pre-transitional conditions women generally have a major, although inevitably more constrained, economic role.

In this stylized discussion, a country's birth and death rates are high and roughly equal in pre-transitional circumstances, and low and roughly equal in post-transitional circumstances.[22] The age structure, however, has changed from being young to being old. There are few reasons to suppose that this change in age structure has negative consequences for the economy – provided that post-transitional fertility remains near the replacement level (about two births per woman) and that population ageing does not become extreme. For example, in the Swedish case shown in Figure 2.3, there were approximately 70 'dependent' people (here, those aged under 15 or over 60 years) for every 100 people aged 15–59 in *both* the period 1750–1800 and in the year 2010. Of course, in an old population 'dependants' are mainly elderly people, while in a young population they are mainly children. Both of these sections of society involve 'costs'. But with institutional and related change, there is clearly considerable potential for older people to contribute economically and in other ways – for example, by helping to care for young and very old people.

The demographic transition involves a long period during which the total age dependency ratio of the population is reduced. Thus, as fertility declines it brings about a decline in the child dependency ratio, and it is only after some time that this is counterbalanced by a rise in the old-age dependency ratio. Therefore, as is discussed in Chapter 7, the transition provides a potential 'window of opportunity' for improved economic performance. Essentially, this is the period during which there can be an increase in capital deepening. There are reasons to believe that a sizeable proportion of the rapid economic growth experienced by quite a few countries in Asia and Latin America in recent decades can be attributed to this particular aspect of the transition. On the other hand, when the total age dependency ratio rises this can raise challenges compared to the period when it was falling. For example, it is relatively easy to introduce old-age pensions when the dependency ratio is falling, but it is harder to finance them when the ratio is rising (Lee 2003). There certainly can be costs in adapting to population ageing.

As noted, the processes of urbanization and economic growth often interact synergistically. The two processes are usually hard to disentangle, although urbanization can occur in the absence of economic growth. However, urbanization can involve very different rates of urban growth. And there is little doubt that rapid urban growth can produce difficulties – e.g. in terms of the provision of basic infrastructure and the creation of slums – which would be less challenging if urban growth was slower. Therefore, urbanization is probably more beneficial economically if it is achieved with slower rather than faster urban growth.

More generally, however, as the demographic transition proceeds so it is in the growing towns that the economic gains to be had from the division of labour are greatest. It is the towns which provide a larger and more concentrated market for an increasing range of goods and services. And it is in the growing towns that the greatest increases in economic competition, production and trade all occur. The fact that people are increasingly concentrated in urban areas tends to facilitate the matching of the demand for specialized skills with the supply of people who can provide these skills. And the fact that firms are grouped together in towns allows them to share inputs and exchange ideas.

Sustained economic growth involves a marked rise in the demand for manufactured goods and services, which are mostly produced in the urban sector. Indeed, economic growth usually involves only a modest rise in the demand for agricultural products. That said, urban growth does require the production of more food – and, as noted, this tends to stimulate increases in rural productivity. In time, technological and other changes originating in the towns mean that a *much* smaller fraction of the rural population can produce the necessary food and other supplies for the growing urban sector. As a result, rural labour is released to work in the towns – thereby contributing to urbanization. What occurs, then, are processes of cumulative causation (Bloom and Canning 2001). On the one hand, sustained economic growth depends upon an expansion of the initially small urban population. On the other hand, economic growth in the urban sector influences urbanization – most directly, by heightening the attraction of urban life for rural people.

This brings us finally to a consideration of the effect of population growth on economic growth. The fairly modest population growth rates experienced in the early transitions in Europe and Japan do not appear to have had an adverse influence on economic growth. With the advent of industrialization and modern economic growth from early in the nineteenth century, a new economic era had arrived – one based upon the mass exploitation of energy obtained from coal (and, later, oil and natural gas). As a result, economic growth had such dynamism that it was largely unaffected by the rate of population growth. Indeed, in offshoot populations like the United States, population growth – much of it stemming from immigration – almost certainly had a distinctly positive effect on economic growth during the nineteenth century. Population growth helped the US economy by raising the overall level of demand, enabling efficiencies of scale, encouraging innovation, and helping to generate new economic institutions. Here, the context was extremely important – because demographic growth was helping to open up and exploit vast territories that were rich in material resources.

In recent decades, however, many poor developing countries have experienced population growth of quite unprecedented speed and scale – and, other things equal, the implications of this for economic growth have often been negative. Recall that some societies were still largely 'pre-transitional' as recently as the middle of the twentieth century – when they suddenly experienced very substantial mortality decline.

The negative influence of the ensuing rapid population growth on economic growth has probably been greatest in sub-Saharan Africa, and a dry-land belt stretching westwards from Afghanistan, through parts of the Middle East, and on into the countries of the Sahel. In such locations rapid population growth has often produced decreasing returns to labour in agriculture, problems in generating employment, difficulties in raising levels of savings and investment, and negative economic effects deriving from various forms of environmental degradation which are themselves heavily influenced by the occurrence of rapid demographic growth. Here one is thinking of soil degradation, falling water tables, deforestation and increased flooding, for example. In rural areas these kinds of problem have exerted downward pressure on living standards and raised out-migration to the towns – thus contributing to the occurrence of rapid urban growth with its attendant difficulties. Urban living conditions are often atrocious, but people might be even worse off if they remained in rural areas.

The main point, however, is that whether one considers the rural or the urban sector, the improvement of living standards is made more difficult by rapid population growth. These issues are explored in Chapter 7. It will suffice here to say that there is now a widespread consensus among economists that rapid population growth has a strong and distinctly negative influence upon per capita income growth. It is a major factor contributing to both the amount and the severity of poverty (see, for example, Birdsall et al. 2001; Headey and Hodge 2009).

In conclusion, the phenomenon of modern economic growth, which began in north-western Europe in the decades around 1800, would probably not have been sustained in the long run in the absence of the demographic transition. The processes of mortality decline, fertility decline and urbanization must all be regarded as having essentially positive economic effects. And, comparing the start and end of the transition, the effects of population ageing are probably best regarded as neutral. The economic consequences of population growth appear to be variable – depending on the speed of the growth, and the context in which it occurs. The occurrence of sustained and *rapid* population growth in poor countries today, however, is probably having a decidedly negative influence on people's economic welfare. Indeed, in some cases the effects may turn out to be so negative as to largely counterbalance positive economic consequences deriving from other aspects of the transition.

*The emergence of modern democracy* Demography and politics are often entwined. Yet the influence of the demographic transition on political systems is a topic that is seldom addressed. It is unlikely, however, that something as profound and far-reaching as the demographic transition would have left the nature of politics untouched.

Here the argument is that the move from pre-transitional to post-transitional circumstances has underlain the gradual broadening in the basis of political power in society – i.e. the process of democratization. In plain terms: urbanization and population ageing have underpinned the emergence of modern systems of liberal democracy (see Figure 2.1). Of course, these systems have various dimensions (e.g. the rule of law, freedom of speech, etc.). But for present purposes it is probably best to think of them in terms of the principle of 'one person, one vote'.

The rise of modern democratic systems – imperfect though they are – is something that occurred first in the countries of north-western Europe and their main offshoots. It is a process, however, that, even in these societies, has approached its later stages only during recent times. For example, in the United States and Australia the extension of equal voting rights to all adult citizens – irrespective of race – was established only in the 1960s. Democratization is a process which, at the start of the present century, was still not complete in every country of Europe. And, despite the possibility of a population being able to 'jump ahead' of its stage in the demographic transition, it is a process that is still far from finished in most developing countries.

Again, the argument is best made by contrasting pre-transitional and post-transitional conditions. Thus, before the transition, society is rural and dispersed, and a fairly high proportion of the people are children. In these circumstances, it is comparatively easy for a small number of autocratic, often hereditary rulers (e.g. monarchs, emperors, etc.) to control the reins of power. Indeed, this was virtually always the case in pre-transitional populations. The transition, however, concentrates and ages the population. And, as we have seen, society becomes increasingly complex. As these processes unfold they raise the prospect of challenges to autocratic rule. Consequently political power eventually becomes somewhat more evenly distributed in society.

There are *a priori* grounds to consider that a population containing a higher proportion of adults will be more concerned with the distribution of political power than one in which perhaps between 30 and 45 per cent of the population is aged less than 15 years. It may also be the case that the increased confidence which derives from mortality decline makes it more likely that people will become more interested in issues of justice and political fairness. However, urbanization and urban growth are also significant considerations in this context – partly because people in towns tend to have a heightened capacity to influence events and challenge arbitrary rule.

It is clear that in Europe and North America during the nineteenth and twentieth centuries, the demand for reform and popular elections came primarily from the growing urban classes. It was mainly in the towns that people organized, marched and protested to bring about political change. Interestingly, in some places (e.g. parts of Scandinavia) urban growth involved a relatively high degree of socio-economic equality – and the process of democratization is sometimes seen as the natural counterpart of this. Elsewhere, however, urban growth involved conditions of heightened inequality. And, in such circumstances, revolution – or the threat of it – was involved in autocratic rulers losing – or gradually ceding – their hold on power. This is an illustration of how, in different contexts, remote causal processes can unfold in different ways, and with different rationales, but to the same ultimate end.

The basic argument regarding the rise of modern democracy will be elaborated in Chapter 7. But it is worth stressing that – here as elsewhere – we would expect there to be long time lags between the operation of demographic processes and the ensuing political changes. Furthermore, there clearly have been cases where, in terms of the nature of their political systems, countries have been able to 'jump ahead' of their demographic processes. India, for example, has been a democracy since about 1947, despite having a low level of urbanization and a young population. Therefore India is a good example of how basic causal processes can be short-circuited. Moreover, to reiterate, demographic change does not explain everything. Thus, although one can think of cases where modern economic growth has coexisted with autocratic rule – consider contemporary China, for example – there are reasons to believe that aspects of modern economic growth can also help to erode autocratic rule – at least in the long run. Thus sustained economic growth may also produce new bases of power in society, which eventually challenge traditional structures (Easterlin 1996). Finally, it is worth noting that the increase in population scale caused by the demographic transition is a consideration that strengthens the requirement for modern democratic systems to be representative – i.e. working through the existence of political parties – rather than participatory.

## Discussion

The demographic transition has played a fundamental role in world development during the past two centuries. Moreover, the processes and effects of the continuing demographic transition are likely to remain of great importance for the foreseeable future. Several points about the central argument are relevant in concluding.

There is a clear sequence of cause and effect in relation to the transition's main processes. Indeed, there can be few areas of social science where cause and effect are so apparent, and so significant. To reiterate: sustained mortality decline is the initiating process; it causes population growth; in turn, this growth produces various pressures which lead to fertility decline; mortality decline underpins both urbanization and urban growth; and fertility decline causes population ageing. Although these demographic processes overlap and interact, in the very long run this basic sequence appears to be largely independent of other developments, and fairly relentless in its progression. The transition's processes are still not complete in most countries. But, other things equal, it is virtually certain that they will occur.

As noted, the origins of mortality decline lie in the Enlightenment. Therefore, in a very broad sense, the changed way of thinking that came about during the Enlightenment can be said to be the cause of the demographic transition. Having said that, however, a great many considerations have shaped its unfolding.

One consideration is simply the passage of time. The so-called 'late development effect' (Dore 1970) is essentially the capacity of societies that develop later to benefit from the experience of societies that develop earlier. There is no doubt that this effect has influenced the course of both mortality and fertility declines. One way to illustrate this is simply to refer to the many technologies that did not exist in the nineteenth century, but are available today – for example, antibiotics, immunizations and modern contraceptive methods. In this context, however, the late development effect reflects many things besides improvements in technology. In broad terms, when mortality and fertility declines occurred as part of the historical transitions, no one had a clear idea of what was happening, or where things were going, and governments took little interest in the course of events. In the modern world, however, the situation is very different in all of these respects. Indeed, the demographic transition itself provides a framework for what is both expected and normally desired.

In historical terms, mortality decline has generally been a sustained process, once it has begun. The HIV/AIDS epidemic in sub-Saharan Africa is an unusual, but only a limited, exception. The epidemic caused mortality decline in the region to 'stall' (i.e. plateau) between the 1980s and the start of this century. Some countries experienced major falls in life expectancy. It seems likely, however, that no country experienced a decline in life expectancy back to truly pre-transitional levels. Moreover, there has been progress in combating HIV/AIDS – progress that has ultimately stemmed from the results of scientific research. And, early in the present century, the process of mortality decline appears to have resumed in sub-Saharan Africa as a whole (United Nations 2009).

Fertility decline is also a fairly inexorable process, once it has begun. There are strong reasons to think that if a society is able to export some of its own natural increase through migration then, other things equal, this can have a delaying effect on the occurrence of fertility decline. Clearly, in this case the possibility of out-migration is an important part of the overall context of a population. It may also be that rapid economic growth can postpone the occurrence of fertility decline for a while – essentially by delaying the trade-off between living standards and family size that people must eventually face. More generally, fertility declines have occasionally stalled – for example, in Argentina and Chile in the 1950s and 1960s, and in Bangladesh in the 1990s (Bongaarts 2008). Such mid-transition stalls, however, have tended to happen at moderate levels of fertility, and hitherto they have eventually come to an end. For various reasons, governments have also tried to delay, or reverse, the process of fertility decline by introducing policies designed to bolster fertility. But such policies have seldom had much success in long-run perspective. Fertility decline is generally a fairly unfaltering process.

Governments have also attempted to restrict urban growth and urbanization. Again, however, viewed in relation to the long run, their efforts have been unsuccessful. For example, in apartheid South Africa the government tried to confine people to so-called 'homeland' areas, and it imposed severe restrictions on movement to the major towns. But there was a large rise in rural-to-urban migration in the early 1990s, following the collapse of the apartheid regime (Dyson 2003). Another example is China, where since 1947 the government has employed measures designed to restrict movement to the towns. Between 1947 and 1980 these efforts had some success – the level of urbanization rose only from around 13 to about 20 per cent. There were limits, however, to how much urban growth and urbanization could be restrained. By 2010 about 45 per cent of China's people were living in urban areas (United Nations 2008).

Governments can certainly influence the processes of the demographic transition. For example, their actions can accelerate mortality decline, and in some circumstances it seems that government policies have been able to accelerate fertility decline. However, attempts by governments to work *against* the flow of events – i.e. to stem or reverse the course of the transition's main processes – are invariably unsuccessful in the long run.

Turning to what we have termed the transition's 'societal' effects, it is clear that some of them are very closely related to the transition itself. In the case of these effects, if the transition occurs, then the effects will almost certainly occur as well. For example, this is probably true in relation to the increasing role of vertical kin relationships – and the diminishing importance of horizontal ones – as the transition proceeds. It is probably true in relation to the fundamental changes in human psychology that occur as a result of mortality decline. And, to some extent, it is probably true in relation to the increase in societal complexity that accompanies the increase in population scale (especially in urban areas) that is generated by the transition.

That said, the pace and extent to which the transition brings about reductions in gender differentiation, for example, may be more variable. The position of women with respect to men is certainly becoming more equal in much of the world. But in some societies the prevailing institutional structures may obstruct the process severely. Moreover, even in relation to the most demographically advanced societies, to say that gender differentiation is diminishing is not to say that all such differentiation will disappear. A similar point can be made with respect to democratization. It is obvious that other considerations can arise to stall, or even reverse, this process. For example, in Europe between 1920 and 1990 the growth of democracy was severely restricted by fascist and communist political regimes.

A repeated refrain here has been that the processes of the demographic transition have often contributed greatly to modern economic growth. Indeed, the two phenomena have sometimes been so intimately entwined that it can be extremely hard to disentangle their effects. It is a fact, however, that the transition can occur in poor settings. The idea – still widespread – that a major rise in living standards is required for fertility decline to occur is plainly incorrect.

That is not to say that economic decisions do not feature in the central argument. They are represented here in two respects. The first is in relation to the decision to adopt birth control, which is almost always based on people's realization that they, and perhaps equally importantly their children, will be better off if they have fewer births.[23] The second pertains to the decision of some people to migrate from rural to urban areas – a decision that must be as old as the existence of the urban sector itself. This decision too often has an economic dimension – in that some people conclude that they would be better off if they moved to the towns.[24]

Both of these decisions, however, can be made in both poor and rich settings. And in both cases the decision can be made largely irrespective of whether the economy is growing or contracting. Of course, the proximate explanation that people give to account for their decision will vary according to the particular context. Thus, in countries where living standards are improving, people may say that they are having fewer births partly because there are now other things apart from children that they want to enjoy. And in countries where living standards are deteriorating, people may explain exactly the same decision with reference to their worsening economic circumstances.

Mirroring this, social scientists have commonly 'explained' fertility declines in terms of economic growth. They have done this because fertility decline and economic growth have tended to go together. In other contexts, however, researchers have tried to account for fertility decline in terms of falling living standards – so-called 'poverty-induced' fertility declines (see, for example, Basu 1986). In both cases these explanations miss the underlying, remote causal process that is actually bringing fertility decline about – namely prior, and to some extent concurrent, mortality decline.

Recall what was said above in relation to democratization in Europe. In some countries growing socio-economic equality in urban areas was used to account for the emergence of democracy. But in other countries growing inequality in the urban sector appears to have had the same effect. The point is that, in different places, remote causal processes can unfold very differently, but to the same eventual effect.

There is an associated point of methodology here. It is that researchers have tended to search for the causes of fundamental demographic processes by studying the differentials that prevail at one moment (or period) in time. Indeed, this approach has been common in trying to explain fertility decline. Thus, for example, research often focuses on fertility variation between different countries, or between different households within the same country. The variation in fertility is then 'explained' in terms of variation in the accompanying socio-economic characteristics of the countries or households (e.g. the level of per capita income, or the level of education).

Procedures designed to analyse differentials, however, may not be appropriate in accounting for change in the overall level of a variable. Thus if fertility decline – or urbanization – occurs in *every* society sooner or later, then studying the reasons for variation in it may miss the fundamental processes that are actually at work. Focusing on differentials may help to account for differences in the timing and speed of demographic change, while contributing little to explaining its occurrence per se. In relation to the major changes of the transition, we are dealing with processes that are likely to be universal in the very long run (see Lieberson 1985; Ní Bhrolcháin and Dyson 2007).

It should be clear that the demographic transition promises some good things that can be enjoyed by societies that are still fairly poor in economic terms. In many ways, the effects of the transition are beneficial. But there can be negative effects. For example, urban growth may involve the emergence of new forms of pathological behaviour. And, perhaps more importantly, rapid population growth can make economic growth much harder to achieve. Moreover, the expansion of the world's population as a result of the demographic transition may contribute to major challenges with respect to the environment. This brings us to some words on the future.

*The future* This book is chiefly concerned with examining past developments. But the relationships considered should have relevance for the future – although they are unlikely to always unfold at a steady pace, and given other factors they may not always be assured.

For the world and its major regions, it is possible to make some fairly firm statements regarding *broad* population trends during the next few decades. Thus it is expected that mortality will continue to improve in most countries – perhaps with occasional setbacks – and that fertility will continue to fall in all societies where it has not yet reached a low level. In most developing countries death rates are already quite low, and therefore they cannot fall much further (although mortality will continue to improve). Birth rates, however, are still relatively high in many of these countries, and in such places there are good reasons to believe that they will continue to fall. As a result, rates of population growth in developing countries will continue to fall. The next few decades will see population ageing in most societies. Indeed, some developing countries will experience particularly rapid ageing because of their particularly rapid experience of fertility decline. There are equally firm reasons to suppose that urban growth and urbanization will continue apace in most developing countries.

The major processes inherent in the demographic transition are expected to continue until, at some point during the second half of the present century, the world's population will have low and approximately equal death and birth rates. The human population will be appreciably larger then – perhaps somewhere between nine and ten billion. It will be much older and much more urban. That is certainly the *direction* of change – although it is doubtful that the world's population will ever reach a 'steady state'.

Looking at the developing world as a whole, it seems reasonable to conclude that the continuation – and eventual completion – of the demographic transition will contribute to some significant and beneficial societal effects (in the long run, and other things equal). Thus, in addition to the fact that people will generally be enjoying longer and healthier lives, and having fewer children, the continuing demographic transition should mean that: people's sense of personal agency will tend to increase; the importance attached to formal education will continue to rise; women will become more independent with respect to men; countries will generally become more open and democratic; and societies will continue to become increasingly complex in a multitude of ways. Many countries should benefit economically as a result of the processes of the demographic transition. However, although the transition will contribute to these and other dimensions of development – and strengthen their base – it is important to emphasize that there are now many other influences that help to bring such changes about.

The transition is also contributing to new challenges and problems. It is a phenomenon to which societies *must* adapt. If conditions of low fertility give more freedom to women, and alter the nature of the relationship between them and men, then, in turn, this raises new issues in relation to the production of children – and ultimately the reproduction of society. Such changes may well lead to a gradual renegotiation of gender roles – one which results in a more equal distribution of parental responsibilities, for example. Also, while the demographic transition may contribute to the future spread of democracy, it is unlikely that the ensuing political changes will always be smooth. It has been noted too that urban growth and urbanization can produce increased levels of crime and disorder. Moreover, in the future many of the world's major urban centres are going to be truly extraordinary in terms of their size, and this too will bring new challenges.

The unprecedentedly rapid population growth experienced by many poor countries in recent decades has generally had a negative economic effect. Of course, the influence of population growth can be offset by other factors. But in much of Africa, and parts of Asia, rapid natural increase seems likely to continue to have negative economic consequences in the coming decades. And the situation may well be worsened by deteriorating environmental conditions. Tellingly, poverty reduction targets are usually framed in terms of reducing the proportion – rather than the number – of people living in poverty.[25] Clearly, this is partly because reducing the *number* of people living in poverty is a more difficult target to achieve. Moreover, relatively high fertility and population growth in poor countries will continue to play a major role in contributing to the maintenance of very large numbers of people living in poverty.

The fact that the demographic transition is at very different stages in different world regions will certainly cause changes in the regional composition of humanity. And it will also condition patterns of international migration. In the future, as in the past, societies going through the transition are likely to exhibit an increased tendency to export their people – as a result of the pressures brought about by population growth. Moreover, because of the population growth that results from the continuing transition there will be a tendency for the number of people in most types of migration stream to rise. In general, the occurrence of the demographic transition tends to stimulate migration.

Lastly, a word is required about the transition's consequences for the global environment. The period since about 1800 has been termed the 'Anthropocene' because of the huge impact which people have had on the world's environment (see Crutzen and Stoermer 2000). The massive rise in $CO_2$ and other greenhouse gas emissions is especially important here – because it threatens calamitous climate change. In simple terms, it's a question of both what we do, and how many of us there are. Population growth has played – and it will continue to play – a significant underlying role in this connection. Again, however, the *context* is important. Thus, if the population of North America grows substantially in the coming decades – as is generally expected – then, other things equal, this will have a large effect in raising global emissions. However, the effect of rapid population growth in sub-Saharan Africa, for example, will be small in terms of increased emissions (Dyson 2005).

That said, and partly because of population growth, there is little chance that the world's emissions of greenhouse gases will be reduced in the next few decades – despite all the palaver. Indeed, there are reasons to think that total emissions will rise. Relatedly, there is an unknown but significant chance that humanity will face some form of serious climate change later in this century or the next. Should this happen, then past experience may be a poor guide with which to assess future mortality trends. Should this happen, then other things will not be equal.

In relation to this, and many other issues, an appreciation of aggregate demographic trends is helpful. Therefore it is to the world population situation – within the context of the transition – that we now turn.

# 3 · World population and the transition

We live in an age of remarkable demographic diversity and change – so much so that it can be difficult to keep abreast of every significant development (and that is certainly not the intention here). Nevertheless, an appreciation of the broad facts relating to the world's population – past, present and future – is important in itself, and it provides background for what follows.

This chapter focuses on population trends and characteristics at both the world and world regional levels. The growth of the human population over the past two or three centuries has been a direct consequence of the demographic transition. Moreover, current demographic variation between different parts of the world can only really be understood within the context of the transition. The chapter uses population estimates and projections made by the United Nations. And it introduces some basic concepts and measures (for further details, see the Glossary). With reference to circumstances around the year 2010, the chapter also provides examples of countries that are in very different positions with respect to the transition.[1]

The chapter begins by considering the past growth of the world's population. It then examines present demographic variation between the world's main regions. This is followed by a short consideration of projected future trends. The chapter ends with a brief summary and discussion.

## Past growth of the world's population

If the word 'population' has meant one thing in the study of population and development during the period since 1945 – i.e. the end of the Second World War, when the modern era of 'development' really began – then that one thing has been population *growth*. The reason is that there has been extraordinary population growth – most of it occurring in the so-called 'developing' world. This growth is best considered in long-run perspective.

*The growth in human numbers* Figure 3.1 plots growth in the world's population over the last two thousand years. Although estimates of the size of the population in the distant past are very rough, the basic picture shown is certainly correct. This is because the changes indicated for more recent times have been so enormous as to dwarf any inaccuracies in the estimates for earlier periods (Brass 1970).

For most of human history the world's population has grown very slowly indeed. The world's death rate was certainly very high. Therefore, on average, the birth rate must have been just a tiny bit higher.[2] The result was that, on average, an adult couple were only just about able to replace themselves – in the sense of two of their children managing to survive into adulthood to become potential parents themselves.[3] This explains why the world's population grew so very slowly. Of course, if couples had *not* been able to replace themselves in this way, then the human population would have eventually dwindled away.

Starting from some time in the eighteenth century, however, there was a marked acceleration in the population growth rate of the world (see Figure 3.1). For example, using the estimates compiled by Maddison (2007), the average rate of population growth between the year 1 and the year 1700 was only about 0.06 per cent per year – i.e. a rate that was

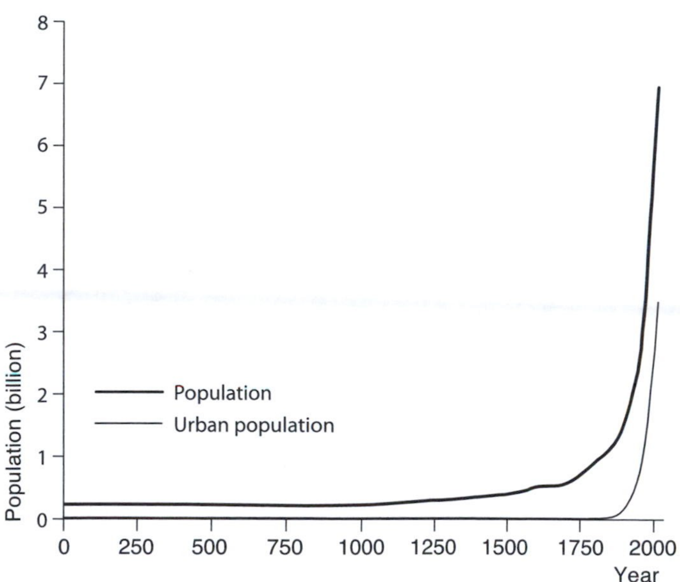


*Principal sources*: Grauman (1977), Maddison (2009), United Nations (2008, 2009)

**Figure 3.1 World population and urban growth over two millennia – the recent influence of the demographic transition**

TABLE 3.1 Summary of world population estimates, 1800–2010

| Year/ period | Population (million) | Growth rate (% per year) | Increment per decade (million) | Death rate | Birth rate | Life expectancy (years) | Total fertility (births per woman) | Median age (years) | % urban |
|---|---|---|---|---|---|---|---|---|---|
| 1800 | 954 | – | – | – | – | – | – | 24.7 | 5.3 |
| 1900 | 1,650 | 0.6 | 70 | 40.3 | 46.0 | 25.0 | 5.7 | 24.3 | 13.6 |
| 1950 | 2,529 | 0.9 | 185 | 34.1 | 43.3 | 30.0 | 5.5 | 24.0 | 29.1 |
| 1960 | 3,023 | 1.8 | 494 | 18.4 | 36.3 | 48.1 | 4.9 | 23.2 | 32.9 |
| 1970 | 3,686 | 2.0 | 663 | 14.4 | 34.2 | 54.3 | 4.8 | 22.1 | 36.0 |
| 1980 | 4,438 | 1.9 | 752 | 11.1 | 29.6 | 59.2 | 4.1 | 23.0 | 39.1 |
| 1990 | 5,290 | 1.8 | 852 | 10.0 | 27.6 | 62.5 | 3.5 | 24.4 | 43.0 |
| 2000 | 6,115 | 1.4 | 825 | 9.2 | 23.6 | 64.6 | 3.0 | 26.7 | 46.6 |
| 2010 | 6,910 | 1.2 | 795 | 8.5 | 20.7 | 67.0 | 2.6 | 29.1 | 50.6 |

*Notes*: All figures are approximate. The population, per cent urban and median age figures are for the exact years shown. The remaining figures are averages for the preceding *periods* (e.g. 1800–1900, 1900–50, 1950–60, etc.). Thus the death rate for the 1950s of 18.4 is shown on the 1960 line. See the Glossary for information on technical terms. The death rates and birth rates are expressed per thousand population. For the world, the population growth rate is the birth rate minus the death rate, and it is expressed as a percentage.

*Sources*: Figures for before 1950 are derived from Biraben (1979), Hauser (1971) and Grauman (1977). Figures for 1950 and later are from the United Nations (2008, 2009).

positive, but close to zero. But between 1700 and 1800 the growth rate was appreciably higher, at around 0.46 per cent per year.[4]

It is thought that there were roughly 770 million people alive in 1750, and that the population reached 1 billion very early in the nineteenth century (Biraben 1979). There appears to have been a further modest increase in the rate of population growth during the nineteenth century. But it took over a century for the world's population to arrive at 2 billion – which it did around 1930.

Table 3.1 provides estimates of past trends relating to the world's population. We know that there were about 2.5 billion people in 1950. Then, in the space of just sixty years, an *additional* 4.4 billion people were added – taking the total to around 6.9 billion by 2010. This implies an average annual growth rate of about 1.7 per cent per year. The remarkable increase between 1950 and 2010 amounts to the addition of an extra billion people every fourteen years. This addition represents 'natural increase', i.e. the surplus of births over deaths. In terms of the timescale used in Figure 3.1, the recent growth of the human population has been almost vertical.

Notice from Figure 3.1 that growth of the world's urban population has been strongly related to the expansion of the total population. Moreover, the world is urbanizing. That is, the proportion of humanity living in urban areas has risen, and is continuing to rise. It has been estimated that only about 5 per cent of the world's population lived in towns and cities in 1800, but by 1900 the figure had increased to around 14 per cent (Grauman 1977). The estimates of the United Nations suggest that by 2010 the proportion had reached nearly 51 per cent (see Table 3.1). In recent times the urban population growth curve in Figure 3.1 is actually steeper than the total population curve. Thus whereas between 1950 and 2010 the world's population grew at an annual rate of 1.7 per cent, the urban population grew at 2.6 per cent.

*Explaining the growth in numbers* The unprecedented increase in the size of the human population over the past two or three centuries is the direct result of the demographic transition. The key change in this context has been the fall in the world's death rate. The fall in the death rate has occurred because of mortality decline – a process which is often represented in terms of an increase in life expectancy at birth (LEB).

Table 3.1 indicates that during the period 1800–1900 the world's death rate was slightly lower than the birth rate. The estimates for this period are especially rough. Nevertheless, the birth rate is thought to have been in the vicinity of 46 births per thousand population per year, while the death rate was about 40 per thousand. Therefore, the world's population was growing at an average annual rate of about 0.6 per cent per year, i.e. (46–40)/10. Life expectancy is believed to have averaged around 25 years during this time. This figure is extremely low by modern standards, but it may have represented a slight improvement in world mortality compared to earlier periods.

Average life expectancy during 1900–50 is thought to have been about 30 years, and the world's death rate had fallen to about 34 deaths per thousand population. With an average birth rate of perhaps 43 per thousand, the world's population grew at around 0.9 per cent per year during the first half of the twentieth century (see Table 3.1).

Following the Second World War, the late 1940s and early 1950s were a period of very considerable mortality decline (i.e. improvement). This was particularly true in the world's so-called 'developing' regions – i.e. essentially Latin America, Africa and Asia (with the exception of Japan). This was when the modern phenomenon of rapid population growth – conventionally taken as being growth at an annual rate of 2.0 per cent per year or more – began to occur in many developing countries.

Table 3.1 shows that by the 1950s the average level of life expectancy in the world had risen to around 48 years. The death rate was about 18 per thousand – a figure roughly half that of the first half of the twentieth century. As a result, in the 1950s the population grew at about 1.8 per cent per year – double the rate of the first half of the century. Table 3.1 shows that mortality has continued to decline in subsequent decades. Life expectancy is estimated to have reached 54 years in the 1960s, with a corresponding death rate of around 14 per thousand. The world's population growth rate peaked at about 2 per cent per year during the 1960s. It is estimated that in the first decade of this century (i.e. 2000–10) average life expectancy was in the vicinity of 67 years, with a corresponding death rate of around 8.5 per thousand (see Table 3.1).

However, while there was a major reduction in the world's death rate – especially, but not only, in the decades immediately following the Second World War – the birth rate initially fell at a much slower pace. The main reason for this was that the world's total fertility rate (TFR) remained at a comparatively high level. Thus Table 3.1 shows that during the nineteenth century women had an average of about 5.7 births each. But even as late as the 1950s and 1960s the level of total fertility was still nearly 5 births per woman, with a corresponding birth rate of around 34–36. Inasmuch as there had been a fall in the world's birth rate by the 1960s, it had happened mostly because of the major fertility declines that had occurred by then in the world's more developed regions – i.e. essentially Europe, North America, Australia/ New Zealand and Japan. It was not until the 1970s that the average level of total fertility per woman in the developing regions began to fall at an appreciable pace – so bringing about a really significant decline in the global level of total fertility. By 2000–10 the world's TFR had fallen to about 2.6 births per woman – approximately half the level of the 1950s and 1960s. Related to this, the world's birth rate had declined to around 21 per thousand by 2000–10 (see Table 3.1).

The fall in total fertility per woman that has occurred in recent decades, however, has not been matched by an equal fall in the birth rate. For example, compared to the 1960s, the total fertility rate had fallen by 46 per cent by 2000–10, whereas the birth rate had fallen by only 40 per cent. The explanation is that the birth rate depends upon the age structure of the population, as well as the level of total fertility. In this context, the age structure of the world's population has been, and remains, fairly young. Thus in 1970 the median (i.e. central) age of humanity was about 22 years (see Table 3.1). This young age structure has meant that falls in total fertility per woman have been partly offset by rises in the number of women coming into the reproductive (i.e. childbearing) ages.[5] And this has acted to slow the fall in the world's birth rate (see below).

Also note from Table 3.1 that although the world's age structure is still quite young, it is nevertheless getting older. Thus in 2010 the median age of humanity had risen to about 29 years. This process of 'population ageing' has happened – and is happening – because of the fall in fertility. And population ageing helps to explain why the world's death rate has fallen only slightly in recent decades (e.g. from about 11 per thousand in the 1970s to 8.5 during 2000–10). In fact, world mortality has continued to improve – recall that average life expectancy had risen to 67 years by 2000–10. But a population's death rate is also influenced by its age structure. And, in general, older people tend to die at higher rates than younger people. The relative constancy of the death rate in recent decades shown in Table 3.1 reflects the fact that, although mortality is continuing to decline (i.e. life expectancy is rising), the composition of the world's population is getting older.

A final comment in this connection is that, of course, if the world's death rate is roughly constant, and the birth rate is falling, then the rate of population growth must be falling as well. Table 3.1 shows that this is indeed the case. By 2000–10 the population growth rate had fallen to about 1.2 per cent per year.

In summary, until the 1960s the world's death rate fell faster than the birth rate, with the result that the population growth rate increased. Starting from the 1970s, however, the birth rate fell faster than the death rate, with the result that the rate of population growth has decreased. That said, it is important to note that while the *percentage* rate of growth peaked in the 1960s at about 2 per cent per year, the *absolute* addition to the world's population peaked during the 1980s – when approximately 852 million people were added to the global population. These numbers underscore a simple but important point – namely, that both the percentage and the absolute changes should be kept in mind when considering population growth. The decade 2000–10 will see the addition of roughly 800 million people (see Table 3.1).

*The historical and contemporary transitions* The world population trends discussed above reflect the confluence of two broadly distinct demographic transitions. The rise in the rate of population growth during the eighteenth and nineteenth centuries largely reflects the onset of the historical demographic transitions in the countries of the world's more developed regions. And the population growth that has occurred during the twentieth century has largely been due to the contemporary transitions that are still under way in the rest of the world.

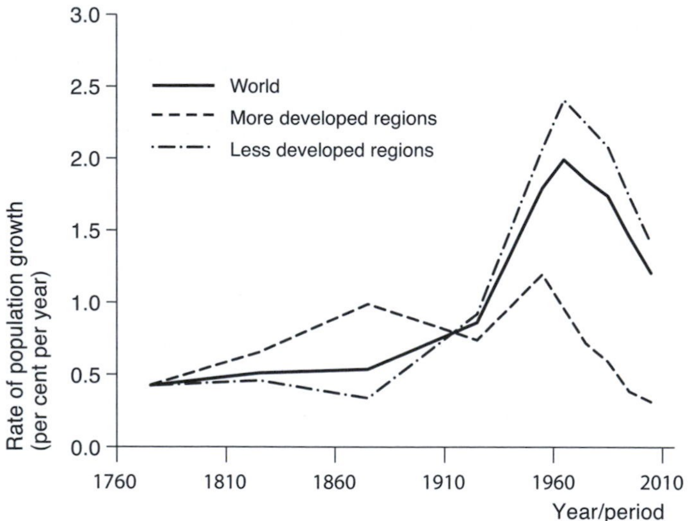


*Note*: The growth rates for before 1950 are for periods of fifty years; the rates for after 1950 are for periods of ten years.

*Principal sources*: Brass (1970), Maddison (2009), United Nations (2009)

**Figure 3.2 Population growth rates for the world and its more and less developed regions since the eighteenth century**

In this context Figure 3.2 compares population growth rates for the countries of the world's developed and developing regions since the second half of the eighteenth century. It shows that the average growth rate of the developed countries increased in the nineteenth century. It fluctuated during the twentieth century – due partly to the influence of the two world wars – and it then fell fairly sharply during the second half of the twentieth century. Notice that the population growth rate for the developed countries never went much higher than 1.0 per cent per year, and that by 2000–10 it had fallen back to roughly the level of the late eighteenth century.

In contrast, the average population growth rate of the developing regions began to increase from the decades around 1900.[6] It rose sharply in the middle decades of the twentieth century, and stayed above 2.0 per cent per year between 1950 and 1990. The growth rate has been falling since about 1970, although it remains at a comparatively high level. And because the developing regions contain most of humanity – about 82 per cent in 2010 – it is trends in these regions

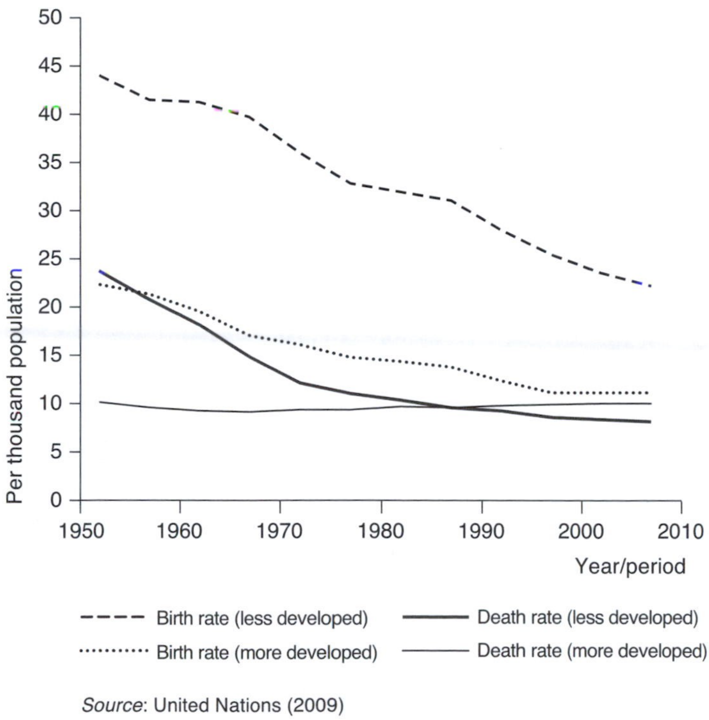


*Source*: United Nations (2009)

**Figure 3.3 Crude death and birth rates for the world's more and less developed regions, 1950–2010**

TABLE 3.2 Demographic estimates for the world's regions around the year 2010, with projections to 2050

| Region | Population (million) | Growth rate (% per year) | Death rate | Birth rate | Life expectancy (years) | Total fertility (per woman) | Median age (years) | % urban | Projected population (million) | |
|---|---|---|---|---|---|---|---|---|---|---|
| | 2010 | 2005–10 | 2005–10 | 2005–10 | 2005–10 | 2005–10 | 2010 | 2010 | 2030 | 2050 |
| Sub-Saharan Africa | 820 | 2.4 | 13.9 | 38.6 | 51.5 | 5.1 | 18.6 | 37.3 | 1,247 | 1,677 |
| Middle East | 446 | 1.8 | 6.1 | 24.2 | 69.5 | 2.9 | 24.6 | 59.1 | 589 | 693 |
| South-Central Asia | 1,780 | 1.5 | 8.1 | 23.7 | 64.0 | 2.8 | 24.5 | 32.2 | 2,232 | 2,495 |
| South-East Asia | 590 | 1.2 | 6.5 | 19.4 | 70.0 | 2.3 | 27.8 | 48.2 | 706 | 766 |
| East Asia | 1,564 | 0.6 | 7.2 | 13.0 | 74.1 | 1.7 | 35.2 | 48.5 | 1,666 | 1,600 |
| Latin America | 589 | 1.1 | 6.0 | 19.0 | 73.4 | 2.3 | 27.7 | 79.4 | 690 | 729 |
| North America | 352 | 1.0 | 7.8 | 13.8 | 79.3 | 2.0 | 36.9 | 82.1 | 410 | 448 |
| Oceania | 36 | 1.3 | 7.0 | 17.4 | 76.4 | 2.4 | 33.0 | 70.6 | 45 | 51 |
| Europe | 733 | 0.1 | 11.4 | 10.5 | 75.1 | 1.5 | 40.2 | 72.6 | 723 | 691 |
| World | 6,910 | 1.2 | 8.6 | 20.3 | 67.6 | 2.6 | 29.1 | 50.6 | 8,308 | 9,150 |

*Notes*: Here the Middle East refers to the countries of North Africa (including Sudan) and West Asia; Latin America is inclusive of the Caribbean. The growth rates include the effects of migration. See also the notes to Table 3.1.

*Sources*: United Nations (2008, 2009)

which have dominated changes at the global level, especially in recent decades (see Figure 3.2).

Lastly in this section, Figure 3.3 compares death rates and birth rates for the countries of the developed and developing regions over the period 1950–2010. In the developed regions the birth rate has fallen to almost the level of the death rate. Therefore, migration aside, a long period of population growth that stretches back into the late eighteenth century has effectively come to an end. In contrast, in the developing regions the average birth rate remains appreciably higher than the death rate.[7] As a result, there is still considerable natural increase – although the rate of natural increase (i.e. the *gap* between the birth rate and the death rate) is now diminishing with time. This brings us to a consideration of contemporary demographic variation at the regional level.

## Contemporary demographic variation

Table 3.2 presents United Nations demographic estimates for the world's major geographical regions around the year 2010. Clearly, there is considerable demographic variation within most of the regions. Broadly speaking, however, the first six regions can be regarded as developing while the remaining regions are developed.[8] The order in which the regions are listed corresponds roughly to the degree to which they have progressed through the demographic transition – starting with sub-Saharan Africa, which has seen least progress. The following discussion draws on UN estimates for the period since 1950. But it is important to emphasize that all regions, and almost all countries, had experienced some mortality decline before 1950 – although to varying degrees.

*Sub-Saharan Africa* Sub-Saharan Africa contained about 820 million people in 2010 – i.e. around 12 per cent of the world total. The most populous countries were Nigeria (with an estimated 158 million), Ethiopia (85 million), Democratic Republic of Congo (69 million), South Africa (51 million), Tanzania (45 million) and Kenya (41 million). Average life expectancy for the region during 2005–10 was about 51 years – a figure that had been more or less constant during the previous two decades, owing mainly to the HIV/AIDS epidemic. However, while this new infectious disease has caused big falls in life expectancy in some countries – especially in southern Africa – in many others its spread has been limited, and therefore mortality has continued to improve (i.e. life expectancy has continued to rise). The net effect for the region as a whole has been a stagnation in the level of mortality, rather than a reversal. Moreover, even a life expectancy of 51 years represents a big improvement compared to earlier times.

Sub-Saharan Africa is probably the region to which the phenomenon of mortality decline came last. The death rate of about 14 per thousand during 2005–10 was much higher than for any other developing region, and a similar statement applies to the birth rate. That said, the level of total fertility began to fall from around the 1990s, and in 2005–10 it was about 5 births per woman (compared to a figure above 6 during the 1980s and before). High fertility, of course, produces a young age structure – in 2010 the median age of the region's population was approximately 19 years (i.e. about half the population was aged less than 19). The high birth rate – of about 39 per thousand – underpinned the region's rapid rate of population growth of 2.4 per cent per year during 2005–10. Finally, Table 3.2 shows that about 37 per cent of the region's people lived in urban areas in 2010.

*The Middle East* The Middle East – taken here as comprising the countries of North Africa and West Asia – had a population of about 446 million in 2010, i.e. about 6 per cent of the global total. The most populous countries were Egypt (84 million), Turkey (76 million) and Sudan (43 million). This region has experienced considerable mortality decline. Thus in 1950–55 average life expectancy was about 43 years, but by 2005–10 it had increased to about 69. The region as a whole has experienced a significant fall in fertility – especially since the early 1980s. In 1950–55 total fertility was about 6.6 births, but it is estimated to have fallen to approximately 2.9 by 2005–10. Nevertheless, the fact that fertility was high until the 1980s means that the region's population was still reasonably young in 2010 – the median age being around 25 years. In 2005–10 a fairly high birth rate of 24 per thousand, and a low death rate of 6, combined to produce a relatively high rate of population growth of 1.8 per cent per year. However, the growth rate is falling because the birth rate is falling and, with a fairly young population, the region's death rate is so low that it cannot fall much further. Table 3.2 shows that the Middle East is a fairly urbanized region. In 2010 about 59 per cent of the population lived in urban areas – up from 27 per cent in 1950.

*South-Central Asia* South-Central Asia contained about a quarter of the world's population in 2010. This region consists mainly of countries in the Indian subcontinent. India's population alone was in the vicinity of 1.21 billion. Pakistan (185 million), Bangladesh (164 million) and Iran (75 million) are the region's other major countries. South-Central

Asia has also experienced considerable mortality decline. Average life expectancy in the early 1950s was around 39 years – itself representing a substantial improvement compared to earlier times. By 2005–10 life expectancy had risen to approximately 64 years. There has also been a significant decline in fertility – which was close to 6 births per woman in the late 1960s. By 2005–10, however, total fertility had roughly halved – to about 2.8 births. As in most developing regions, early in the present century the death rate is more or less constant, while the birth rate is falling. Therefore, the rate of population growth is falling as well. During 2005–10 a birth rate of about 23 and a death rate of 8 produced a population growth rate of around 1.5 per cent per year. Again, the region's age structure in 2010 was still quite young – the median age being about 25 years. As elsewhere, however, declining fertility means that the population is steadily getting older. Lastly, the estimated level of urbanization is the lowest of any region in Table 3.2. The figure of 32 per cent is, however, certainly influenced downwards by the particular way in which settlements in India are classed as urban.[9]

*South-East Asia* The population of South-East Asia was around 590 million in 2010 – i.e. approximately 9 per cent of the world total. Indonesia (233 million), the Philippines (94 million) and Vietnam (89 million) were the most populous countries. This region is even more advanced in demographic terms. Thus during 2005–10 life expectancy was about 70 years (compared to 41 in 1950–55). Total fertility fell from about 6 births per woman in the early 1950s to around 2.3 births during 2005–10 – a decline which really gained pace in the 1970s. In conditions of low (i.e. favourable) mortality, a TFR of 2.3 is only slightly higher than the replacement level – which in modern circumstances is often approximated by the figure of 2.1 births per woman.[10] With a birth rate of about 19 and a death rate of 7, South-East Asia's population was growing at about 1.2 per cent per year during 2005–10 – although, again, this growth rate is falling. Around 48 per cent of the population was classed as living in urban areas in 2010 (Table 3.2).

*East Asia* In 2010 the population of East Asia was about 1.56 billion – i.e. 23 per cent of humanity. China was the world's most populous country, with 1.35 billion people. China comprised 87 per cent of the region's population, and Japan (127 million) an additional 8 per cent. This region is even further advanced in demographic terms. Thus during 2005–10 average life expectancy and total fertility were estimated at about 74 years and 1.7 births respectively. Clearly, these figures largely reflect conditions in China. In 1950–55 China's life expectancy and total fertility rate were about 40 years and 6.2 births. The country made great progress in reducing mortality from the early 1950s onwards, but the level of fertility remained high. Then, in the 1970s, the Chinese government introduced *very* strong measures to reduce fertility – and, as a result, the TFR fell from about 6 births in 1969 to just over 2 in 1980 (State Statistical Bureau of the People's Republic of China 2000). During 2005–10 fertility in China, and therefore East Asia as a whole, was well below the replacement level. Because of the influence of age structure, however, the birth rate was still higher than the death rate. The estimates in Table 3.2 suggest that the region's population was growing at about 0.6 per cent per year during 2005–10. But, again, this growth rate is falling, and the population is also getting older at a fast pace – reflecting its earlier fast fertility decline. By 2010 the median age was already as high as 35 years, and about 48 per cent of the population was residing in urban areas.

The two main countries of East Asia are particularly interesting in terms of the demographic transition. Thus, outside of Europe and North America, Japan was the first major society to experience the phenomenon. And few countries today are more demographically advanced than Japan. In addition, China represents a remarkably rapid example of the transition – especially given its enormous size.

*Latin America* Latin America (including the Caribbean) had a population of about 589 million in 2010 – around 9 per cent of the global total. Together, Brazil (195 million) and Mexico (111 million) contained about half of the population. Latin America is also relatively advanced in demographic terms. In 2005–10 average life expectancy was around 73 years (compared to 51 in 1950–55) and total fertility was about 2.3 births (compared to 5.9 in 1950–55). The region's death and birth rates in 2005–10 were estimated at 6 and 19 per thousand respectively. In fact, some countries – notably Chile and Argentina – began to experience mortality decline from late in the nineteenth century, and this helps to explain the region's comparative advancement. In terms of fertility decline, however, Latin America has clearly been overtaken by East Asia. Nevertheless, as Table 3.2 shows, Latin America has a very high level of urbanization – about 79 per cent in 2010. This may partly reflect the fact that some countries classify very small settlements as 'urban'. Nevertheless, there is no doubt that the region's population is predominantly urban. This brings us to a consideration of the world's more developed regions.

*North America* There were about 352 million people in North America in 2010 – most of them in the United States (318 million) with the rest in Canada (34 million). This region contained about 5 per cent of humanity. At 79 years in 2005–10, life expectancy was the highest of any region. And at 2.0 births per woman, total fertility was marginally below the replacement level. The median age of the population was high, at about 37 years. And the level of urbanization was very high, at 82 per cent. It is worth emphasizing that, even in such an advanced region, both mortality and fertility have tended to decline during recent decades. For example, in the early 1950s life expectancy in North America was about 69 years, and total fertility was slightly above 3 births per woman. Notice that during 2005–10 the region's birth rate was higher than the death rate. Together these two vital rates imply an annual rate of natural increase of about 0.6 per cent. The population growth rate shown in Table 3.2, however, is significantly greater than this – at 1.0 per cent. The difference between these two rates (i.e. +0.4) is explained by substantial migration into North America.

*Oceania* Oceania's population is tiny in global terms. The region includes a lot of small developing island nations. But Australia (22 million) and New Zealand (4 million) contained about 72 per cent of the population in 2010. It will suffice to say here that the demographic characteristics of these two countries are broadly similar to those of the United States and Canada. Indeed, in what follows these four countries constitute what are referred to as the main European 'offshoot' populations. And a relatively high proportion of their population growth has come from migration.

*Europe* This brings us finally to Europe, which had a population of about 733 million in 2010, i.e. roughly 11 per cent of humanity. The most populous countries were Russia (140 million), Germany (82 million), France (63 million) and the United Kingdom (62 million). Life expectancy averaged about 75 years in 2005–10, and total fertility was exceptionally low at around 1.5 births. A history of relatively low fertility means that Europe's population is exceptionally old – the median age was approximately 40 years in 2010. The continent's old – and still ageing – population does much to explain its comparatively high death rate of about 11 per thousand in 2005–10. Note from Table 3.2 that this death rate was almost as high as that prevailing in sub-Saharan Africa (13.9 per thousand), although, of course, the levels of mortality in these two regions – as gauged by life expectancy – were very different. Note too that in 2005–10 Europe's death rate was slightly higher than its birth rate – implying negative natural increase of about –0.1 per cent per year. Because of a modest amount of in-migration, however, the region's population growth rate was slightly positive.

*Discussion* These regional sketches provide only a flavour of contemporary demographic variation. Although they have been framed in relation to the year 2010, the broad relative picture should remain fresh for a considerable period.

As noted, as one moves downwards in Table 3.2 so, in general, life expectancy rises, total fertility falls, and the population growth rate declines. Also, the populations tend to become both older and more urban in their composition. To a considerable degree, the differences between regions reflect differences in the timing of their experience of the demographic transition. Thus it is fair to say that the transition came last to sub-Saharan Africa; and Europe and North America were the first to experience the phenomenon.

Notice that differences in population growth rates between the regions are largely explained by differences in the *birth rates* rather than in the death rates. Thus the range of variation in the birth rates in Table 3.2 is some 28 points (i.e. 38.6 – 10.5) whereas the range of variation in the death rates is only about 8 points (i.e. 13.9 – 6.0). Therefore, it is birth-rate variation which accounts for most of the variation in contemporary rates of natural increase, and therefore rates of population growth.

It is difficult to say exactly when a population has completed going through the demographic transition – because its completion can be defined with respect to several different characteristics.[11] The first six regions in Table 3.2, however, are certainly still experiencing the transition in various ways. In particular, they are all experiencing natural increase (i.e. higher birth rates than death rates), although only to a modest degree in East Asia. The level of fertility is also declining in these regions, again with the exception of East Asia, where fertility is already very low. The populations of all six regions are steadily getting older. Furthermore, these regions – including Latin America – are still experiencing urbanization. Indeed, to the extent that there are anomalies in relation to the relative levels of urbanization in Table 3.2, they are partly explained by differences of classification.[12]

In contrast, however, Europe, North America and Australia/New Zealand within Oceania have really completed the demographic transition. Thus these populations have low death and birth rates compared to pre-transitional conditions. They have low levels of mortality and fertility. They are fairly old and highly urbanized. Also, the fact that they have low and roughly equal death and birth rates means that international migration can influence the rate of population growth to a considerable extent. Indeed, through such migration, the populations of these regions are growing partly from the natural increase generated by demographic transitions under way elsewhere in the world.

We have seen that world population growth and urban growth have been strongly related in time (see Figure 3.1). It is also worth noting that differences in population growth rates between regions exert a strong influence on differences in how fast their urban populations are growing. Thus in 2005–10 sub-Saharan Africa's population was growing at the fastest annual rate, and this region also had the fastest urban population growth rate of 3.7 per cent per year. At the other end of the scale, North America and Europe had the slowest rates of population growth, and they also experienced the slowest rates of urban growth – at 1.3 and 0.2 per cent respectively during 2005–10 (United Nations 2008).

Despite its poor relative position, it is worth emphasizing that sub-Saharan Africa is some way into its demographic transition. There has been considerable mortality decline. Indeed, for this developing region – as for the others – there was almost certainly significant mortality improvement before 1950 (recall that pre-transitional life expectancy for the world as a whole appears to have been as low as 25 years – see Table 3.1). Although mortality decline in sub-Saharan Africa has recently been interrupted by HIV/AIDS, the UN estimates that, starting from around 2005–10, the process of mortality decline has resumed. Also, fertility decline is now occurring in sub-Saharan Africa, and therefore there are the first tentative signs of population ageing. The region is also urbanizing.

Finally in this discussion, these regional sketches point to some important factors which can intervene to complicate – either delay or accelerate – the main processes of the demographic transition. Thus, clearly, HIV/AIDS had a delaying effect in relation to mortality decline in sub-Saharan Africa. And China's experience during 1970–79 provides a striking example of how government intervention accelerated the process of fertility decline.

*Country examples* Figure 3.4 illustrates contemporary demographic variation using data for six countries with a combined population of 1 billion in 2010. To facilitate comparison, the age distributions are all expressed in percentage terms. The rough pairing of countries

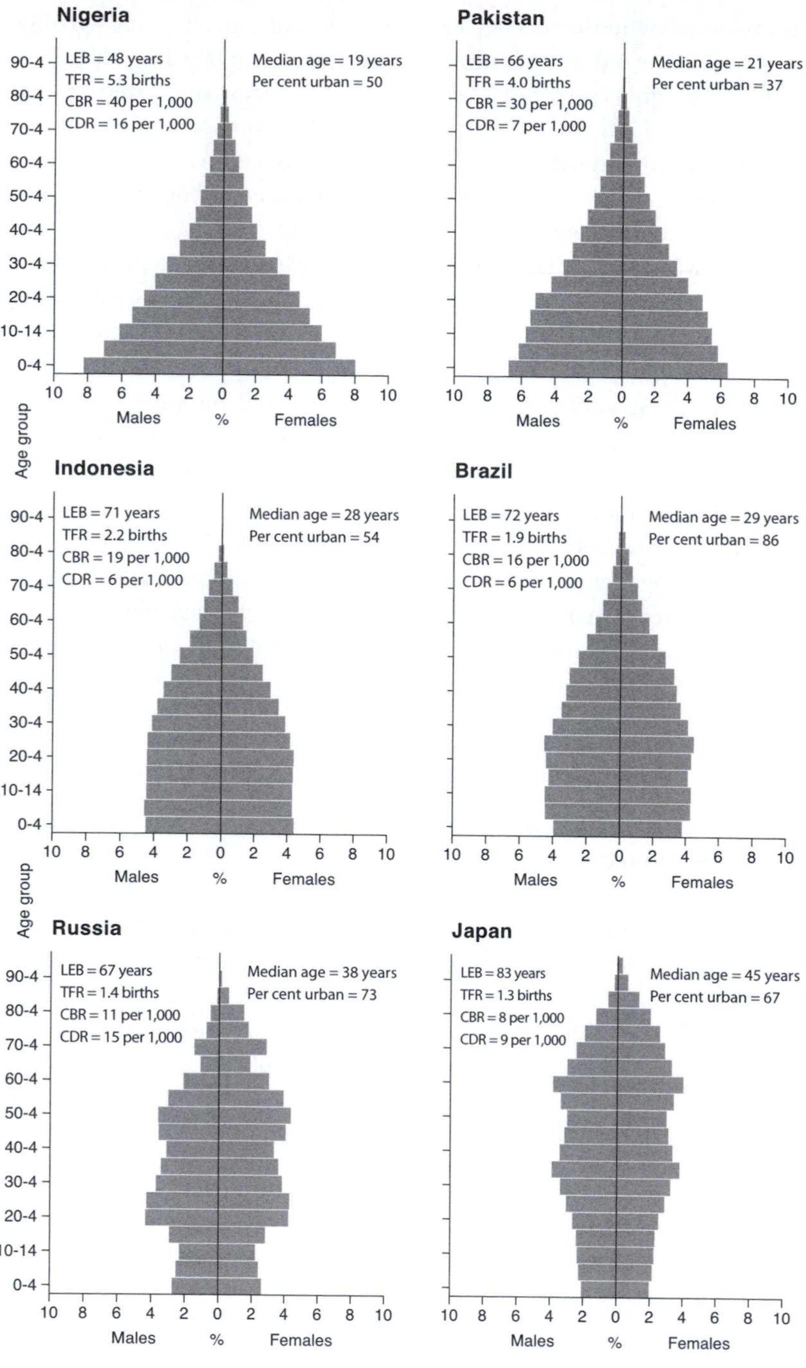


*Sources*: United Nations (2008, 2009)

**Figure 3.4 Percentage age distributions, and associated demographic estimates, selected countries around 2010**

underscores the fact that, in terms of the transition, there can be broad similarities between populations in different regions – just as there are differences between countries within the same region.

Nigeria is the least developed of these countries in demographic terms. According to the United Nations, life expectancy at birth (LEB) rose from around 36 years in the early 1950s to reach about 48 years in 2005–10. As in most countries, the average level of life expectancy which prevailed before the demographic transition is unknown. There is little doubt, however, that it was lower than 36 years. Therefore Nigeria has experienced substantial mortality decline, although at a slow pace. The total fertility rate (TFR) remained around 7 births per woman until the late 1980s, but it has fallen somewhat since – reaching about 5.3 births in 2005–10. This history of high fertility (and falling mortality) produces a very young age structure. Thus in 2010 the median age of the population was about 19 years, and 42 per cent of the population was aged under 15. In turn, this young age structure means that the number of women coming into the reproductive ages in the coming decades is certain to grow greatly (see below). Put differently: Nigeria's age structure embodies considerable 'population momentum'. With a birth rate of about 40 per thousand and a death rate of 16, the population was growing at about 2.4 per cent per year during 2005–10.

Pakistan is somewhat more advanced in terms of the transition. Mortality has declined to a significantly greater extent than in Nigeria, and by 2005–10 life expectancy in Pakistan was around 66 years. There has also been a greater decline in fertility – with total fertility falling from over 6 births per woman in the late 1980s to about 4 during 2005–10. Nevertheless, the country's age structure is still fairly young. The median age was about 21 years in 2010, with around 37 per cent of the population being aged under 15. Therefore Pakistan's age structure also has a fair amount of momentum (although less than in Nigeria). In 2005–10 the death rate was around 7 per thousand and the birth rate was 30 – implying a rate of natural increase of about 2.3 per cent per year.

Indonesia and Brazil have both progressed appreciably further in terms of the demographic transition. Life expectancy in Indonesia in the early 1950s was about 37 years – i.e. a similar level of mortality to that which prevailed in Nigeria and Pakistan at that time. However, by 2005–10 Indonesia's life expectancy had increased to around 71 years. Life expectancy in Brazil in 2005–10 was similar – although in this case there was even more mortality decline before the early 1950s. Indonesia and Brazil have also experienced considerable fertility decline – with total fertility in 2005–10 being close to the replacement level in both countries. Notice from Figure 3.4 that by 2010 the age structures of these countries showed very clear evidence of fertility decline – with the proportion of the population aged 0–4 being similar to the proportion aged 20–24. In other words, the proportional age structures had 'drawn in' at the base to a considerable degree (especially in Brazil). The median ages of both populations had risen to about 28–29 years. Nevertheless, despite the attainment of low average levels of fertility per woman, the age structures of both countries meant that in 2005–10 the birth rates were still appreciably higher than the death rates, and both populations were growing at roughly 1 per cent per year – overwhelmingly due to a modest degree of population momentum.[13]

Lastly in Figure 3.4 there is the pairing of Russia and Japan. Both countries can be regarded as having passed through the demographic transition. Life expectancy in Russia in 2005–10 was only about 67 years. This relatively low figure (by current standards) reflects the difficult socio-economic conditions experienced both before and after the collapse of communism in 1990. Nevertheless, it represents a huge improvement compared to the pre-transitional situation. In Japan in 2005–10 life expectancy was about 83 years – an extremely high figure. Both of these countries experienced most of their fertility decline relatively early in the twentieth century. Indeed, Japan has experienced below-replacement fertility since the late 1970s. Russia's experience of this has been more recent – dating from around 1990. Both countries had *very* low TFRs during 2005–10. Not surprisingly, then, the age structures show the effect of sustained very low fertility – being severely drawn in at the base. In 2010 only about 13–15 per cent of these populations were aged under 15 years. In Russia about 13 per cent of the population was aged 65 years and over, while in Japan, with its very high life expectancy, the figure was 23 per cent.[14] Notice that in Japan the median age of the population had reached 45 years. Clearly, these countries have very old age structures. Both have low death rates and low birth rates. Indeed, in both countries there was negative natural increase during 2005–10 – particularly in Russia.

According to the UN estimates, all six countries in Figure 3.4 became significantly more urban between 1950 and 2010 (United Nations 2008). As noted, the level of urbanization partly reflects how areas are defined as 'urban' – and this may help to explain the exceptionally high level of urbanization indicated for Brazil. Even so, it is generally the case that the level of urbanization rises as one proceeds from pairing to pairing.

In summary, Figure 3.4 shows societies at very different stages of demographic transition. As before, in general in the comparisons made mortality improves, fertility declines, and the level of urbanization rises. But mortality decline begins before fertility decline. And the age structure of the population influences trends in both the birth rate and the death rate. Thus the essential contrast shown is between populations that in 2010 still had relatively high fertility, young age structures and were growing rapidly (i.e. Nigeria and Pakistan), and populations that had low fertility, old age structures and were diminishing in size (i.e. Russia and Japan, both *post*-transitional societies). Indonesia and Brazil were in intermediate positions, although nearer to the transition's end.

## Future demographic change

The preceding discussion is strongly suggestive of dynamic causal relationships which unfold through time. Partly as a result, in general terms, and other things equal, the issue of what will happen in the future can be addressed with a fair degree of confidence. The following discussion briefly explores future demographic change with reference to the world, regional and country levels.

*The global level* Table 3.3 summarizes the United Nations 'medium' variant (i.e. central) population projection for the world out to the year 2050. The life expectancy and total fertility rate figures shown are essentially assumptions – based on past experience – as to how fast mortality and fertility will decline in the future. Naturally, the further ahead one looks, the more uncertain the assumptions – and therefore the results of the projection – become. Nevertheless, it is very likely that the general trends revealed by the projection – e.g. in relation to the world's death and birth rates, the growth rate and the median age – will occur. Moreover, it is worth adding that the UN has a pretty good record of population projection at the global level.

The projection in Table 3.3 is essentially concerned with the latter reaches of the world demographic transition. It is envisaged that by mid-century (i.e. 2050) average life expectancy will have risen to about 75 years, and total fertility will have fallen to slightly below the replacement level. The world's death rate is unlikely to change much between 2010 and 2050 – indeed, with population ageing it may rise a little. The decline in total fertility produces significant population ageing – the median age of humanity increases by about nine years. Indeed, the projection suggests that between 2010 and 2050 there will be little change in the size of the population aged 0–14. Put differently: almost all of world population growth in the period to 2050 will occur at adult ages.[15] The decline in fertility also brings about a considerable reduction in the

TABLE 3.3 World population projections to 2050

| Year/ period | Population (million) | Growth rate (% per year) | Increment per decade (million) | Death rate | Birth rate | Life expectancy (years) | Total fertility (births per woman) | Median age (years) | % urban |
|---|---|---|---|---|---|---|---|---|---|
| 2000 | 6,115 | 1.4 | 825 | 9.2 | 23.6 | 64.6 | 3.0 | 26.7 | 46.6 |
| 2010 | 6,910 | 1.2 | 795 | 8.5 | 20.7 | 67.0 | 2.6 | 29.1 | 50.6 |
| 2020 | 7,675 | 1.1 | 765 | 8.3 | 18.8 | 69.4 | 2.4 | 31.5 | 54.9 |
| 2030 | 8,309 | 0.8 | 634 | 8.4 | 16.3 | 71.6 | 2.3 | 34.2 | 59.7 |
| 2040 | 8,801 | 0.6 | 492 | 9.0 | 14.7 | 73.5 | 2.1 | 36.6 | 64.7 |
| 2050 | 9,150 | 0.4 | 349 | 9.8 | 13.7 | 75.2 | 2.0 | 38.4 | 69.6 |

*Notes*: See also the notes to Table 3.1

*Sources*: United Nations (2008, 2009)

birth rate. On these assumptions, by the decade 2040–50 the world's death and birth rates are around 10 and 14 per thousand respectively, with a corresponding growth rate of about 0.4 per cent per year. The resulting natural increase of the human population during the same decade is put at about 350 million.

The projection suggests that the world's population will grow to almost 9.2 billion in 2050 (Table 3.3). This would represent a rise of nearly 50 per cent compared to the year 2000, and nearly 33 per cent compared to 2010. More speculative projections by the United Nations for the period beyond 2050 suggest that the human population may eventually peak at about 9.5 billion some time around the year 2075.[16] However, although the population may stop growing at about that time – i.e. the death and birth rates may become equal – the processes of population ageing and urbanization will probably still be occurring. Moreover, some populations are likely to be reducing in size, while others will still be expanding.

Although total fertility still has some way to fall in several regions – notably sub-Saharan Africa – much of the coming demographic growth for the world as a whole will be due to population momentum (i.e. the influence of age structure). Figure 3.5 sheds light on this using UN estimates and results from the medium variant projection (see also Merrick 1994). The total fertility rate (TFR) falls in the projection to 2.0 births per woman by 2050. But the *number* of women in the reproductive ages (i.e. those aged 15–49 years) increases throughout the period to 2050. This increase is essentially inevitable, because it arises largely from the world's *current* – still fairly young – age structure (i.e. that holding around 2010). As a result of these offsetting influences, the number of births occurring in the projection falls only slowly from decade to decade. In short, the rising number of women of childbearing age will act to slow the rate at which the world's birth rate falls.

Nevertheless, the speed at which the TFR declines in the future will-have a significant influence on how much the world's population will grow. In this context the UN makes alternative population projections. In the 'high' variant projection total fertility is assumed to be around 2.5 births per woman in the decade 2040–50. As a result, the population reaches 10.5 billion in 2050, and is still increasing at an annual rate of about 0.8 per cent at that time. In the 'low' variant projection total fertility falls to about 1.6 births in 2040–50. As a result, the world's population at mid-century is around 8.0 billion and beginning to decline in size.

The fact that even in the low projection – in which total fertility reaches

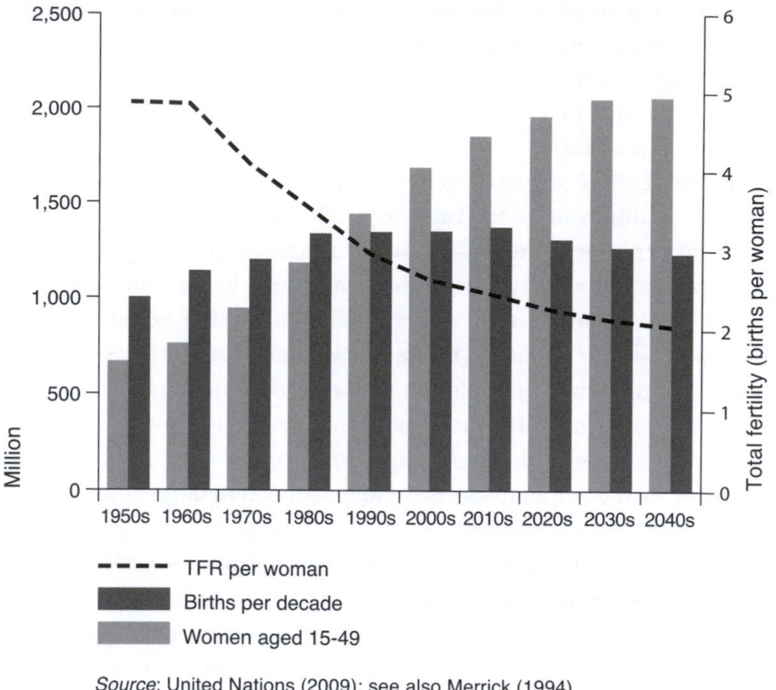


*Source*: United Nations (2009); see also Merrick (1994)

**Figure 3.5 Estimates and projections for the world of total fertility, the number of women of reproductive age, and the number of births, 1950–2050**

2.0 births as early as 2015–20 – the world's population still increases to peak at 8.0 billion underscores the large role that momentum will play in future population growth. The range of variation between the UN's high and low projections is almost entirely dependent upon the speed at which fertility falls in the developing regions of the world.

Table 3.3 indicates that there will be a steady rise in the level of urbanization. The projected figure of 69.6 per cent urban for 2050 should be regarded as especially rough. Nevertheless, when combined with the medium variant population total of 9.2 billion for mid-century it reflects an important likely fact – namely that the future growth of the world's population will either occur as a natural increase in the world's urban areas (where by 2010 half of humanity already lived) or it will end up living there – through migration from rural to urban areas. Therefore, the UN projections suggest that between 2010 and 2050 the size of the world's rural population will *fall* from about 3.4 billion to around 2.8 billion. But the world's urban population will rise from about

3.5 billion to 6.4 billion. To reiterate, at the global level either future natural increase will occur in urban areas or, through migration, those constituting it will end up living there. The absolute size of the world's rural population seems set to decline in the coming decades.

*The regional level* The UN medium variant population projections assume that mortality will continue to decline in all regions, and that fertility will continue to decline in all those regions where it is still above the replacement level. For populations where fertility is already very low it is assumed that there will be an *increase* in total fertility towards a figure of 1.85 births per woman. One consequence of these assumptions is that all regions will experience population ageing in the coming decades, although to differing degrees. Table 3.2 gives the projected regional population totals for 2030 and 2050.

Sub-Saharan Africa faces a future of considerable population growth. The high birth rate ensures this growth. Table 3.2 shows that this region's population is projected to roughly double in size between 2010 and 2050. Moreover, it is likely that even at mid-century the population will still be growing at an appreciable pace – for example, the UN's *low* variant projection puts the population growth rate for 2045–50 at 0.8 per cent per year. The Middle East will also experience considerable, though lesser, growth. The medium variant projection puts the population at about 693 million in 2050 – a rise of 247 million (i.e. 55 per cent) compared to 2010. The projection for South-Central Asia suggests a rise of about 715 million (i.e. 40 per cent). And for South-East Asia and Latin America the corresponding rises are 176 and 140 million (i.e. 30 and 24 per cent respectively). By 2050, however, natural increase in South-Central Asia, South-East Asia, and Latin America will be nearing its end.

East Asia is a particularly interesting case. The medium variant projection implies growth of only about 100 million between 2010 and 2030 (see Table 3.2). This is followed by a period of sustained population decline – reflecting the assumption that fertility will remain below the replacement level in China (as well as Japan). Moreover, the fact that China experienced a particularly rapid decline in fertility ensures that population ageing will happen at a particularly fast rate. By 2050 it is projected that half of East Asia's population will be aged 46 years or more. The different population trajectories envisaged for South-Central Asia and East Asia in Table 3.2 reflect the fact that, around the year 2025, India is expected to overtake China to become the world's most populous country.

The UN projections suggest that the populations of North America and Oceania will continue to increase at a fairly significant rate, partly because of immigration. North America's population is projected to grow by about 96 million between 2010 and 2050. In contrast, with lower fertility and a lower rate of immigration, Europe's population is projected to fall by about 42 million (i.e. 6 per cent) over the same period (see Table 3.2). This fall happens even though it is assumed that the level of fertility will rise somewhat in the future. Clearly, if this does not happen then the continent's population may decrease by more than 6 per cent. The medium variant projection suggests that by 2050 about half of Europe's population will be aged 47 years or more.

It is important to add a good dose of caution when considering these projections. After all, recent history provides a case (sub-Saharan Africa) where a region's mortality decline has been much slower than was generally anticipated, and a case (East Asia) where fertility decline occurred at an unexpectedly quick pace. Therefore, looking at the period to 2050, we might expect that there will be other instances where a region's experience deviates significantly from the assumptions contained in the projections. Also, future trends in migration are especially difficult to foresee – and this could be important, for example in relation to Europe's anticipated population decline.[17]

Nevertheless, and despite these caveats, the *broad* relative picture revealed by these projections will almost certainly turn out to be correct. Thus sub-Saharan Africa will experience very considerable growth. There will be significant – though lesser – population growth in most of the other developing regions. Demographic growth in East Asia, however, is probably nearing its end. With their long histories of immigration, the populations of North America and Oceania are likely to continue to expand. Europe's demographic future is certainly one of little growth, or even significant decline. Moreover, different population growth rates between different regions mean that the composition of humanity is changing. For example, whereas in 1950 Europe's population was around 22 per cent of the world total, by 2050 it is projected to comprise about 8 per cent (see Table 3.2).

Finally, the UN projects that urbanization will continue to occur in all regions (United Nations 2008). In most regions it is envisaged that by 2050 the absolute size of the rural population will be appreciably smaller than it was in 2010. The main exception to this is sub-Saharan Africa – where there is likely to be a significant further rise in the size of the rural population. Even in sub-Saharan Africa, however, most of the projected population growth is expected to be living in the urban sector in 2050.

*Country examples* Returning to the six countries addressed in Figure 3.4, the UN medium variant projections suggest that between 2010 and 2050 the populations of Nigeria and Pakistan will increase by 83 and 81 per cent respectively.[18] Future growth will almost certainly differ from these figures. The main point, however, is that both countries are sure to experience considerable growth. As we have seen, both Indonesia and Brazil have low and falling levels of total fertility, and falling rates of population growth. Not surprisingly, therefore, their projected growth for the period 2010–50 is appreciably lower – at 24 and 12 per cent respectively. As noted, this growth will be almost entirely due to momentum. And, of course, both countries will experience significant population ageing.

Turning to Japan and Russia, the projections suggest population reductions of 20 and 17 per cent respectively over the period 2010–50. It is worth noting that these reductions occur despite the assumption that the level of total fertility will increase towards a figure of 1.85 births. Put simply: the age structures and fertility levels of Japan and Russia in Figure 3.4 augur the *reverse* of population momentum – i.e. circumstances in which very low levels of fertility per woman lead to smaller and smaller numbers of women entering the childbearing ages, where they then experience very low levels of fertility, leading to still smaller numbers of women entering the childbearing ages. Provided total fertility remains well below the replacement level, then the ensuing process of population decline will eventually become rapid and self-sustaining. It should be clear, however, that such a scenario takes us well beyond the end of the demographic transition.

Lastly, Figure 3.6 illustrates some of the dynamic effects of the transition through a comparison of Russia and Nigeria (see also Demeny 2003). Notice that the populations are represented on the same scale, and in *absolute* rather than in percentage terms. Between 1950 and 2000 Russia's population grew from about 103 to 147 million. But natural increase ceased towards the end of this period (indeed, it became negative) and the country's population had become appreciably older. The projected age distribution for 2050 shows an ageing and diminishing Russia – the population is put at about 116 million. In contrast, Nigeria was still in the early stages of the demographic transition in 1950. Its population was very young. Between 1950 and 2000 the population grew from around 37 to 125 million, because of mortality decline. Although Nigeria's population was smaller than that of Russia in 2000, a comparison of the two age structures reveals an important difference at the base. Thus there were 21 million Nigerian children aged 0–4 in 2000,

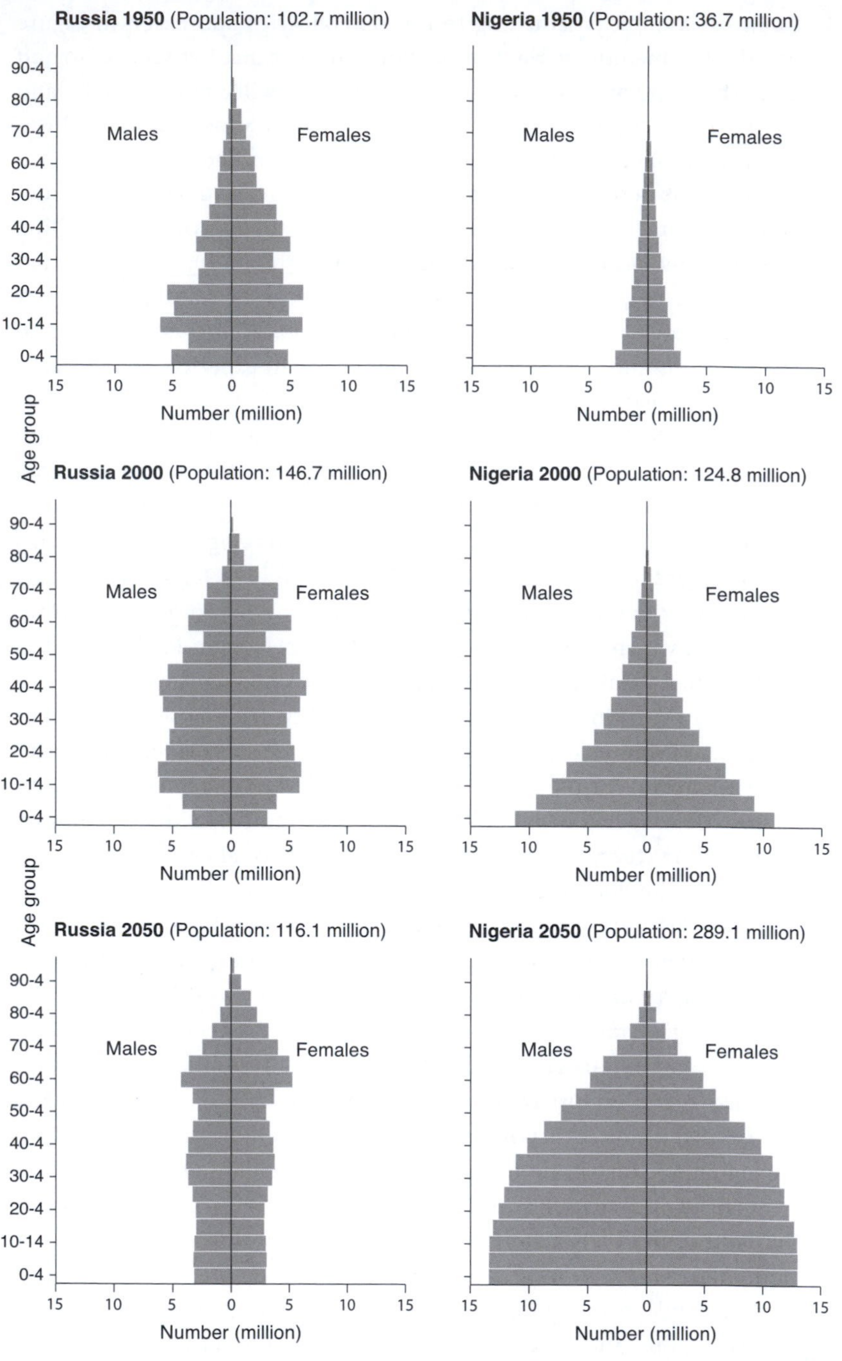


*Sources*: United Nations (2009); see also Demeny (2003)

**Figure 3.6 Population size and age distribution, Russia and Nigeria—estimates and projections for 1950, 2000 and 2050**

but only 6.5 million Russian children. The UN projection for Nigeria assumes that total fertility will decline to about 2.4 births per woman by 2045–50. The country's population is projected to be around 289 million in 2050 (and rising). Again, the details of the projections are inconsequential. But the broad relative picture is virtually certain. Considerations of population dynamics will ensure that the general contrast shown in Figure 3.6 will occur. The comparison underscores the great demographic diversity that exists in the modern world.

## Discussion

This chapter has covered some important terrain – and points made here will be elaborated in what follows. Some basic measures and concepts have also been introduced.

In summary, the world's population was about one billion at the start of the nineteenth century. It had grown to around 2.5 billion by 1950. It then rose by a further 4.4 billion to reach 6.9 billion in 2010. It is widely believed that the human population will eventually peak – or perhaps roughly stabilize – at somewhere between 9 and 10 billion some time during the second half of this century. All of this population growth is the direct result of the global demographic transition. It seems likely that this transition will be a phenomenon that will have extended over a period of approximately three centuries.

It is impossible to know the size of the world's population at the start and the end of the transition. Indeed, we have only a crude idea of when the start was, and when the end will be. If the world's death and birth rates become approximately equal during the second half of this century, however, and the population has indeed grown to about 9.5 billion, then, very roughly speaking, there will have been a tenfold increase in the size of the human population as a result of the global demographic transition.[19]

Essentially, this unprecedented expansion of the world's population has occurred because the death rate fell earlier than the birth rate. Mortality decline – a process marked by a major rise in life expectancy – has been the main driving force (see Table 3.1). The more developed countries were the first to experience mortality decline, which probably began in the eighteenth century. Most developing countries began to experience mortality decline at some time in the first half of the twentieth century.

Mortality decline is continuing today, and – barring some major and unanticipated development or event – it is a process that seems certain to continue. However, mortality decline is no longer producing a fall in the world's death rate. But the birth rate is falling because of fertility decline. Therefore, the world's population growth rate is falling. Fertility decline and a slowing rate of growth also seem certain to continue at the global level (see Table 3.3). And the same is true of population ageing and urbanization – processes that can be regarded as virtually universal and unstoppable. The coming growth of the human population will occur almost entirely at adult ages, and it will be concentrated in the urban sector.

Yet although most countries are still experiencing the transition in various ways, there is also remarkable demographic variation in the contemporary world. This is true, for example, with respect to rates of population growth – where some countries are growing rapidly, while others, having passed through the transition, are beginning to experience negative natural increase and therefore population decline. There is also great variation with respect to population structure (see, for example, Figure 3.4). Essentially, contemporary variation in demographic characteristics reflects the fact that different populations are at different stages of the demographic transition. Fertility variation is especially important in this context. Moreover, we have seen that population projections – such as those of the United Nations – are informed by, and conducted within, the framework that is provided by the demographic transition.

It is clear that the demographic transition is a phenomenon which can sometimes involve very considerable momentum – through the influence of age structure. And it is evident that time lags are involved as well. Moreover, because the processes of population ageing and urbanization involve changes in a population's composition, they take longer to complete than the changes in mortality and fertility that do so much to bring them about. For example, fertility decline can occur very rapidly – as it did in China. But this influences the age structure of the population only at the base. Therefore, it takes much longer for the full process of population ageing to occur. Such delayed effects mean that even in countries where vital rates are low and equal, the processes of ageing and urbanization may not be complete.

The chapter has pointed to the almost inexorable nature of the main processes of the demographic transition. It has also underscored the importance of context, however – different countries and regions, for example, having very different experiences. Moreover, we have noted cases where factors that can be regarded as 'external' to the transition itself – e.g. a new disease, or a government policy – have intervened to influence the timing and speed of the processes. It is clear too that international migration has the potential to complicate matters. Nevertheless, and despite these qualifications, when dealing with the demographic transition we are focusing on a phenomenon that, in very long-run perspective, is fundamentally uniform.

The chapter has drawn a broad distinction between the 'historical' and the 'contemporary' transitions. We noted that they differ greatly with respect to their accompanying rates of population growth. Thus if the growth multiple for the world's population turns out to be roughly ten, there will be great variation around this figure. In Europe, for example, populations often rose by factors of only about three or four (although there was substantial variation). And if the UN projections prove to be correct then China's population will grow by a multiple approaching four, and India's by a factor of perhaps five or six. In many developing countries, however, growth multiples that are much greater than ten seem likely to apply; figures as high as twenty or thirty are quite possible.[20]

This leads us to a consideration of different experiences of the demographic transition – with particular focus on the progress of death rates, birth rates and the resulting rates of natural increase.

PART TWO

# The processes of the demographic transition

# 4 · The demographic transition – facts and theory

Interest in the demographic transition arose during the first half of the twentieth century. It became clear that the level of fertility per woman had fallen from comparatively high to comparatively low levels in north-western Europe, and some other parts of the world where the people were mainly European in origin. Early writing on the transition often involved classifying countries into groups – with the more or less explicit suggestion that the phenomenon involved a population moving through a series of stages (Thompson 1929; Carr-Saunders 1936). An early attempt at explaining the transition – i.e. the proposal of theory – was Adolphe Landry's book *La Révolution Démographique*, which appeared in 1934. In the literature written in English, however, a 1945 paper by Frank Notestein is often seen as being the first theoretical statement. That said, the contributions of Kingsley Davis (1945, 1963) have also been very influential.

The transition has been described as the central preoccupation of modern demography (Demeny 1972: 153). The explanation of mortality decline has generally been regarded as relatively straightforward. Therefore, from the earliest days, most work has focused on fertility, and the reasons for its decline. Our understanding has increased as more has been learnt about historical cases of the transition – especially in Europe – and as more has become known about the transitions that are still under way in the developing world. Influential writing on the subject has included that of Kirk (1971, 1996), Coale (1973), Caldwell (1976), Coale and Watkins (1986) and Cleland and Wilson (1987). The particular concern with fertility has been strengthened because – given falling death rates – it is high fertility which has been responsible for the unparalleled expansion of the world's population in recent decades. However, one consequence of the focus on fertility is that the demographic transition is seldom addressed in the round – although a notable exception here is the work of Jean-Claude Chesnais (1992).[1]

The present chapter addresses the major falls in death rates and birth rates – and behind them the declines in mortality and fertility – that are central to the demographic transition. There is a reasonably clear distinction between 'fact' and 'theory' in relation to this subject. Accordingly, the chapter begins by considering the facts, and it then turns to matters of theory. In relation to matters of fact, a key issue is the basic sequence (i.e. order) of the two main demographic processes that are involved. In relation to matters of theory, mortality decline is dealt with first, before we turn to the explanation of the decline in fertility. Many factors can influence the timing and speed of fertility decline in a society. However, the argument here is that mortality decline is the remote (i.e. underlying) cause of fertility decline.

## Matters of fact

If the demographic transition is a global phenomenon – i.e. one that is affecting all human populations – then it is desirable to try to illustrate this with examples for all of the world's main regions. However, that is easier said than done. For most developing countries it is difficult to go much beyond the demographic estimates for the period since 1950 assembled by the United Nations and used in Chapter 3. Valuable though these estimates are, they provide only a glimpse of the transition, and for many populations it is inevitably a rather manufactured glimpse at that.[2]

In fact, very few countries have long-run time series of vital rates (i.e. death rates and birth rates) that can be used to depict all – or even most – of the transition, even in rough terms. One reason for this is that very few countries had vital registration systems in operation at the time that the transition began. A modern system of vital registration is one where, for legal and statistical purposes, people are required to register the deaths and births that occur within their households with representatives of the state (usually local registrars). These registration systems emerged in the countries of north-western Europe in the eighteenth and nineteenth centuries from the pre-existing institution of ecclesiastical (i.e. Church) registration of baptisms, marriages and burials. The countries of north-western Europe were also the first to begin to experience the demographic transition. And the fact that societies in this part of the world were advanced both in terms of experiencing the transition, and in terms of collecting information that can be used to illustrate it, is not a coincidence.

When one considers regions other than Europe, then it is much harder to find long-run time series of vital rates to depict even a reasonable fraction of the transition, let alone all of it. Even today, many countries have no vital registration system. In some countries such systems exist, but they are deficient in coverage – i.e. many of the deaths and births that occur are not registered for various reasons.[3] For present purposes, such under-registration is not necessarily a problem – provided that its level does not alter greatly through time. Unfortunately, however, the level of registration coverage does sometimes change – on occasion quite suddenly – and this precludes the use of the resulting vital rates here. There can also be gaps in time series of vital rates (e.g. due to periods of war) and the series can finish rather abruptly. Finally, it should be recalled that, outside of Europe, there are only a few countries where the birth rate has fallen to the level of the death rate – i.e. countries where the transition can be considered as complete in the sense used in this chapter.[4]

The difficulty of finding full illustrations of the demographic transition is hardly surprising – given that it is a phenomenon that stretches over very long periods. Anyhow, vital rates derived from ecclesiastical and modern systems of registration are used here to illustrate the transition from two related perspectives. First, we consider time series for populations where the available data can provide an impression of a good part of the overall transition. Second, we examine how the resulting rates of natural increase have changed through time. Essentially, this involves examining the population growth paths produced by the transition – and, since good examples are rare, we also draw on the vital rates for Sweden and Sri Lanka that were considered in Chapter 2.

*Illustrations of the transition* Figure 4.1 presents six relatively complete examples of the demographic transition – considered here in terms of the progression of vital rates. The cases shown relate to fairly sizeable populations, located in different parts of the world. They all depict a fairly large slice of the transition. Notice that, for reasons of presentation, the examples are plotted on somewhat different scales – especially in relation to time (i.e. on the horizontal axis).[5]

As noted, it is comparatively easy to find relatively full illustrations of the transition for countries in north-western Europe (albeit based partly on ecclesiastical data). We have discussed Sweden already (see Figure 2.2) and France is considered below. North-western Europe is represented in Figure 4.1 by England and Wales (henceforth 'England'). The inclusion of Spain helps to underscore the fact that countries in other parts of Europe generally experienced the phenomenon at somewhat later times. Latin America is represented by Chile. East Asia is represented by Taiwan. For South-Central Asia we have already looked at Sri Lanka (see Figure 2.2), but another case is provided by relatively reliable registration data for a sizeable area of central India.[6] Egyptian

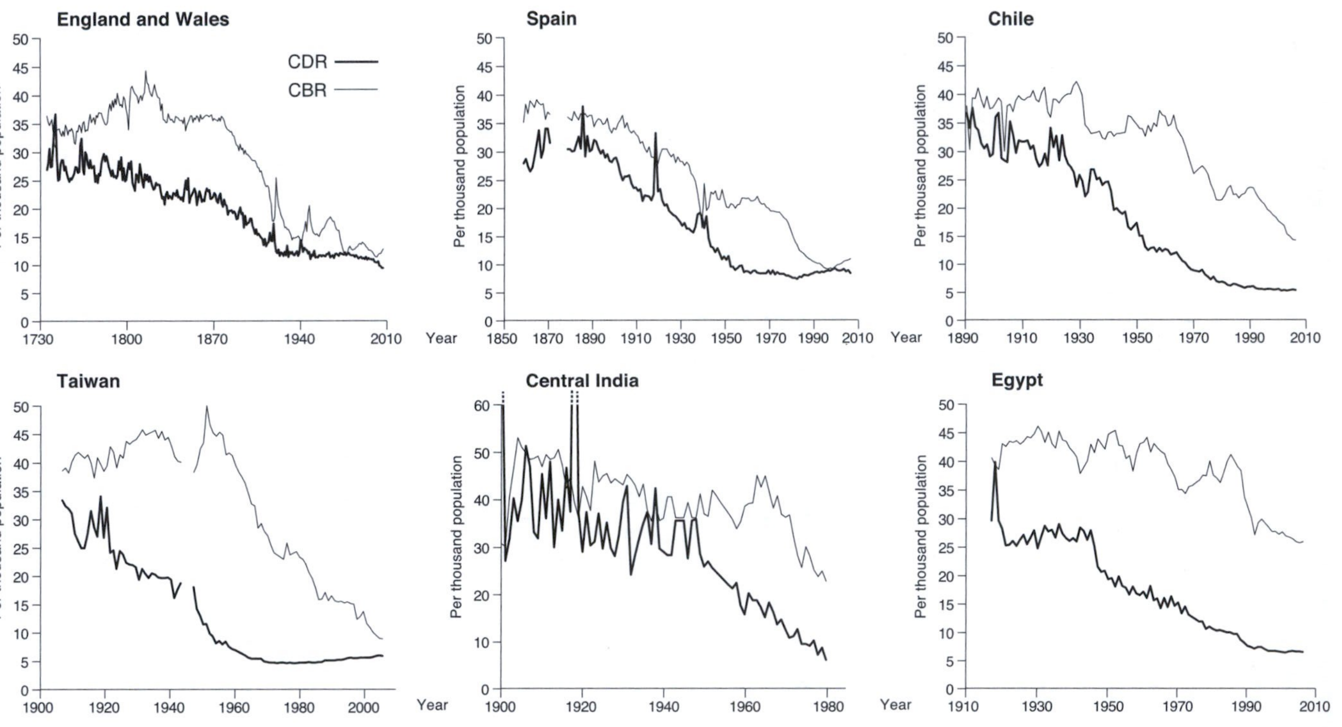


*Principal sources*: England and Wales (Wrigley and Schofield 1981; Chesnais 1992; ONS 2009); Spain (Chesnais 1992); Chile (Mitchell 1983; INE-CELADE 2000); Taiwan (Mitchell 1982; Republic of China 2007); Central India (Dyson 1989); Egypt (Chesnais 1992). Rates were also taken from United Nations *Demographic Yearbook* (various years).

**Figure 4.1 The demographic transition—vital rates in six populations**

data provide the best illustration of the transition for the Middle East. A paucity of registration data means that comparable examples of the transition cannot be presented for North America and sub-Saharan Africa, but both of these regions are considered in the following discussion.

Naturally, the examples in Figure 4.1 vary greatly in their details. That is to be expected, given the very different populations that are represented. The time series for individual populations reflect many comparatively local events. For instance, in Spain the death rate (shown in bold) rose sharply in 1885 owing to an outbreak of cholera. The country's death rate also increased – and the birth rate fell – as a result of the 1936–39 civil war. In addition, the time series in Figure 4.1 reflect the effects of several worldwide events – which often had broadly similar effects in different places. For example, the vital rates for both Egypt and central India reflect the influence of the Second World War.[7] Note too that in England the death rate rose and the birth rate fell during both world wars, and that both of these conflicts were followed by 'baby booms'. That said, perhaps the best illustration of the effect of a short-term global event in Figure 4.1 is that the death rate increased in every population because of the influenza pandemic of 1918/19.

Nevertheless, the main point of Figure 4.1 is to demonstrate that the demographic transition appears to have the same *essential* form, irrespective of its context and timing. Thus, although none of the time series shown is entirely reliable, and several are incomplete, all six cases give the same general impression of the sequence of processes. In short: the death rate starts to decline first; the birth rate starts to decline somewhat later; there is an extended period during which the birth rate is higher than the death rate; therefore there is an extended period during which natural increase occurs (i.e. the population grows); the death rate eventually flattens out at a low level; the birth rate continues to fall until it becomes low and approximately equal to the death rate. At that point, in terms of vital rates, the transition is more or less complete. Mortality and fertility have declined from high to low levels. And the size of the population has increased.

Actually, only the illustration for England depicts nearly all of the sequence from beginning to end.[8] An early sign of mortality decline in England was a reduction of fluctuations in the death rate during the 1700s (Figure 4.1). A similar initial dampening of volatility in the death rate is apparent in the Indian example – although the reduction occurred in the 1920s and 1930s.[9] However, we can be reasonably confident that if the time series for the other populations in Figure 4.1 could be extended farther back in time, then they would all show

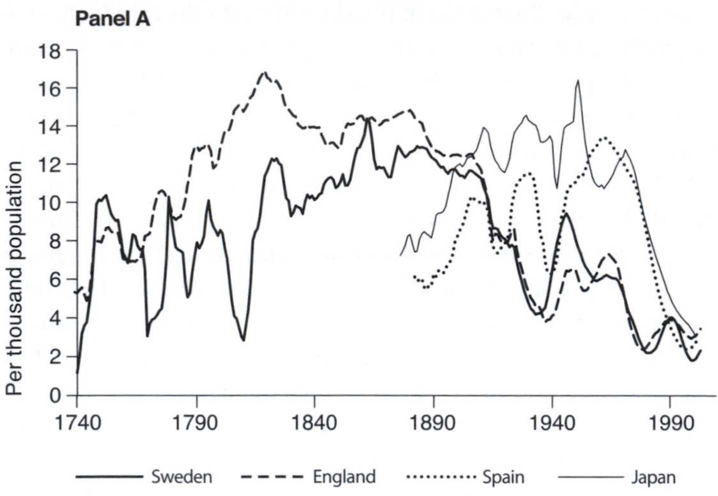


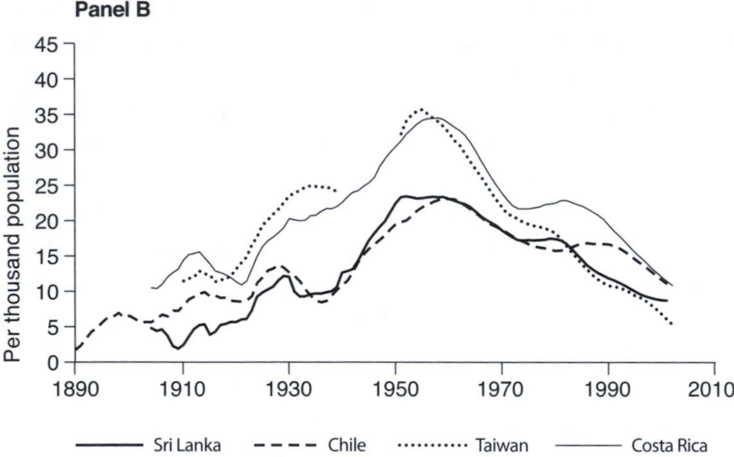


*Principal sources*: Costa Rica (Mitchell 1983); Japan (Japan Statistical Association 1987). Rates were also taken from the United Nations *Demographic Yearbook* (various years). See also the sources cited in Figures 2.2 and 4.1.

**Figure 4.2 The rate of natural increase—selected historical and contemporary transitions**

that major fluctuations in the death rate were once quite frequent. Notice that Spain is the only other population to show the completion of the transition in terms of vital rates. The end of Spain's transition, in this sense, happens in the 1990s. However, in England it is harder to say when the ending occurs – a case can be made for both the 1930s (when fertility per woman first fell below the replacement level) and the 1970s.[10] Although it is difficult to say exactly when the transition in England starts and ends, a total duration of almost two centuries seems quite plausible. In Spain, however, the duration may have been somewhat shorter.

In general, the non-European populations in Figure 4.1 also seem to have experienced somewhat shorter demographic transitions. At the start of the twenty-first century, Taiwan was closest to completion (in the present sense). The fall of Taiwan's death and birth rates also seems to have been relatively fast. At the start of this century the transition was also fairly advanced in Chile. It will not be too long before the country's birth rate is in the vicinity of its death rate. In central India, however, the time when the birth rate is similar to the death rate is probably somewhat further off.[11] Finally, despite the fact that Egypt's death rate probably began to fall during the nineteenth century, the decline in the country's birth rate appears to have been fairly delayed.

Therefore, although the cases in Figure 4.1 reveal the same basic sequence of processes – i.e. the same essential form – they also show substantial secondary variation in terms of form. Considerations of context are obviously important here.

*Paths of natural increase* Figure 4.2 illustrates how the rate of natural increase – i.e. the difference between the birth rate and the death rate – changes as a result of the transition. The figure compares trends in the rate of natural increase for eight populations that have progressed through all – or most – of the transition. Panel A shows examples we have examined where the phenomenon can be regarded as complete in the present sense. Notice that Japan – an almost unique case of a complete transition for a non-European population – is also included. Panel B relates to transitions that can be regarded as well advanced, though not yet finished. Notice that Costa Rica – which provides a rare case of a nearly complete transition outside of Europe – is also included.[12] Finally, it should be mentioned that all of the time series have been smoothed with a nine-year moving average in order to help emphasize their basic features.

Figure 4.2 suggests that the path of the rate of natural increase produced by the transition is often very roughly symmetrical in form (see also Chesnais 1992: 280–83).[13] This has already been implied – more or less – by the illustrations in Figure 4.1. The rates of natural increase for the two countries in north-western Europe followed a similar long-run trajectory from around the middle of the nineteenth century (see Panel A).[14] In Sweden and England the rate of natural increase was very low during the first half of the eighteenth century, and at the end of the twentieth century. In both countries the rate of natural increase was relatively high around 1860–90. In the English case, however, any impression of rough symmetry is dispelled because of the relatively high rate of natural increase that seems to have prevailed in the first decades of the nineteenth century. Turning to Spain and Japan, the beginnings of the transition are much harder to discern (owing to lack of data). About all we can say is that in both countries it may have begun in the early-to-middle decades of the nineteenth century. Spain's rate of natural increase appears to have peaked in the 1950s and 1960s. The peak in Japan seems to have happened between 1930 and 1950. The interpretation of the series for these two countries is complicated by the influence of major wars. Nevertheless, we can probably conclude that the paths of natural increase in Spain and Japan were more concentrated in time (compared to Sweden and England). Thus in Spain and Japan the rate of natural increase appears to have risen quite steeply in the

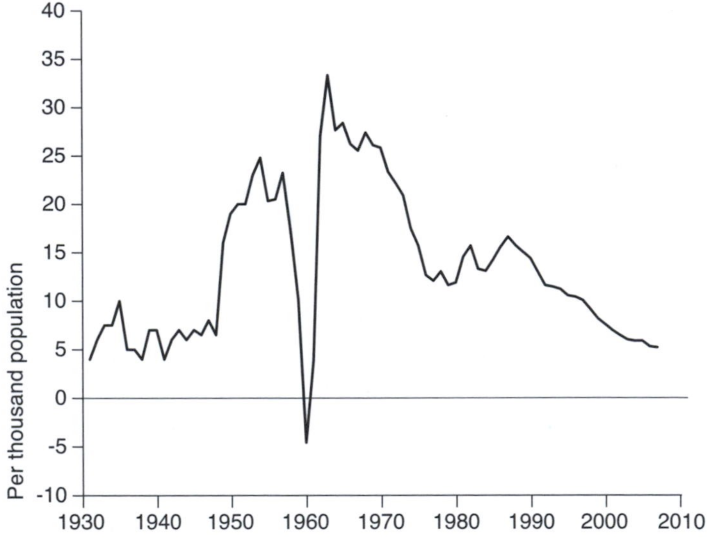


*Note*: See the text for discussion of the figures for 1931-48. Figures for subsequent years are crude rates of natural increase.

*Sources*: 1931–48 (Chesnais 1992), 1949–2007 (National Bureau of Statistics of China 2008)

**Figure 4.3 The rate of population increase in China since 1931**

late nineteenth century. And it certainly fell quite steeply – reflecting a fairly rapid fall in the birth rate in both countries – during the second half of the twentieth century.

Turning to the comparatively advanced – but not yet complete – transitions addressed in Panel B of Figure 4.2, we see a greater suggestion of symmetry. Although they are sometimes classed as 'developing' populations, Sri Lanka, Chile, Taiwan and Costa Rica are all unusual because they have vital registration data which can be used to depict much of the transition. This suggests that actually they are all fairly 'developed' in certain key respects. In these four cases the start of the rise in the rate of natural increase seems to have happened around the end of the nineteenth century. In each population the peak rate of natural increase occurs around 1955–60. In each case the birth rate has been falling since 1955–60 (from somewhat earlier in Chile). And in each case, at the start of the present century, the rate of natural increase is falling towards zero. Again, these four examples of demographic transition will probably be appreciably more compressed (i.e. shorter) compared to those experienced in north-western Europe. Indeed, they may be slightly more compressed in time than the cases of Spain and Japan.

That said, the developing-country transitions in Panel B of Figure 4.2 involve much higher rates of natural increase. The natural increase curves for the more developed populations in Panel A rarely exceed 14 per thousand (i.e. 1.4 per cent per year). All of the curves in Panel B, however, exceed a rate of 20 per thousand (i.e. 2.0 per cent per year) – most of them by a significant margin, and for several decades.

Finally, to broaden the geographical scope still further, Figure 4.3 presents annual rates of population increase for China. Annual death and birth rates are available for the country starting from 1949. However, Chesnais (1992: 265) presents annual population growth rates for 1931–48.[15] These rates agree with other sources in suggesting that the rate of population growth in China in the 1930s was very low (see Barclay et al. 1976: 621). Therefore, given the country's importance, they have been used here. The massive dip in the natural increase rate shown for around 1960 reflects the rise in the death rate, and fall in the birth rate, caused by the major famine of 1959–61. Otherwise, however, Figure 4.3 reflects the fact that there was both a very rapid fall in the death rate in the late 1940s and 1950s, and a very rapid fall in the birth rate in the 1970s. Notice that for some of the 1950s, and most of the 1960s, the rate of natural increase exceeded 20 per thousand. Again, there is a (very) rough intimation of symmetry. China's population is expected to stop growing around the year 2035. On this basis it seems reasonable to say that the country's demographic transition will probably have lasted for about a century – perhaps a little less.

*Claimed exceptions* Clearly, different examples of demographic transition exhibit what we have termed 'secondary' variation in form. But we have also said that all cases involve the same essential sequence – in particular, that mortality decline precedes fertility decline. Yet there are occasional claims that some populations have experienced fertility decline before they have experienced mortality decline (see, for example, van de Walle 1986; Klein 2004: 77–9). It is important to address this matter before we turn to the task of explanation.

Sub-Saharan Africa certainly provides examples where the level of total fertility fell from high to low levels without an improvement in mortality. For example, areas of the Democratic Republic of Congo, the Central African Republic and Gabon experienced big falls in fertility during the first half of the twentieth century. In such places the birth rate fell from high to low levels, while the death rate remained high. Therefore, some areas experienced population decline in the early decades of the twentieth century (see Romaniuk 1980; Frank 1983; Larsen 2000).

However, these were not cases of 'fertility decline' in the usually accepted sense. Instead, they resulted from the spread of sexually transmitted diseases (STDs). The disruption to traditional ways of life brought about by the intrusive activities of various European colonial powers produced conditions – e.g. labour migration and family breakdown – which were conducive to the spread of STDs like chlamydia and gonorrhoea. These diseases cause tubal scarring and infertility. And, as their prevalence increased, so many women (and men) became sterile. In some areas around a fifth of all women remained childless at the end of their reproductive years – i.e. they had no births at all (Romaniuk 1980). Moreover, many women who did have children later became sterile, and so were unable to have any more. That such cases of fertility decline were neither intended nor desired is demonstrated by the fact that fertility has subsequently increased, as antibiotics have become available.

Turning to true examples of fertility decline – i.e. ones where reductions in marriage, and especially increases in the use of birth control, have been responsible – then the United States and France are sometimes cited as cases where fertility decline preceded mortality decline (see, for example, Klein 2004: 77–9). However, assessment of the issue is not straightforward, partly because mortality and fertility data for the relevant periods are often either lacking or questionable.

Registered vital rates for the United States are available only from around 1900. But it is known that the birth rate fell considerably from early in the nineteenth century – indeed, perhaps from late in the eighteenth century. However, conditions in the United States were exceptional. Compared to most of Europe, the level of mortality in eighteenth- and early-nineteenth-century America was low (i.e. favourable). This reflected a plentiful supply of land, fairly secure supplies of food, and low population densities which acted to limit the spread of infectious diseases. It is also important to appreciate that the fall in the birth rate in the first half of the nineteenth century occurred from a very high level. Thus in 1800 American women were having about seven births each (Klein 2004: 78). The favourable material circumstances of eighteenth-century America meant that men and women were able to get married and establish their own homesteads while they were still very young.[16] And because people did not use any form of birth control, women ended up having a lot of births (i.e. an average of about seven in 1800).

The fall in the US birth rate during the first half of the nineteenth century appears to have occurred because – faced with a decline in the availability of land along the country's eastern seaboard – young people were forced to delay the age at which they got married (Klein 2004: 80–1). In turn, this meant that the age at which women started having children was postponed, and as a result they ended up having somewhat fewer children. By 1850 the average had fallen to about 5.5 births per woman. This sort of *limited* fall in fertility – i.e. one caused by a delay in the age at which women get married, and perhaps an increase in the proportion of women who remain single – was a fairly normal response to more difficult economic times in north-western European countries (from which most of the US population had originated). Therefore, it is questionable whether the fall in the birth rate during the first half of the nineteenth century represented the onset of sustained fertility decline within the context of the demographic transition. Instead, it probably reflected the typical response of such a population to tightening economic circumstances. In contrast, the fall in the birth rate during most of the *second* half of the century can indeed be seen as reflecting fertility decline within the context of the transition.

So there is little in the experience of the United States which contradicts the view that mortality decline precedes fertility decline. The exceptional circumstances of the United States – a young frontier country, populated mainly by immigrants and their descendants – makes it

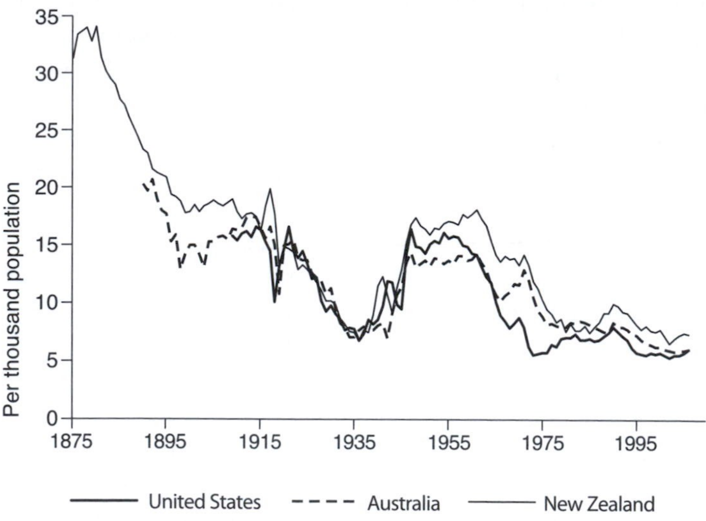


*Principal sources*: United States (Chesnais 1992, United States Census Bureau 2009); Australia (Mitchell 1983, Australian Bureau of Statistics 2008); New Zealand (Mitchell 1983). Rates were also derived from vital rates taken from the United Nations *Demographic Yearbook* (various years).

**Figure 4.4 The rate of natural increase in the United States, Australia and New Zealand**

inappropriate for purposes of comparison with the experience of long-established settled populations elsewhere in the world.

Almost certainly, a similar conclusion applies to the other 'offshoot' populations from north-western Europe – i.e. those of Canada, Australia and New Zealand. These countries also enjoyed exceptional economic conditions by European standards. In this context, Figure 4.4 compares the annual rates of natural increase for the United States from 1900 onwards, with corresponding rates for Australia and New Zealand. It is important to appreciate that these three countries experienced relatively low crude death rates throughout the period in question. Accordingly, the trends shown in Figure 4.4 mainly reflect variation in the *birth rates* of these populations. The similarity of experience – as these three English-speaking countries were affected by the events of the twentieth century – is extremely clear. The general trend is downwards – reflecting falling birth rates. Notice that the series for Australia and New Zealand extend further back in time (i.e. before 1900). And they convey an impression of what we know also happened in the United States during most of the nineteenth century.[17] In short, the birth rate – which was much higher than the death rate – fell from an exceptionally high level. Therefore, there was a major fall in the rate of natural increase. The fall in the birth rate during the *later* decades of the nineteenth century involved increasing use of birth control, and therefore should be seen within the context of the transition. Interestingly, Chesnais (1992: 281) describes this pattern as a 'demi-transition'. The point being that, in a sense, it mainly reflects the *second* half of the transition – during which, because of declining fertility, the path of natural increase falls towards zero.

France would be a more difficult case to explain *if* it could be shown that fertility decline preceded mortality decline. France's population was the first in the world to turn to some form of conscious birth control on a mass scale. We do not know exactly what this new form of behaviour was (see, for example, van de Walle and Muhsam 1995). It has become customary to attribute it to the practice of 'withdrawal' (i.e. of the penis prior to ejaculation) although there are other possibilities (e.g. mutual masturbation).

The spread of birth control in France was a truly momentous development in human affairs. Really for the first time in history, the fertility of a major society came to be controlled *within* marriage – rather than through variation in marriage itself (i.e. through changes in the age of women at marriage and/or changes in the proportion of women remaining single). In most of the rest of north-western Europe, and its offshoot populations, deliberate control of fertility within marriage did not begin to become widely adopted until the 1860s and 1870s. In France, however, it began from around the 1790s, i.e. the decade of the Revolution. This very early timing has helped to support the suggestion that fertility decline may have preceded mortality decline.

Figure 4.5 presents annual vital rates for France for the period since 1740. It also shows the path of the rate of natural increase, using a nine-year moving average. There is little evidence here that the birth rate came down before the death rate. Perhaps a better description might be that both rates declined more or less in tandem from the last decades of the eighteenth century. One consequence of this was that the annual rate of natural increase remained exceptionally low – at just under 7 per thousand (i.e. 0.7 per cent) – as France progressed through the demographic transition. The moving average in Figure 4.5 remains positive between about 1750 and 1910 – meaning that the death rate was generally below the birth rate for the whole of this time. Therefore, the experience of France does not appear to have been unusual in that the death rate was lower than the birth rate. Note too that the moving average peaks in the middle of this period – i.e. around 1820. Lastly, it

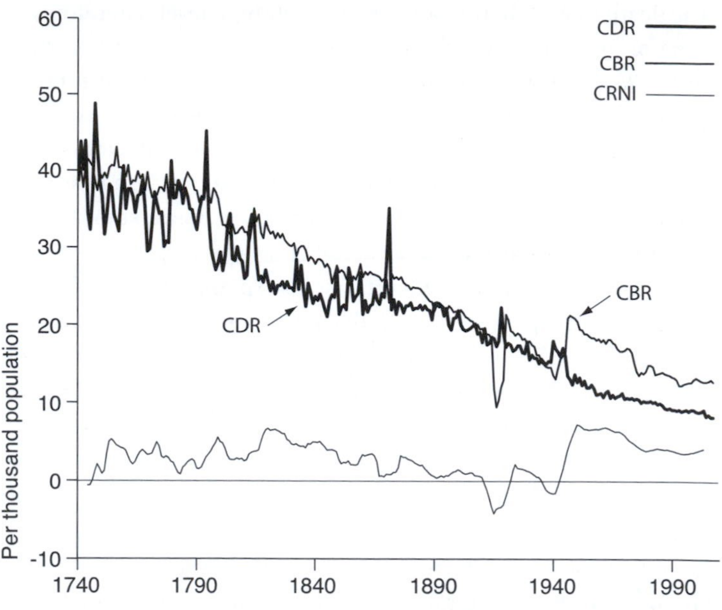


*Principal sources*: Chesnais (1992), United Nations *Demographic Yearbook* (various years)

**Figure 4.5 Vital rates in France since 1740**

is difficult to decide exactly when the transition in France came to an end. Exceptional circumstances meant that the rate of natural increase was negative during both world wars. As perhaps in England, however, the attainment of replacement-level fertility during the 1930s might signify a more appropriate ending – in which case the country's transition lasted for about 180 years.

In fact, although data to evaluate the issue are sparse, there are reasons to believe that mortality decline in France may well have preceded fertility decline by a little. This issue cannot be resolved using crude death and birth rates (as in Figure 4.5). However, according to Chesnais (1992: 354), between 1740 and 1780 average life expectancy in France rose by about six years. And, according to Wrigley, between the 1780s and the 1820s life expectancy increased from about 28 to around 39 years. This represented a major decline in mortality compared to experience elsewhere in Europe. Indeed, in proportional terms the increase in life expectancy was huge – equivalent to the entire rise that was experienced in France over the following century (Wrigley 1987a: 287). It seems, then, that France is probably not an exception to the principle that mortality decline precedes fertility decline (see also Chesnais 1992: 353–4).

Finally, a word is required in relation to the experience of England – because it too is sometimes depicted as a case where mortality decline may not have preceded fertility decline (see, for example, Woods 2000: 20). Thus the vital rates in Figure 4.1 suggest that during the late eighteenth and early nineteenth centuries there was a major rise in the country's birth rate, and that this was the main reason why the rate of natural increase rose at that time. The vital rates for this period are derived mainly from ecclesiastical records. And, essentially, the burial and baptism rates for the late eighteenth and early nineteenth centuries have been adjusted upwards to obtain the vital rates shown in Figure 4.1 – on the assumption that the level of ecclesiastical registration deteriorated significantly (Wrigley and Schofield 1981). The view that the level of mortality in England had not improved much by the late eighteenth and early nineteenth centuries (compared to the first half of the eighteenth century) depends to a large degree upon the upward adjustment to the ecclesiastical rates. A smaller (or no) adjustment to the rates would imply that more of the increase in the country's rate of natural increase was due to a decline in the death rate (and mortality decline), and less to a rise in the birth rate (and fertility). Given issues of data, the matter may never be resolved. However, it is important to note that there is a substantial body of research which questions the assumption that ecclesiastical registration deteriorated so much, and which therefore concludes that the level of mortality in England did improve significantly at this time (see, for example, Lindert 1983; Vallin 1991; Razzell 1993, 2007). Furthermore, even the rates shown in Figure 4.1 are indicative of some mortality decline in the period before the 1870s – i.e. the time when birth control in England began to be adopted on a mass scale and there was sustained fertility decline.[18]

To conclude this section, the experience of the United States in the early nineteenth century was so special in relation to the overall context that it does not really constitute an exception. There are reasons to believe that mortality decline in France preceded fertility decline by a little. And there are grounds to think that there was mortality decline before the occurrence of fertility decline in England. In no case has it really been established that a major population experienced fertility decline in the absence of some prior mortality decline. That is not to deny that both processes can occur concurrently to some degree – indeed, that is invariably the case (see Figure 4.1). And, to some extent, changes in ways of thinking about personal behaviour may exert a simultaneous downward influence on both mortality (especially that of young children) and fertility.[19] However, these points aside, almost all researchers accept that mortality decline precedes fertility decline (see, for example, Kirk 1996: 385; Chesnais 1992: 7; Cleland 2001; Casterline 2003: 214). The position is captured well by David Reher's statement, based on analysis of data for 145 countries, that 'everywhere, without exception, mortality decline appears to have preceded fertility decline in a clear-cut way' (Reher 2004: 24).

*Further remarks on fertility decline* We noted that the first sign of mortality decline is a dampening of fluctuations in the death rate. Because mortality crises and their causes – epidemics, famines, wars – also tend to depress the birth rate (with a lag of about nine months) the reduction in death rate fluctuations is invariably accompanied by a reduction in fluctuations in the birth rate. This early development – i.e. an increase in the stability of the birth rate through time – can probably be regarded as a general feature of the demographic transition. For example, analysis of the time series for central India in Figure 4.1 shows this dampening effect very clearly (see Dyson 1989).

Another fact raised by some of the examples in Figure 4.1 is that – before it starts to decline – there is often a relatively short-lived *rise* in the level of total fertility. This can occur either because of an increase in marriage (e.g. a fall in the age of women at marriage) or because of an increase in the level of marital fertility (i.e. the level of fertility within marriage). Increases in marital fertility can happen, for example, because of reductions in breastfeeding (e.g. if infants and young children are increasingly fed with breast-milk substitute) or because of increases in the frequency of sexual intercourse within marriage (e.g. if traditional restrictions on having sexual relations diminish with time).[20]

Irrespective of its cause, however, a pre-decline rise in fertility may not be apparent from the trend in a population's birth rate. In particular, the early stages of mortality decline usually involve sizeable reductions in the death rates of infants and young children. By saving many *young* lives, these reductions often produce an initial temporary youthening of the population's age structure. In turn, this reduces the proportion of the population that is in the reproductive ages (for women, ages 15–49). And this change in age structure can cause a minor fall in the birth rate, other things equal. Such a series of events can obscure the upward influence on the birth rate that would come from a pre-decline rise in fertility.

That said, there frequently *is* a pre-decline rise in total fertility per woman within the transition. Thus to the extent that there was an increase in the birth rate in England in the period before 1815 this seems to have reflected a decline in the age of women at marriage (see Figure 4.1 and Szreter and Garrett 2000). Note too that the birth rate in central India rose sharply during the late 1950s and early 1960s – i.e. immediately before it began to decline (see Figure 4.1). During this period the estimated level of total fertility increased from about 4.5 to 6.1 births per woman. In this case possible explanations for the rise include reductions in widowhood – brought about by mortality decline – and reductions in breastfeeding (Dyson 1989).

It is likely that other populations in Figure 4.1 also experienced pre-decline rises in fertility – although this may not always be apparent from the birth rate. When data from vital registration, censuses and surveys are considered together it is common to find signs of a pre-decline rise. This is true for historical transitions, and it is true in relation to more recent examples. There appear to have been especially pronounced pre-decline fertility rises in Latin America between about 1935 and the 1950s, after which the trend was reversed. During this time there were widespread falls in the average age of women at marriage. Also, although the evidence is fragmentary, there are reasons to believe that many countries in sub-Saharan Africa experienced substantial rises in fertility, and birth rates, at times during the twentieth century. One cause of these rises was a fall in the prevalence of sexually transmitted diseases – as antibiotics became available. Reductions in breastfeeding, and the relaxation of restrictions on women engaging in sexual intercourse in the year or two after giving birth, probably also contributed (Dyson and Murphy 1985). Such pre-decline fertility rises have sometimes contributed to increases in rates of natural increase within the demographic transition – although this should not obscure the dominant role played by falling death rates.

It is usually the case that a reduction in marriage – reflected, for example, by a rise in the age of women at marriage – plays some role in the overall process of fertility decline. This was generally true in the historical transitions. For example, the initial fall in the birth rate in England after about 1815 reflected a rise in the age of women at marriage. It was only from the 1870s that the fall in the birth rate reflected an increase in the use of birth control within marriage. Considering more recent examples of fertility decline, since the middle of the twentieth century almost every developing country has experienced an increase in the age of women at marriage. Indeed, there are reasons to believe that – by raising the ratio of women to men in the age range at which people usually get married – mortality decline has contributed to this almost universal rise in the age of women at marriage.[21] However, regardless of why it has occurred, it is something that has led to a fall in fertility among women aged in their teens and early twenties.

Looking at the process of fertility decline as a whole, however, the main proximate cause of the decline – and the consequent fall in the birth rate – is that populations move from circumstances where there is little or no control of fertility by 'married' couples to circumstances where most people employ some form of birth control when they engage in sexual relations. Essentially, fertility moves from being uncontrolled to being controlled. In this move, it is older people of reproductive age – e.g. women in their forties and late thirties – who are usually the first to change.[22]

There is debate as to the practice of birth control in pre-transitional populations (see, for example, Wrigley 1987b; Santow 1995). However, if it was practised, then it was on a fairly small scale, and only among limited sections of society. The crucial role of increased birth control in the process of fertility decline can be illustrated using estimates of contraceptive prevalence for countries represented in Figure 4.1. Thus, as of around 2007, the percentages of women aged 15–49 who were in stable sexual unions, and who reported that they were using some form of contraception, were: England and Wales (82), Spain (74), Chile (61), India (56) and Egypt (59).[23] These figures are only broadly indicative. Nevertheless, they imply a revolution in the nature of the prevailing reproductive regimes. In each country, the percentages would have been close to zero before the onset of fertility decline.

*How the transition has changed* Several additional observations of a factual kind must be made in relation to the occurrence of the demographic transition more generally – drawing both on the preceding discussion and other work.

It is clear that in the earliest examples of the transition in north-western Europe, both the mortality declines and the fertility declines were relatively gradual affairs, and they were spread out over especially long periods of time. We have seen that, compared to later examples, the historical transitions involved much lower rates of natural increase. Part of the explanation for this was that the gap between the start of mortality decline and the start of fertility decline was often comparatively short (Reher 2004: 23).[24] The French case is particularly suggestive of both vital rates declining together with only a brief lag.

However, it also seems that the birth rates (and fertility levels) that prevailed in these European populations at the start of their transitions were *moderate* – i.e. they were not particularly high.[25] This point is supported by the examples shown in Figures 4.1 and 4.5 (see also Figure 2.2). Thus in these European countries the birth rate rarely exceeded 40 per thousand. And women might have an average of only about four or five live births each during the course of their reproductive lives. The fact that pre-transitional levels of fertility were generally moderate also helps to explain why the rates of natural increase experienced in the historical cases of transition were comparatively low.

In general, more recent demographic transitions in developing countries have involved faster falls in both mortality and fertility (see, for example, Kirk 1971; Chesnais 1992; Reher 2004). However, usually there has been a longer lag between the start of the fall in the death rate and the start of the fall in the birth rate. Also, fertility appears to be falling from somewhat higher levels in most contemporary examples of the transition. Thus most developing countries appear to have experienced birth rates of 40 per thousand or higher for extended periods of time. Again, an impression of this can be obtained from the examples in Figure 4.1 (see also Figure 2.2). Anyhow, the result of more rapid mortality decline and an apparently higher starting level for fertility has generally been significantly higher rates of natural increase in more recent transitions.

It is worth noting that some of the earliest writers on the transition – such as Warren Thompson and Adolphe Landry – believed that declines in death rates and birth rates would probably become faster in the future (Kirk 1996: 361–3). That is, they foresaw that these demographic processes would probably occur more rapidly in populations that experienced them later. Also, there was a relatively early appreciation that because later cases of mortality decline were occurring faster, countries would tend to experience higher rates of natural increase as a result. In addition, because some of the early writers recognized that they were addressing a phenomenon that would eventually affect *all* of humanity, much of their writing reflected the idea that the many differences – economic, cultural, political, etc. – that characterize different societies would ultimately *not* stand in the way of the occurrence of the transition. Landry, for example, was explicit in stating that death rates could be reduced without there being much improvement in the standard of living of a population – an observation which Dudley Kirk describes as 'strikingly modern' (Kirk 1996: 363).

In relation to populations that have progressed through most, or all of the transition, Kirk also remarks that a new balance between mortality and fertility has not yet materialized (Kirk 1996: 383). Thus all European countries, and an increasing number elsewhere in the world, have gone on to experience levels of fertility that are below the replacement level. We saw in Chapter 3 that the prospect of death rates that are higher than birth rates – and population decline – is now a real one in some countries. It is important to note, however, that it was probably rare for there to be more than a rough degree of balance between birth and death rates in pre-transitional populations. Therefore, we should probably expect no more than a rough degree of balance to apply in most post-transitional populations.

In conclusion, the overarching similarity of the demographic transition in its various manifestations is clear. However, with the passage of time, the phenomenon has tended to become more rapid in several different ways. And, beyond these considerations, we have seen that there can be important secondary differences in the form of the transition. With this as background, it is to matters of explanation that we now turn.

## The explanation of mortality decline

Mortality decline is the principal driving force within the demographic transition. But accounting for the process in any given situation is complex – and only a brief explanation of some of the more important factors involved can be given here. It is worth stressing that in all cases of decline, it is death rates at younger ages (i.e. among children, and then infants) which tend to fall first. Indeed, to a considerable extent, mortality decline consists of the progressive reduction of death rates at young ages. Declines in adult mortality tend to become more important later in the overall process.

The process of mortality decline in different societies is never exactly the same – either with regard to the facts, or their explanation. For one thing, the conditions that influenced death rates in pre-transitional circumstances were variable (e.g. in terms of diseases and climate). And the factors that contribute to mortality decline can combine in different ways. Nevertheless, there are several theoretical approaches to explaining the process (see Hill 2008). Some emphasize the importance of economic growth – working especially through improvements in nutritional status. Other accounts stress the role of public health measures – such as the introduction of clean water supplies and better systems of sewage disposal. Other explanations highlight the role of behavioural change informed by greater knowledge about disease transmission – illustrations here include advances in household cleanliness and the boiling of drinking water. Still other accounts emphasize the contribution of medical progress – i.e. improvements in preventive and curative medicine. Of course, all of these developments can interact with each other, and they benefit from wider changes in society – such as improvements in social stability and increasing levels of education.



*Mortality decline in Europe* The initial dampening of death-rate fluctuations in north-western Europe in the eighteenth century (and even before) reflected many developments associated with the gradual emergence of the modern nation-state. Thus advances in systems of administration, transport and trade contributed to the decrease in famine. Measures were developed which helped to control epidemics. For example, restrictions on movement (e.g. the quarantining of ships) assisted in the conquest of plague (Livi Bacci 2000: 61–90). And smallpox inoculation – a practice introduced through contact with Asia – spread in Europe during the second half of the eighteenth century. Then, in 1796, Edward Jenner demonstrated vaccination (with cowpox). This was the first effective and safe measure that could provide long-lasting protection, on a mass scale, against a major infectious disease. It spread rapidly across Europe and was soon taken to other parts of the world. That said, it would be several decades before vaccination began to have a truly global impact.[26]

There is little doubt that the mortality decline that occurred in Europe (and its offshoots) during the nineteenth century did reflect to some degree the rising living standards that arose eventually from the Industrial Revolution.[27] The argument that nutritional improvements – resulting from better living standards – explained the fall in mortality from infectious diseases at this time is associated with the work of Thomas McKeown (see, for example, McKeown 1976; McKeown and Record 1962). It is an argument that has received some support in work by Robert Fogel (1997, 2004). However, it is an argument that may have been overdone. There is a substantial body of research which indicates that the role of nutritional improvement in mortality decline in Europe has been overstated – especially in relation to the first half of the nineteenth century (see, for example, Livi Bacci 2000; Schofield et al. 1991).

There is considerable agreement, however, regarding the significant contribution that advances in water supplies and sanitation made to mortality decline in Europe (and its offshoots) – especially in urban areas – during the second half of the nineteenth century (see, for example, McKeown 1976; Szreter 1998). And this period also saw major progress in attitudes and behaviour towards infants and young children. For example, mothers became increasingly educated in relation to matters of breastfeeding, food preparation and the care of their children (see, for example, Woods 2000: 247–309).

It is generally agreed that – with the exception of vaccination against smallpox – medical progress played little part in reducing death rates in these societies until the first decades of the twentieth century (see, for example, Livi Bacci 2000: 146–7). However, helped by the development of the microscope, the last decades of the nineteenth century saw major scientific advances in the understanding of infectious diseases which were to have enormous implications for mortality decline during the twentieth century. For example, here one is thinking of the contributions of Louis Pasteur (e.g. in relation to the establishment of the germ theory of disease), Robert Koch (who discovered the bacteria responsible for both tuberculosis and cholera) and Ronald Ross (who identified the role of the mosquito in malaria transmission). These and many other scientific advances eventually had a huge impact everywhere – for example, through the development of vaccines, therapeutic drugs and a host of preventive health strategies. They also helped to substantiate changes like the increasing use of antiseptic procedures, the training of midwives, and the introduction of improved infant feeding practices.

*Mortality decline in developing countries* Turning to the developing world, the significant but relatively modest mortality decline that occurred in many countries during the first half of the twentieth century was based on the introduction of fairly basic procedures (see, for example, McNeill 1976: 217–68). For instance, in India there was: a decline in the frequency of major famines – mainly due to the development of more adequate policies of famine relief; some fall in mortality from diseases like smallpox (due to vaccination) and cholera (e.g. through efforts to improve water supplies); a decline in plague – perhaps partly reflecting policy measures (e.g. quarantine, and efforts to control rats); limited success in the control of malaria in certain locations – for example, through attempts to reduce mosquito breeding by draining freshwater pools and using larvicides. These and other procedures were often introduced in a limited and piecemeal way. Nevertheless, in India, and many other places, they produced some decline in mortality, and prepared the ground for what was to happen after 1945.

The major falls in death rates that have occurred in most developing countries since the end of the Second World War have also reflected the influence of many different factors. It is important to note that in the late 1940s there was previous experience – not all of it for developed countries – which demonstrated that considerable mortality reduction could be achieved. Also, in the 1940s and 1950s several relatively affordable and effective new health technologies became available. Here one is thinking of antibiotics, sulphonamide drugs and perhaps especially the spraying of DDT to help in the control of mosquitoes and other insects that transmit diseases like malaria and yellow fever. In addition, more and more countries assumed responsibility for their own health conditions – i.e. with the process of decolonization. This has underpinned the increased commitment of many national governments to establishing basic systems of healthcare (and education).

Several other considerations need to be mentioned in the context of mortality decline in the developing world since 1945. Thus this period has seen greatly increased coordination and commitment in the international community to improve health conditions. The activities of bodies like the World Health Organization have been one expression of this. Also, in the late 1970s it became clear that China – poor, overwhelmingly rural, and containing almost a quarter of humanity – had been able to achieve very substantial mortality decline using fairly basic approaches. These approaches included the provision of elementary healthcare and education to all of the population (i.e. there was stress upon universal access). While China's experience was unique in many respects – and rarely easy to copy – it nevertheless contributed to the growing realization that a reasonably high life expectancy could be achieved in poor settings and at relatively low cost (see, for example, Halstead et al. 1985; Caldwell 1986).

Another far-reaching development, starting from the 1970s, has been the international promotion of well-tried vaccines that protect children against major killer diseases like tuberculosis, diphtheria, measles, whooping cough and tetanus. Large-scale, and often subsidized, immunization programmes have played a big part in reducing levels of infant and child mortality in many poor countries. Other low-cost health interventions which have also played a role include oral rehydration and the improvement of latrines. The spread of mass education has certainly assisted in the reduction of mortality. Indeed, few indicators are more closely associated with the level of child mortality in households (and populations) than the level of women's education. Relatedly, the second half of the twentieth century almost certainly saw a significant secularization of attitudes towards disease and illness. In earlier times people tended to interpret episodes of sickness primarily in supernatural terms. Increasingly, however, they recognize that something practical can be done to improve the situation (see, for example, Caldwell et al. 1988). These and many other developments – including, to differing degrees, rising living standards, improvements in water and sewage, and advances in curative medicine – have all contributed to the transformation of mortality that has occurred in most developing countries since about 1945.

*Discussion* To simplify, in Europe and its offshoots, mortality decline was largely what Reher (2004: 30) describes as an *autochthonous* process – i.e. one that occurred mainly from within these societies (taken as a whole). This helps to explain why the first examples of mortality decline were relatively gradual. In contrast, the improvement in mortality that has happened in developing countries since 1945 has resulted from a whole battery of measures that have been introduced in just a few decades. Most of these measures – many of them, such as childhood vaccines, extremely effective – came largely from outside, although it is important to stress that they were often paid for by the developing countries themselves. These considerations help to explain why more

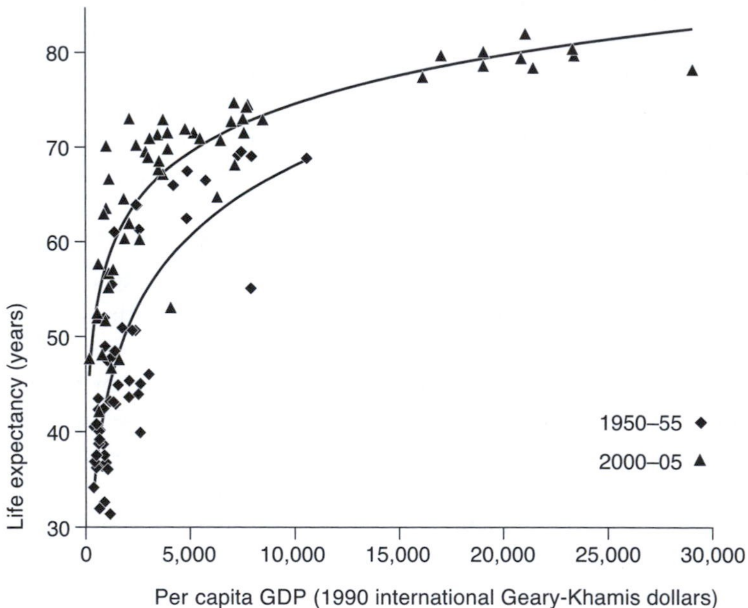


*Sources*: Maddison (2009), United Nations (2009)

**Figure 4.6 The changing relationship between per capita income and life expectancy, fifty-six countries, 1950–55 and 2000–05**

recent examples of mortality decline have usually been much more rapid than earlier examples.

It should be emphasized that in all cases of mortality decline – historical and contemporary – the bulk of the decline has resulted from falls in *infectious* (and sometimes parasitic) diseases. For example, Samuel Preston (1980) has estimated that between 1900 and 1970 roughly 70 per cent of the total mortality improvement that occurred in developing countries was due to reductions in deaths from just the following diseases: influenza, pneumonia, bronchitis, respiratory tuberculosis, diarrhoea, enteritis, gastroenteritis and malaria. Of course, the estimate of 70 per cent *is* rough – Preston provides a range of 60–80 per cent. But the basic point is clear. Infectious diseases have become comparatively easy to prevent and treat. It is only later in the process of mortality decline – when life expectancy reaches a fairly high level – that chronic, degenerative ailments, such as cancers and heart disease, tend to predominate. Of course, degenerative ailments largely affect adults, and they are harder to prevent and more expensive to treat. To a considerable extent, however, mortality decline results from the reduction of deaths from infectious diseases; this reveals a more stubborn core of chronic degenerative ailments. The overall process has been referred to as the 'epidemiological transition' (Omran 1971).[28]

A related point is that economic growth made a rather limited contribution to mortality decline during the twentieth century. Here Preston (1975) examined the changing international cross-sectional relationship between per capita income and life expectancy. He found that countries with higher incomes tended to experience higher life expectancies. But the relationship had shifted greatly over time. Thus, for any level of per capita income, a population could expect to experience a much higher life expectancy in the 1960s compared to the 1930s. Of course, this reflected the impact of the many *other* factors that help to determine the overall level of mortality in a population. Preston concluded that only about 16 per cent (range 10–25 per cent) of the overall rise in life expectancy that had occurred in the world between the 1930s and the 1960s was due to increases in national income per se (see also Bloom and Canning 2001: 176–9). More recently it has been observed that some countries that have experienced modest – or even negative – economic growth have nevertheless experienced large rises in life expectancy (Soares 2007).

In this context, Figure 4.6 shows the international relationship between levels of per capita income and life expectancy using estimates for both 1950–55 and 2000–05. The major upward shift in the relationship is very clear.[29] In 2000–05 there were quite a few populations with very low incomes which nonetheless had life expectancies of 60 years or more. Countries with low incomes in 2000–05 which had relatively low life expectancies – i.e. in the range 40–50 years – were chiefly those affected by warfare and/or HIV/AIDS. It is worth emphasizing, however, that even a life expectancy of 40 years was very rare for a pre-transitional society.[30] It is also worth noting that the country with the highest per capita income in 2000–05 was the United States. But, as can be seen from Figure 4.6, life expectancy in the United States was slightly lower than in several countries with lower levels of per capita income. In short, many factors besides income determine a country's level of mortality. In recent decades most mortality decline has had little direct connection with rising incomes.

Finally in this discussion, it is important to note that during the second half of the demographic transition the process of fertility decline *itself* makes a significant contribution to mortality decline. Indeed, this is probably a universal feature of the transition. There are several reasons why it occurs – most of them related to improvements in infant and child mortality (see, for example, Hobcraft, McDonald and Rutstein 1983, 1985; United Nations 1994; WHO 1995). Thus, in a pre-transitional situation of relatively high fertility, a disproportionate number of deaths happen among infants and young children who are either born at short birth intervals (e.g. of less than 24 months) or are borne by women who are themselves either very young or fairly old in terms of their reproductive age (i.e. in their early teens, or in their late thirties and forties). Births to such women tend to be more difficult physiologically, and they also tend to involve babies that are of low birth weight, and hence at greater risk of dying.

However, as we have seen, fertility decline involves a rise in the age of women at marriage, and a major increase in the use of birth control. Consequently fewer births occur at very short birth intervals – i.e. births tend to become better spaced. Also, fewer births happen to women who are either very young or relatively old in reproductive terms. Therefore, the overall level of mortality in the population declines because fewer children (and mothers) die. This is probably an inevitable benefit of fertility decline within the transition. Also, other things equal, parents can probably care for their children better if there are fewer children around. The overall effect of fertility decline on mortality decline can be appreciable. For example, Soares (2007: 272) cites a study in Bangladesh where between 1966 and 1981 increased use of family planning is estimated to have reduced the population's death rate by the admittedly exceptional figure of 50 per cent. This takes us to the explanation of fertility decline.



### Explanations of fertility decline

We have seen that fertility decline usually involves a reduction in marriage – either through its postponement, or through a rise in the proportion of women remaining single. In the long run, however, the main proximate mechanism is that people turn to the use of some form of birth control – almost always some form of contraception.

Again, examples of fertility decline are never exactly the same – either with regard to the facts or their explanation. But that is only to be expected, given the very different circumstances in which the process occurs. Here, we need to stand back and address broader themes – such as the reasons why more recent fertility declines have tended to occur more rapidly. However, the key task is to explain why people adopt birth control in the first place.

*Early theories* The first explanations for fertility decline were proposed in relation to the presumed experience of countries in western Europe and their main offshoots – especially the United States. The work of Notestein (1945, 1953) was particularly influential here. He provided what became known as the 'classical' theoretical statement of why people adopted birth control. In many ways, however, this statement was more descriptive than analytic.

Notestein's account was framed chiefly in relation to the emergence of 'urban industrial society' and it contained many considerations that were presumed to be causal in some way. For example, he stated that the conditions of urban industrial life stripped the family of many of its functions. He emphasized the rise of factory employment, and the growing anonymity that people experienced in the expanding towns. He stressed the increasing importance of individualism and rising personal aspirations. He located the process within a context of a growing demand for skilled labour, and therefore a rising need for formal educational qualifications. As a result of these and other considerations 'the cost of child-rearing grew and the possibilities for economic contributions by children declined. Falling death rates at once increased the size of the family to be supported and lowered the inducements to have many births' (Notestein 1953, cited in Kirk 1996: 364). Therefore Notestein's was a multifaceted account of fertility decline, and it refers to many factors – including falling death rates – that have subsequently been studied by social scientists in this context. It seems reasonable to say that he regarded fertility decline as being caused by a complex of socio-economic changes that accompanied and arose out of industrialization.

Another important contribution on the subject came from Kingsley Davis (1963). He too was concerned with trying to explain the experience of Europe and North America. However, writing in the early 1960s, to these examples he was able to add Japan. Davis also regarded fertility decline as something that happened as a society moved from being mainly rural and agricultural to being mainly urban and industrial. However, his approach was distinct in that it placed particular emphasis on the role of mortality decline within the transition. The approach has been described as the theory of 'multi-phasic' response (Friedlander 1969: 359).

In brief, Davis noted that mortality decline meant that couples were faced with having to deal with larger numbers of surviving children, that adults themselves lived longer, and that there would be a higher rate of natural increase in the population as a result. He argued that these demographic changes produced various strains in society. For example, within households there would be more mouths to feed; and within communities there might be heightened pressure on agricultural land. Faced with such strains, a population could respond in a variety of ways. The various responses were not mutually exclusive, and the extent and timing of their adoption would vary according to the circumstances. In the short run, social and economic responses might be able to offset the increasing strains. For example, a rise in agricultural productivity might be possible in order to produce more food. However, in the longer run there were limits to the relief that social and economic responses could provide.[31] Therefore, behind them, there were three major demographic responses. These were (i) *out-migration*, for example from rural to urban areas, or perhaps to another country, (ii) a *reduction in marriage*, for example through a delay in the age of marriage, and (iii) *increased birth control* within marriage, mainly through the use of contraception, but possibly through the use of induced abortion, as had been the case in Japan.

Davis regarded out-migration as being a comparatively easy response for a society to take – provided that the opportunities for it were available. He recognized that a reduction in marriage was a common initial response to rising pressure on resources; indeed, it was the traditional response in much of north-western Europe to try to maintain living standards. Davis considered that, because it involved changes in sexual behaviour, increased use of birth control within marriage was often a rather difficult step for people to take. Nevertheless, because there were limits to what could be achieved through out-migration and reductions in marriage, he considered that increased birth control was essentially the backstop response – i.e. it was *inevitable* in the long run. It seems fair to say that Kingsley Davis considered that mortality decline was the underlying cause of fertility decline (Cleland 2001).

*Lessons from Europe* In the 1960s and 1970s an increasing body of research shed new light on the nature of the fertility declines that had occurred in Europe (see, for example, Coale and Watkins 1986). This led to a reconsideration of the factors that had been involved in the process. Perhaps the most important realization to emerge was that in many countries cultural variables – such as language, religion and ethnicity – performed quite well in explaining variation in the timing and speed of fertility declines. For example, birth rates in Belgium fell earlier in the rural French-speaking areas than in the Flemish (i.e. Dutch-speaking) areas that contained the major towns (Lesthaeghe 1977). In general, maps of cultural variables were at least as helpful in explaining variation in fertility decline as were maps of socio-economic variables – such as the level of urbanization or the degree of industrialization.

A similar point arose from comparison of the experiences of England and France (see Figures 4.1 and 4.5). In economic terms, England was much more developed than France during the eighteenth and nineteenth centuries. After all, England is often considered to be the birthplace of the Industrial Revolution. It was where the phenomenon of 'modern economic growth' – i.e. a sustained rise in the average level of per capita income – is thought to have begun. Compared to France, per capita incomes were appreciably higher in England throughout the nineteenth century (Maddison 2007: 382). Moreover, England was also much more urbanized. Chesnais (1992: 329) notes that when the English turned to birth control in the 1870s around three-quarters of the population lived in towns. However, when the French began to employ birth control in the 1790s, only about a quarter of France's population lived in towns. So, clearly, being an 'urban industrial' society was *not* necessarily very important.

Interestingly, accounting for the different experiences of England and France has involved making use of the theoretical approach provided by Davis. As we have seen, there was considerable mortality decline in France before the Revolution. The ensuing population growth put pressure on agricultural resources – especially land. In late eighteenth-century France, however, there were few chances for people to migrate out of rural areas – either overseas (e.g. Quebec had been lost in 1759) or to the country's comparatively small urban sector. Also, by the 1790s people in France were already marrying at a relatively late age, and a fairly high proportion of them were remaining single. Given these considerations, it is easier to appreciate why the French resorted to birth control at a very early time (see, for example, Livi Bacci 2000: 151–7). In contrast, in England there were greater prospects for overseas migration (e.g. to North America) and the occurrence of the Industrial Revolution in the country's expanding towns also provided rural people with opportunities to migrate. These considerations help to explain why recourse to the use of birth control occurred much later in England (see, for example, Chesnais 1992: 321–43; Friedlander 1969). Moreover, it is possible that England's relatively dynamic economic performance during the nineteenth century worked to delay people having to confront the essential choice between controlling their births and accepting a deterioration, or slower rate of improvement, in their living conditions.[32]

*Lessons from the developing world* For much of the period since 1945 it was widely assumed that fertility decline would occur in developing

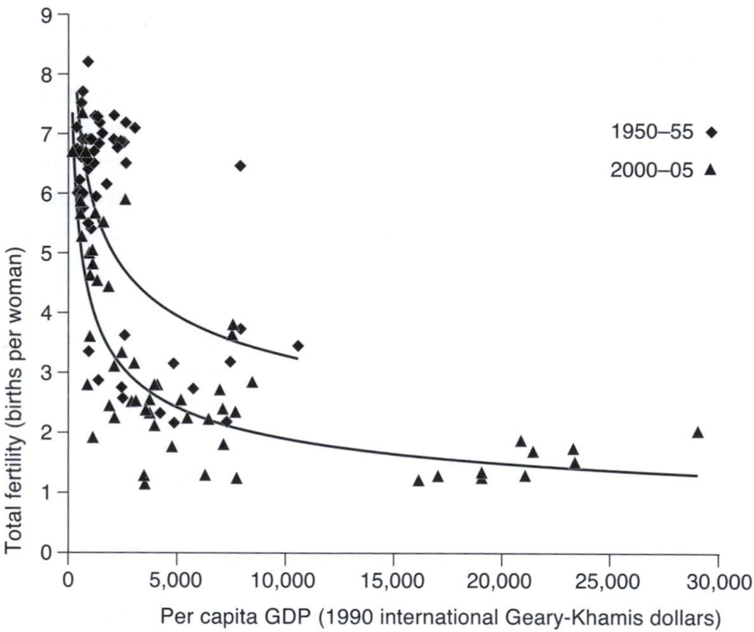


*Sources*: Maddison (2009), United Nations (2009)

**Figure 4.7 The changing relationship between per capita income and total fertility, fifty-six countries, 1950–55 and 2000–05**

countries as a natural outcome of economic growth and associated developments – such as industrialization, urbanization and rising incomes. In recent decades emphasis has also been placed on the role of education (especially of women) in reducing fertility. And it has long been argued that government family planning programmes are needed to help in the reduction of birth rates.

It took some time for it to be realized that – starting from around the 1960s – many developing countries *were* experiencing fertility decline. Early evidence came from relatively small populations, such as Sri Lanka and Taiwan. A prescient paper by Dudley Kirk, published in 1971, argued that a 'new' demographic transition was occurring in the developing world. It was known that the death rate had fallen very rapidly in many poor countries. However, Kirk noted that – after a period of 25 years in which no country had begun to experience fertility decline – there suddenly appeared to be a growing number of societies that were undergoing the process. He stated that there seemed to be 'an acceleration of the rate at which countries move through the demographic transition from high to low birth rates' and that birth rates appeared to be falling 'among peoples of very different cultural backgrounds and ways of life'. Referring to the influence of socio-economic variables, he observed that 'quite different levels and kinds of development are associated with fertility reductions' in different regions of the world (see Kirk 1971: 125, 146). Later experience has only served to strengthen support for Kirk's observations. By the 1980s it was evident that fertility declines were under way in most of Asia and Latin America, and parts of the Middle East (e.g. Turkey and Tunisia).

It is true that all populations that have become 'urban industrial' have eventually experienced fertility decline. However, many populations that are not – or were not – urban and industrial have also experienced substantial fertility decline. Countries that have experienced a major fall in fertility while still being largely rural, agricultural and poor include: Bangladesh, China, North Korea, India, Indonesia, Myanmar (i.e. Burma), Peru, Philippines, Thailand and Vietnam. These countries all had levels of total fertility of about 3 births per woman, or lower, during 2000–05 (United Nations 2009).

In this context Figure 4.7 shows the changing international cross-sectional relationship between per capita income and total fertility – again, using estimates for 1950–55 and 2000–05.[33] Most countries experienced a rise in per capita income over this period. However, a very large downward shift in the curve is clear – most of it due to falls in fertility after 1960–65 (see also World Bank 1985: 29–31). In other words, holding the level of per capita income constant, a population could expect to experience an appreciably lower level of fertility per woman in 2000–05 than in 1950–55. The curve for 2000–05 is exceptionally steep at very low levels of income. Many poor countries have reduced their total fertility rate from high to low levels. Moreover, as we have noted, fertility decline is now under way in nearly every developing country. The world appears to be moving towards a future situation in which fertility is low almost everywhere – largely *irrespective* of the level of per capita income, or indeed virtually any other consideration.

The fact that fertility decline has occurred in a huge variety of different settings has led to a change in the dominant approach to explaining the process. Aggregate considerations such as economic growth, rising incomes, industrialization and urbanization are no longer put at the centre of the stage.[34] The prevailing approach is now more focused, more clinical. There has been a rediscovery of the idea that mortality decline is probably the underlying cause of fertility decline. In this context, it is important to distinguish the *remote* cause of the process from the host of factors that can *condition* it.

*Factors conditioning fertility decline* Many factors condition the process of fertility decline. After all, every population has its own social structure and history. The following comments are selective. Moreover, it is difficult to be precise about the influence of any particular factor.

*Government policies* can influence the nature of fertility decline. China provides a clear case. The sudden introduction of a set of highly coercive measures reduced the level of total fertility from about 5.8 to 2.2 births per woman between 1970 and 1980. This was the fastest major fertility decline in history. It happened in a poor and overwhelmingly rural population. It is generally agreed, however, that fertility in China would have fallen anyway, sooner or later (Scotese and Wang 1995; Sen 1997; McNicoll 2006). What the government policy did was bring about an earlier and faster decline than would otherwise have occurred.

More generally, government family planning programmes were invented in Asian countries (e.g. India, South Korea, Taiwan) in the 1950s and 1960s. They have been adopted to differing degrees in other parts of the world. Assessing their effectiveness in reducing fertility is difficult; and opinions vary as to their effects (see, for example, Pritchett 1994; Bongaarts 1997). However, although family planning programmes may well accelerate fertility decline, they are certainly not required for the process to occur. Birth rates have fallen in many countries (e.g. in Latin America) where there is no government programme. And the fertility declines that happened in Europe and North America in the past occurred without such measures – indeed, the politicians of the time were often hostile to the spread of birth control.

*The range of available contraceptive technologies* can influence fertility decline. The birth control methods available in the nineteenth century were limited – although, with the vulcanization of rubber, modern condoms became increasingly available in the second half of that century. However, in the second half of the twentieth century, many highly effective and low-cost birth control technologies were developed – e.g. hormonal contraceptives (pills, injections, implants), intrauterine devices (IUDs) and several types of male and female sterilization. Clearly, fertility decline can happen without these modern methods. But it is likely that they facilitate the process. Studies consistently find higher levels of contraceptive use in societies where a wider range of contraceptive methods is available (see, for example, Potts 1997).

*The spread of mass education* has facilitated the process of fertility decline.[35] This was true in Europe in the past, and it has applied in many developing countries more recently (see, for example, Cochrane 1979; Caldwell 1980; Woods 2000: 157–66). To a limited degree, education may reduce the birth rate by delaying the age at which young women marry. However, research usually finds that better-educated married women are also more likely to use birth control. There are many possible explanations for this. For example, better-educated women may be more aware of contraception, and in a better position to discuss its use with their partner. They may also take a more secular and instrumental attitude towards the control of their own fertility.

However, while more educated women may lead in the adoption of birth control within a society, there is little reason to think that less educated women are any less capable of using it eventually. For example, most of the fertility decline that has occurred in India in recent years has been among women with little or no education (see, for example, Bhat 2002; McNay et al. 2004). Such women, and their partners, can reduce their fertility – although it generally takes them somewhat longer to adopt birth control. The fact that studies often find an inverse association between levels of education and fertility is largely a consequence of differences in the *timing* of the move towards birth control within society.

*Different forms of communication* condition the nature of fertility decline. This is because the process always entails the diffusion of new ideas and practices. Indeed, some scholars have approached fertility decline largely from the perspective of 'ideational change' (see, for example, Cleland and Wilson 1987). Pamphlets and newspapers helped to raise knowledge about contraception during the nineteenth century – as, of course, did simple word-of-mouth. In more recent times, however, the influence of the media (radio, television, etc.) has expanded greatly. Indeed, one reason why better-educated women adopt birth control earlier is that they are more exposed to modern forms of communication. The diffusion of new ideas about the family (and sexual behaviour) can be pervasive and subtle. And it can have a strong international dimension – as the following statement by Caldwell about conditions in Nigeria in the early 1970s suggests:

> 'The family', as taught by the school, is almost entirely the Western family. Textbooks either come from England or are local products modelled on English prototypes. Readers, used in the first years of schooling, are very much concerned with the family and generally tell of a house with a father who goes out to work [and] a mother who stays home and looks after the children [...] All cinema films, most television films that portray family life, much of the magazine content, and a considerable proportion of the newspaper feature content are imported [...] from the West. The same message of nuclear family structure is relayed as is imparted by the schools. (Caldwell 1976: 353–54)

*Cultural considerations* can influence fertility decline. As we have noted, this was true in Europe. But it is also suggested by more recent experience in developing countries. For example, populations of Confucian culture seem to have adopted birth control relatively quickly. A study of Latin America found that countries where a larger proportion of the people were of European origin tended to experience earlier fertility declines (Beaver 1975). And, within countries, Muslims often have somewhat higher fertility than non-Muslims. That said, 'culture' has many dimensions and correlates. And it may be hard to distinguish what specific aspect of a culture – if any – is having an independent effect. Nevertheless, the fact that people of the same cultural group tend to interact more with each other is certainly relevant to how new ideas and practices of birth control become diffused within a country. Also understandable in this context is that simple geographical location can play a significant role in conditioning fertility decline. The extent to which a society is integrated with the wider world is almost certainly germane. Landlocked countries feature prominently among the places to which fertility decline has come last.

*The level of urbanization* can condition the process of fertility decline. Historically, and in contemporary developing countries, it is usually the case that people in urban areas have lower fertility than people in rural areas. However, there may be a brief initial period in the process of fertility decline during which fertility is higher in urban areas. There is evidence of this in data for some sub-Saharan countries in the 1960s and 1970s – perhaps reflecting greater disruption to traditional practices of breastfeeding and sexual abstinence in urban areas.[36] However, in general people in towns tend to be relatively advanced both in terms of delaying the age at which they marry, and in adopting birth control. This should not, however, obscure the fact that fertility decline has occurred – and is occurring – in rural populations. In other words, urban conditions are not required for the process to unfold. Again, the fact that studies often find lower fertility in urban areas mainly reflects differences in the timing of fertility decline.

*Possibilities for out-migration* can play a conditioning role – as was suggested by Kingsley Davis. Thus, other things equal, the greater the prospects for out-migration, the later will be the process of fertility decline. We saw that this idea receives support from past experience in Europe (comparing England and France). But it may also help to explain why more recent fertility declines have generally been faster. Thus European countries *were* able to export a sizeable proportion of their natural increase as they went through the demographic transition. For example, during the period 1881–1910 about one fifth of Europe's total natural increase was 'exported' through migration – mostly to North America (World Bank 1985: 29). For most contemporary developing countries, however, the chances of trying to equal this are very limited.[37] Nevertheless, the demographic transition tends to stimulate migration, both internal and external. And there is usually a tendency for societies to export people as they go through the transition.

The interaction of possibilities for out-migration with fertility decline can be used to illustrate the difficulties involved in estimating the influence of any particular conditioning factor on fertility decline – especially in modern circumstances. Thus a study of Puerto Rico during the period 1940–70 found support for the idea that out-migration from the island had acted as an alternative to the adoption of birth control (see Mosher 1980). Other things equal, this should have delayed the occurrence of fertility decline. However, the birth rate actually fell earlier in Puerto Rico than in neighbouring Caribbean islands (Dyson and Murphy 1985). A possible explanation for this is that much of the out-migration from Puerto Rico was to New York City. In New York migrants would have been rapidly exposed to new ideas about the family and the use of birth control. It may well be that these ideas were then transferred back to

Puerto Rico – effectively *short-circuiting* other processes. Therefore, the effects of out-migration cannot always be considered in a straightforward way.

Another illustration of the complexity of accounting for fertility decline in modern circumstances is provided by the Gaza Strip. The people of this small, densely settled Palestinian enclave have experienced considerable mortality decline. The population is almost entirely urban, and the level of education is reasonably high. There are very few possibilities for out-migration. Until the 1990s, however, total fertility remained at the very high level of about 7 births per woman. There has been a slight fall in fertility since the 1990s – with reductions in marriage making an important contribution. We can be sure that fertility decline will continue in Gaza, and that eventually there will be increasing use of birth control (see Khawaja 2003; Khawaja and Assaf 2007). However, the Gaza Strip provides a good example of a more general point which is often neglected by analysts – namely, that 'other things' are rarely equal.[38] Thus in this case, as in others, political considerations are clearly an important conditioning influence.

*Discussion of conditioning factors* In concluding, several comments about conditioning factors are required. First, it is important to emphasize that in any particular situation a huge number of conditioning influences are likely to be at work. Those mentioned above are only a selection.

Second, we have used the neutral term 'conditioning' because variation in these factors can influence fertility in different ways. For instance, governments sometimes introduce 'pro-natalist' policies which are designed to raise fertility, or at least delay or slow its decline. Examples of this in the past have included Algeria, Pakistan, Philippines, Malaysia, Mexico and Zambia (see Lee et al. 1998). Such policies may have worked against fertility decline, to some degree.

Third, it is clear that several of the factors mentioned above are relevant to the explanation of why historical cases of fertility decline tended to be slower than many of those that have occurred more recently. Thus in nineteenth-century Europe there were no family planning programmes, and only a few basic methods of birth control. The power of the mass media to affect people's thinking and behaviour was much less than applies today. Also, the possibilities for out-migration to relieve pressures caused by population growth were significantly greater in Europe. Moreover, it seems reasonable to suggest that the faster rate of death-rate reduction in contemporary transitions is also relevant to the explanation of why their fertility declines have often been faster. After all, the sudden occurrence of major falls in mortality has produced unprecedentedly rapid rates of population growth in many societies. In turn, this has presumably produced greater stresses and strains, other things equal. Therefore, we might expect there to be a more rapid decline in fertility in modern examples of the transition – other things equal, and once the process gets under way.

Finally, all of the conditioning factors mentioned above have been found to be associated with fertility *differentials*, within the context of fertility decline. And the same is true of socio-economic variables, such as the level of per capita income. Thus, whether one is comparing different populations, or different groups within the same population, it is usually the case that higher levels of education, urban living or per capita income are associated with lower levels of fertility. However, that said, it is important to appreciate that such differentials mainly reflect differences in the timing of fertility decline. In the long run, all populations, and all groups within them, are moving towards circumstances of low fertility – irrespective of their level of education, place of residence, level of income, etc.

In sum, fertility decline is essentially a *uniform* process, i.e. one that eventually affects everyone. Various factors can condition the process – some of them, such as female education, speeding it up. But these factors are not its underlying cause. The tendency of research to focus so much on differentials has been unfortunate. Among other things, it has obscured the ultimately homogeneous nature of the process of fertility decline.

## Mortality decline as the remote cause of fertility decline

Among scholars who have considered the issue in depth, there is widespread agreement that mortality decline is the underlying cause of fertility decline (see, for example, Chesnais 1992; Hirschman 1994; Kirk 1996; K. Mason 1997a; Galloway et al. 1998; Wilson and Airey 1999; Cleland 2001; Dyson 2001; Livi Bacci 2001). A key reason for arriving at this conclusion is that '[f]ertility declines have occurred under widely varying social and economic circumstances but virtually never in the absence of mortality decline, and this can be taken as strong evidence that mortality decline is the primary cause of fertility decline' (Casterline 2003: 213–14).

It seems that there has never been a case of fertility decline in the absence of mortality decline. But fertility declines *have* occurred in the absence of other factors that are sometimes suggested as causing the process. Thus, to reiterate, fertility declines have occurred in populations that are not urban and industrial; they have occurred in populations where per capita incomes and educational levels are low; they have occurred in the absence of family planning programmes and modern methods of contraception.

Mortality decline as the cause of fertility decline has also been shown to perform well using several criteria that are helpful in assessing possible examples of causation. For instance, in all cases where the facts can be established with reasonable clarity, the start of mortality decline precedes the start of fertility decline (i.e. the cause precedes the effect). In all cases, the magnitude of mortality decline is similar to the magnitude of fertility decline in terms of vital rates (i.e. the cause and the effect are roughly proportional in terms of their scale). And, in all cases, the duration of the cause – i.e. the period during which the death rate falls – appears to be similar to the duration of the effect – i.e. the period during which the birth rate falls (see Ní Bhrolcháin and Dyson 2007).

Within the demographic transition, the lag between mortality decline and fertility decline is the period during which intermediate social and economic processes occur as a result of improving mortality. It is important to emphasize that people do *not* adopt birth control because they 'see' that mortality has improved. Rather, mortality decline leads to various stresses and strains in society which gradually evince themselves in people's lives, and it is to these newly emerging social and economic pressures that people eventually respond. Such pressures can include: the increased costs involved in raising larger numbers of surviving children; increasing difficulties in endowing marriages; a lengthening of the time before landholdings are passed on to younger generations; reductions in the average size of the landholdings that are inherited; downward pressure on wage levels due to increasing numbers of people entering the labour force. This list can easily be extended (see Cleland 2001). Notice that the stresses and strains can include considerations that operate within households (e.g. increased levels of crowding) and considerations that operate beyond the household in the wider community (e.g. increased problems in finding gainful employment). Therefore, in the long run, men and women of reproductive age are faced at more or less the same time with increasing pressures on two fronts.

To reiterate, the strains produced by mortality decline are almost always expressed in terms of the economic circumstances that individuals confront in their daily lives.[39] Of course, that is the context in which all of us – you and me included – live. The basic issue people face is the emergence of an incompatibility between the maintenance of high fertility on the one hand, and the achievement of their economic aims on the other (Macunovitch 2000). In this context, their 'economic aims' might be to improve their living standards, to maintain their living standards, or to slow the rate at which their living standards are falling. It is important to emphasize that the basic dilemma will emerge eventually, largely irrespective of whether per capita incomes are high or low. It will arise largely irrespective of whether economic conditions are improving or getting worse. In short, the explanation that 'we can't afford to have any more children' can be used in almost any context. People turn to birth control unaware of the remote causal process – i.e. mortality decline – that has caused them to change their behaviour.

Both historically and in contemporary developing countries, fertility has often declined in circumstances where average incomes have been rising. Therefore the process has often been attributed to economic growth. It has also been argued that in poor societies children are net contributors to the household economy, and that with rising incomes their economic contribution falls and the costs of raising them increase – leading to a fall in the demand for children. There are, however, all sorts of difficulties with these arguments as the fundamental explanation of fertility decline – not least the lack of evidence that children really are net contributors to the household economy in poor societies (see, for example, Cassen 1976; Cleland and Wilson 1987; Dyson 1991; Vlassoff 1991; Kirk 1996). It is notable too that in other contexts social scientists have 'explained' fertility decline in terms of falling per capita incomes – so called 'poverty-induced' fertility declines (see, for example, Harrison 1979; Basu 1986; Swartz 2002). In both situations, however, the 'explanation' for fertility decline is largely a rationalization of what has occurred. There is no reason to think that economic growth and higher incomes bring about fertility decline in themselves. On the contrary, we might expect improving economic conditions to delay the occurrence of fertility decline, other things equal.[40] Indeed, the fact that the world economy grew at an extraordinarily fast pace in the 1950s and 1960s may help to explain why contemporary fertility declines have tended to occur with a longer lag on mortality decline.[41]

That said, the critical decision that people make to adopt birth control and limit their fertility *is* framed largely in economic terms. It occurs within the context of household circumstances. And, in justifying the decision, people naturally refer to the costs of having children. Ultimately, however, the spread of birth control in any society is an *adaptive* response to the fundamental alteration in circumstances that is brought about by mortality decline. And, within that context, birth control can be seen as an attempt to *maintain* family size, rather than letting it rise to, and remain at, levels that are unprecedentedly high (Reher 2004: 25).

## Conclusions and discussion

The basic message of this chapter is surely very clear: fertility decline is caused by mortality decline. It is not caused by the emergence of 'urban industrial' society. It is not caused by economic growth. It is not caused by any factor other than mortality decline.

The process of fertility decline is essentially a lagged adaptive response to mortality decline. As Chris Wilson has stated:

> Fertility decline must be viewed as a path-dependent process of adjustment. The most significant factor in such a process of fertility decline lies in earlier and concurrent declines in mortality [...] The socio-economic and cultural characteristics of a population determine the nature and speed of this process of adjustment [but t]hey are not the prime movers, and different factors are critical in different societies. Thus the search for universalist explanations for fertility decline in terms of these characteristics is pointless. (Wilson 1995: 23)

Therefore, one demographic process – i.e. mortality decline – is ultimately responsible for another – i.e. fertility decline. It is worth adding that purely demographic interactions play a significant part in other aspects of the transition as well – again, largely independently of the characteristics and conditions of the particular societies involved. For example, we have noted that mortality decline has implications for both the age of women at marriage and the extent of widowhood in society. And an even more important illustration of the point is the fact that in all transitions, once it is under way, fertility decline itself makes some contribution to further mortality decline (e.g. by reducing births to women at very young and old reproductive ages).

Essentially, then, the demographic transition is a macro-level phenomenon that has been 'set off' by mortality decline in a wide variety of different contexts all around the world. The final result – i.e. the movement to low fertility through the use of birth control – is virtually certain, although the manner in which it is achieved is highly variable.

Viewed as an adaptive response, the fertility declines of different populations can be regarded as more or less successful. Thus in France the process of fertility decline was closely associated with the process of mortality decline, and therefore the country's population did not even double in size as it went through the transition.[42] The experience of other countries in Europe was variable. Insofar as it can be assessed, however, the average population 'growth multiple' for Europe was probably in the vicinity of four, although England and the Netherlands, for example, experienced appreciably higher multiples.[43] In the case of China, the country was able to engineer both a very swift decline in the death rate and – after a brief period of rapid population growth – a very swift decline in the birth rate. A growth multiple somewhere between three and four may be reasonable. In these and other examples, we have seen that there are intimations of symmetry between the two fundamental processes involved. The nature of the first process (i.e. mortality decline) may provide some intimation as to the likely nature of the second (i.e. fertility decline).

If this is indeed the case, then it may not augur well for fertility decline in those populations – particularly, but not only, in sub-Saharan Africa – where mortality decline, although it has produced rapid population growth, has nevertheless been relatively lagging and fitful by modern standards. The capacity of warfare and social instability to slow, and indeed halt, the process of mortality decline is worth noting in this context. Such considerations account for much of the uncertainty about the future pace of fertility decline in some areas of the world. Some developing countries may actually experience slower fertility decline than applied in certain countries in Europe. Relatedly, we cannot be sure as to whether all future examples of the transition will be relatively compressed in terms of their overall length.

Finally, there is the question: what is the cause of the demographic transition? Essentially, this amounts to addressing the origins of mortality decline. The thrust of the argument in this book is that, in the final resort, demographic causal processes within the transition operate independently of other aspects of society. In the main, however, mortality decline – the process that sets off and underpins so much of the transition – is not attributable to demographic factors. Here we must take a much broader view.

To answer the question we must go back to eighteenth-century Europe, especially the continent's north-west. This was the time and place of the Enlightenment. Key characteristics of this movement were a growing belief in reason and the possibility of progress, and the expanding influence of both secularism and science (see, for example, Easterlin 1996: 15–29; Mokyr 1990; Porter 2000). Enlightenment ideas informed many key events of the eighteenth century – for example, the American and the French Revolutions. And in England a focus on applied knowledge underpinned the Industrial Revolution and the new phenomenon that was modern economic growth. Ultimately, then, it was changes in the intellectual sphere – in particular the increased recognition that human beings could alter the forces of nature – which caused the demographic transition. In north-western Europe these intellectual changes produced a mortality decline that, especially in its early stages, was both piecemeal and slow. As we have seen, however, by the nineteenth century there were major developments – not least in the understanding of infectious diseases – which eventually had a huge impact everywhere.

To consider just why these intellectual changes of the Enlightenment happened in north-western European societies, and their North American offshoots, during the eighteenth century would take us far beyond our present concerns.[44] Here it will suffice to say that *if* the capacity to reduce death rates from high to low levels had initially developed somewhere else in the world – for example, in East Asia – then the resulting mortality decline would have led to natural increase (i.e. population growth), before fertility fell from high to low levels, and there was population ageing as a result. In other words, the basic causal processes of the demographic transition are not dependent upon any particular context. Moreover, precisely the same statement applies to the remaining process of the transition – namely urbanization, to which we now turn.

# 5 · Urbanization and the transition

Urbanization is a central fact of the contemporary world. In its modern form – in which a population's composition moves from being mainly rural to being mainly urban – the process originated in north-western Europe in the decades around 1800. Today, different parts of the world are at different stages of urbanization. Moreover, most countries are experiencing urban growth (i.e. growth of the urban population), and in many cases this growth is rapid. The projections discussed in Chapter 3 suggest that the world's urban population will expand by about 80 per cent between 2010 and 2050. Indeed, at the global level, all population growth in the period to 2050 is either expected to take place in urban areas as natural increase or, through rural-to-urban migration, end up living there. The number of people residing in rural areas seems set to decrease in most world regions. These facts raise major challenges in terms of improving living conditions in urban areas.[1] The consequences of urbanization for fundamental aspects of development – e.g. for societal complexity, economic growth, and the distribution of political power – will be addressed in the following chapters. Here it will suffice to say that the impetus for most dimensions of development occurs within the urban sector. Indeed, it has even been claimed that '[u]rbanization equals modernization' (Berger 1971: 174).

The main purpose of this chapter is to examine the causal mechanisms through which the process of urbanization comes about. This turns out to be another instance where, because economic growth has often accompanied a demographic process, it is sometimes rather uncritically assumed to be its principal cause. Now it is clearly the case that economic growth often contributes to urbanization. After all, factories and offices benefit from workforces and markets that are concentrated together in towns. However, the argument that economic growth causes urbanization has no more to commend it than the argument that urbanization causes economic growth. And while it is true that all countries that have experienced sustained economic growth have experienced urbanization, it is not true that all countries that have experienced urbanization have experienced sustained economic growth.

Several mechanisms are involved in bringing about urbanization (and urban growth). However, simplifying somewhat, the remote force that underpins the process is mortality decline – especially the control of infectious diseases which occurs within the context of the demographic transition. No population that has experienced a reduction in its death rate from a high level to a low level has failed to urbanize. Given the advent of mortality decline in any pre-transitional society, it is almost inevitable that urbanization will occur – largely irrespective of economic or any other conditions. Indeed, the relationship is so close that urbanization is regarded here as being a *part* of the demographic transition, rather than an outcome of it. The basic facts of the case have long been known. However, they are frequently unrecognized – partly because research is often concerned with change over relatively short time periods. As a result, research tends to become preoccupied with surface movements and fails to see the underlying forces that are actually at work.

The chapter has four parts. The first provides background. It considers conceptual issues and includes a brief history of urbanization in its modern form. The second part discusses economic aspects of urbanization. It criticizes the commonly held view that the process is caused by changes in the structure of employment, as economic development proceeds. It also considers the reasons for rural-to-urban migration. There is a tendency for people to migrate out of rural areas in almost any circumstances; therefore accounting for this is important. The chapter's third part sets out, and illustrates, the demographic changes that contribute to urbanization (and urban growth) within the context of the transition. In the end, a population can urbanize *only* through the operation of three variables – i.e. mortality, fertility and migration. And it is a consideration of how these variables unfold as the transition proceeds which lies at the heart of this chapter. Finally, we summarize the main conclusions and consider some of their implications.

## Background

Some preliminary remarks are required regarding basic conceptual issues, and the history of urbanization.

*Conceptual issues* In what follows, the term *urbanization* is used to refer to the process whereby an increasing *proportion* of a population comes to live in the urban sector (i.e. urban areas, the towns). And the term *urban growth* is used to refer to growth in the total *number* of people who live in urban areas. In theory, it is possible to have urban growth in a country without urbanization. This happens if the urban population is increasing, but at either the same or a slower rate than the rural population. In the modern world, however, such circumstances are rare. Urban growth is happening in almost every country, but urbanization is occurring as well. This means that the urban population is growing at a faster rate than the rural population. Indeed, many countries with low rates of natural increase (i.e. those near the end of the demographic transition) are experiencing a decrease in the size of their rural population – as people migrate out of the rural areas to live in the towns.

The rates of natural increase that have prevailed in the urban and rural areas of most countries in recent decades have tended to be roughly similar in magnitude (White et al. 2004; UNPD 2008). Countries with relatively high rates of natural increase in urban areas tend to have relatively high rates of natural increase in rural areas, and vice versa. However, owing to lower fertility and birth rates in urban areas, it is often the case that the rate of natural increase is a little lower in the urban than in the rural sector of a country – despite age structural effects brought about by migration which might work in the opposite direction.[2] Anyhow, since urbanization is occurring in virtually every developing country, it follows that migration from rural to urban areas is the proximate cause of this urbanization. In other words, without such migration urban populations would *not* be growing faster than rural populations (i.e. countries would not be urbanizing). Of course, net rural-to-urban migration raises the urban population growth rate and lowers the rural population growth rate.[3] That said, it is important to note that in most developing countries urban natural increase (rather than rural-to-urban migration) is the first cause of urban growth.[4] So although rural-to-urban migration is the immediate cause of urbanization, it is often the second cause of urban growth (after urban natural increase). These points will be elaborated below. However, it should be clear that we need to address the issue of rural out-migration, i.e. why, on balance, people tend to migrate out of rural areas to live in the towns.

Two other matters of a conceptual kind require mention. They both pertain to how areas are defined as 'urban'. The first is that, despite international efforts to standardize the criteria that are used in defining places as urban, it remains the case that different countries tend to employ somewhat different definitions. Indeed, even within the same country the criteria employed can be changed. Clearly, this can complicate the task of comparison – both between different populations, and within the same population over time. For the most part, however, the following discussion is sufficiently general that such differences of definition can be disregarded. Here we are chiefly concerned with the overall trend of urbanization, rather than with its precise level (whatever that may be).

The second matter is that, even with a constant definition of what constitutes an 'urban' area, urban growth in any country will involve formerly 'rural' areas being *reclassified* as 'urban' areas. For example, this can happen because a settlement that previously had a population smaller than required to be classed as 'urban' grows beyond the required threshold number (e.g. 5,000 people) and is therefore reclassified as urban. Reclassification can also occur because a town expands to include previously rural areas within its borders. Again, while it is important to be aware of this matter, it need not concern us too much here. Instead, it will suffice to note that the urban growth that is usually brought about by such reclassification ultimately reflects change caused by natural increase and/or rural-to-urban migration. And it is with these last two 'real' contributors to urban growth that we are chiefly concerned here.

Nevertheless, with reference to the issue of reclassification, it is worth presenting a simple example of how natural increase can *by itself* cause both urban growth and urbanization (i.e. in the absence of rural-to-urban migration). Thus consider a hypothetical pre-transitional country in which nearly everyone lives in moderate-sized villages of between three and four thousand people. Using a threshold of 5,000 inhabitants to define a place as urban, the country's population is largely rural. As the country experiences mortality decline within the transition, however, so there will be natural increase, and the size of most of the villages will eventually grow beyond 5,000, i.e. the country will become largely urban. This, of course, is a purely illustrative case. Nevertheless, it raises the essential point that is elaborated below – namely that urban growth and urbanization are ultimately outcomes of mortality decline within the demographic transition.

*A brief history of urbanization* The trend of urbanization at the world level was outlined in Chapter 3. Thus, by some estimates, about 5 per cent of humanity lived in towns in 1800. This percentage had roughly doubled by 1900, and it had more or less doubled again by 1950 (see Table 3.1). Then, between 1950 and 2010, the level of urbanization rose from about 29 to 50 per cent – meaning that for the first time in history as many people lived in towns as in rural areas. That said, we saw that whereas about a third of the people in sub-Saharan Africa and South-Central Asia were estimated to be living in urban areas in 2010, in Europe, North America and Latin America the proportion exceeded

70 per cent (see Table 3.2). These figures provide an idea of what is involved in the modern process of urbanization – typically a sustained rise in the proportion of people living in urban areas from below 10 to over 70 per cent.

Defining an 'urban' settlement as one with 10,000 people or more, Angus Maddison compiled estimates which suggest that in 1800 about 10 per cent of the population of western Europe lived in urban areas. The most urbanized places were the Netherlands (29 per cent), England (20), Belgium (19), Scotland (17) and Italy (15). The Netherlands especially, but Belgium and Italy too, have long histories of being comparatively highly urbanized. The level of urbanization in 1800, however, was appreciably lower in France (9 per cent) and Germany (6). Beyond Europe, perhaps 12 per cent of Japan's people lived in urban areas, and the estimate for China is about 4 per cent (Maddison 2007: 40–43). The level of urbanization in North America was certainly lower than in Europe. Thus, according to the first census of the United States, conducted in 1790, only 3 per cent of the country's 3.9 million people lived in the six towns with 8,000 inhabitants or more (Klein 2004: 91). Historical data for other parts of the world are usually too flimsy to provide estimates. However, with a few scattered and often short-lived exceptions – e.g. peninsular Italy and Egypt during the Roman Empire, the Basin of Mexico at the height of Aztec rule, and perhaps parts of the Middle East (e.g. Iraq, Iran) and coastal China – the level of urbanization everywhere appears to have been extremely low (see, for example, Bairoch 1988; Reader 2005; Maddison 2007).

The modern process of urbanization begins to be discernible in the countries of north-western Europe in the decades around 1800. The taking of regular censuses was only just beginning at this time – for example, France and England held their first modern enumerations in 1772 and 1801 respectively. Therefore, as with respect to the origins of mortality and fertility decline, it is difficult to be precise as to when the process really started.[5] Nevertheless, in England and Scotland there are signs that some urbanization was under way in the second half of the eighteenth century – probably partly reflecting the influence of the nascent Industrial Revolution. In the Netherlands, Belgium and France it may be more appropriate to assign the start of the process to the first decades of the nineteenth century. It then began to occur in other parts of Europe – although it was not until the second half of the nineteenth century that it was affecting countries in the east (e.g. Poland, Romania, Russia). By 1900, however, urbanization was under way throughout all of Europe. Maddison's figures suggest that in 1900 about 30 per cent

TABLE 5.1 Estimates of the proportion of the population living in urban areas, and the rate of urbanization for the world's regions, 1950–2010

| | Per cent urban | | | | Annual rate of urbanization (%) | | |
|---|---|---|---|---|---|---|---|
| Region | 1950 | 1975 | 2000 | 2010 | 1950–75 | 1975–2000 | 2000–10 |
| Sub-Saharan Africa | 11.1 | 21.7 | 32.8 | 37.3 | 2.68 | 1.65 | 1.29 |
| Middle East | 26.7 | 43.7 | 56.4 | 59.1 | 1.97 | 1.02 | 0.55 |
| South-Central Asia | 16.4 | 22.2 | 29.5 | 32.2 | 1.21 | 1.14 | 0.88 |
| South-East Asia | 15.4 | 23.2 | 39.7 | 48.2 | 1.64 | 2.15 | 1.94 |
| East Asia | 16.6 | 23.3 | 40.4 | 48.5 | 1.36 | 2.20 | 1.83 |
| Latin America | 41.4 | 61.1 | 75.3 | 79.4 | 1.56 | 0.84 | 0.53 |
| North America | 63.9 | 73.8 | 79.1 | 82.1 | 0.58 | 0.28 | 0.38 |
| Oceania | 62.0 | 71.5 | 70.4 | 70.6 | 0.57 | -0.06 | 0.03 |
| Europe | 51.2 | 65.7 | 71.4 | 72.6 | 1.00 | 0.33 | 0.17 |
| World | 29.1 | 37.3 | 46.6 | 50.6 | 0.99 | 0.89 | 0.82 |

*Notes*: The rate of urbanization presented here is the growth rate in the urban proportion of the population. The Middle East refers to North Africa (including Sudan) and West Asia; Latin America includes the Caribbean.

*Source*: United Nations (2008)

of the population of western Europe resided in towns. England and Scotland were the most advanced countries – with levels of around 60 and 50 per cent respectively (Maddison 2007; see also Easterlin 1996: 34–5). The level of urbanization in the United States also increased considerably from the start of the nineteenth century. Indeed, by 1910 about 41 per cent of the country's population lived in towns containing at least 100,000 people (Klein 2004: 142). Australia, Canada and New Zealand were also urbanizing during the second half of the nineteenth century, and Japan too began to urbanize at around that time.

Turning to the world's developing regions, it has been estimated that the average level of urbanization rose from about 6 per cent in 1900 to reach 9 per cent in 1925, and 16 per cent by 1950 (see Grauman 1977: 32).[6] A few Latin American countries – notably Argentina and Chile – began to urbanize from the last decades of the nineteenth century (Bairoch 1988; Jones 2003). The first half of the twentieth century saw urbanization occurring throughout Latin America. And the process was also evident in a few places in Asia (e.g. Korea, Taiwan). That said, it seems likely that urbanization was beginning to occur in other parts of Asia and the Middle East during the first half of the twentieth century. Thus United Nations estimates for 1950 put the level of urbanization in China, India and Egypt at 12, 17 and 32 per cent respectively – figures which suggest a likely increase compared to earlier times. The UN estimates indicate that by 1950 about 40 per cent of Latin America's people were living in towns (United Nations 2008). Of course, countries in the world's more developed regions were also continuing to urbanize during the first half of the twentieth century.

Table 5.1 presents UN estimates for the world's major regions which summarize what has happened since 1950. The figures shown – which ultimately reflect many different national definitions of 'urban' areas – should be regarded as only broadly indicative. Nevertheless, it is clear that urbanization has been a virtually universal process in recent decades. Notice that between 1950 and 2000 the level of urbanization in Latin America rose to a similar level to that prevailing in North America and Europe. In general, the *rates* of urbanization in Table 5.1 tend to decline as the overall level of urbanization in each region rises. Related to this, notice that at the start of the present century (i.e. during 2000–10) the rates of urbanization were very low in the world's more developed regions; there is, after all, an upper limit to just how 'urban' any population can become. Nevertheless, it is notable that both East Asia and South-East Asia experienced a major increase in the rate of urbanization in the period after 1975. This is probably a reflection of the comparatively rapid economic development of countries in these regions in recent decades. By 2010, except for South-Central Asia, all world regions had urbanization levels that were similar to, or higher than, the level of Latin America in 1950. Looking ahead, the widespread and sustained nature of the process represented in Table 5.1 suggests very strongly that it will continue in the world's developing regions in the coming decades.

## Economic aspects of urbanization

Clearly, economic considerations are relevant to the explanation of urbanization (and urban growth). In any specific case they are likely to be important in influencing what happens – for example, in relation to the speed of the process. Accordingly, some comments are required about economic aspects of urbanization.

*Structural change in the economy* It is widely held that urbanization results from changes in the structure of employment which occur as part of the phenomenon of modern economic growth. For example, addressing the question of what causes urbanization, it has been stated that '[t]he underlying explanation for urbanization involves changing employment opportunities as structural change takes place in the economy' (Jones 2003: 952). This economic account stresses the movement of the labour force out of agriculture into industry and (later) the service sector which accompanies economic development (see, for example, Easterlin 1996).

In Europe at the time that modern economic growth began – i.e. in the decades around 1800 – it was common for at least 70 per cent of the labour force to be employed in agriculture (Easterlin 1996: 47–51). In a few societies – for example, the Netherlands and England – the figure may have been slightly lower. But in most countries the figure was higher. Moreover, in many of the world's poorest countries it remains the case today that at least 70 per cent of the labour force works in agriculture (UNDP 2009).

The explanation for urbanization that stresses the causal role of structural economic change sometimes depicts urban growth as being built upon a rural base. In particular, increases in agricultural productivity are first required to support urban growth – especially, but not only, in relation to food production. It is also said that increased agricultural productivity 'releases' labour to work in the towns. However, as modern economic growth 'takes off', so factories tend to be located in urban areas in order to take advantage of economies of scale in production, and the existence of a sizeable (and growing) market for manufactured goods. The grouping of factories in towns reduces unit production costs (e.g. in terms of the construction of infrastructure, such as roads and docks). And industries that service consumers (e.g. publishing, printing, catering) also tend to be attracted to urban areas by the growing number of people that reside there. As incomes rise, so most of the resulting increase in demand relates to non-agricultural products that are produced in the towns. Of course, in the past as in the present, the location of natural resources (e.g. energy sources, iron ore, etc.) can be important in determining where factories are built in the first place, and it is possible for a town to then grow up around the industrial plant.[7] Considerations of transport and communication are also important in determining where factories and towns are built (Crook 1997). Key points to acknowledge, however, are (i) that there are many reasons why modern economic growth usually takes off in urban areas, and (ii) that once 'take-off' has occurred, there are many reasons why the economic processes involved tend to reinforce each other.

The occurrence of sustained economic growth in the urban sector increases the employment opportunities that exist there. Urban manufacturing is likely to offer higher wages than rural agriculture. Such developments heighten the attraction of a move to the towns for rural people. This was true historically – for example, it helps to explain the exceptionally rapid urbanization of England and Scotland during the nineteenth century. And it has been true more recently – for example, it helps to explain the rapid rate of urbanization in East Asia (largely China) and South-East Asia (including Indonesia, Malaysia, Thailand and Vietnam) in the period since 1975 (see Table 5.1). There is no doubt that, by encouraging rural-to-urban migration, economic growth tends to hasten both the growth of the towns and the process of urbanization. In the most economically advanced societies today it is usually the case that less than 5 per cent of the labour force is employed in agriculture (UNDP 2009).

*Problems with this explanation* Not surprisingly, this account of urbanization has been heavily influenced by research on what happened in Europe and its offshoots during the nineteenth and twentieth centuries (see, for example, Bairoch 1988; Easterlin 1996; Williamson 1988). In short, these populations experienced industrialization and urbanization at about the same time. Their economies were transformed from being mainly rural and agricultural to being mainly urban and industrial. Furthermore, a similar combination of processes has occurred in many

Latin American and Asian countries in recent decades. Therefore, there has been a tendency to assume that what is being observed is cause (i.e. economic development) and effect (i.e. urbanization).

Because urbanization has often accompanied economic growth (and related shifts in employment), however, does not necessarily mean that it has ultimately been caused by this growth – however attractive such an explanation may seem. We saw in Chapter 3 that the fastest rates of urban growth in recent decades have occurred in sub-Saharan Africa. This world region has also experienced relatively rapid rates of urbanization (see Table 5.1). Yet sub-Saharan Africa has performed poorly in economic terms. Accordingly there has been growing recognition of the fact that urbanization in this region has often taken place in the absence of sustained economic growth, or most of its usual manifestations.

Thus especially, but not only, as regards sub-Saharan Africa, researchers have increasingly noted that urbanization has happened without much economic development (see, for example, White et al. 2004: 93). For instance, Oucho and Gould state that '[i]n sub-Saharan Africa rapid urbanization has preceded industrialization; indeed, the African experience seems to imply that it is completely independent of it' (Oucho and Gould 1993: 275). Research also shows that urbanization in this region has often continued despite protracted negative economic growth – as if carried forward by its own momentum (see, for example, Fay and Opal 1999). There has been some shift in the structure of employment out of agriculture. But to a considerable extent this has occurred simply because people have physically moved out of rural areas. Instead of taking people into a growing industrial sector, such migration has often taken them into employment in the urban informal sector. Indeed, it has frequently taken them into conditions of urban underemployment and outright unemployment.[8]

These conclusions about sub-Saharan Africa – i.e. essentially that there has been urbanization *without* economic growth – are similar to those of earlier research on urbanization in some parts of Latin America during the 1920s and 1930s (see, for example, Davis and Casis 1946; Echavarria and Hauser 1961). More generally, they find echoes in the so-called 'overurbanization' thesis. This is the position, argued initially by Hoselitz (1957), that urban populations in developing countries are often associated with much smaller industrial labour forces compared to what applied in developed countries in the past.

If urbanization and urban growth occur essentially for some reason other than economic growth, there will still be a change in the structure of employment – i.e. a move out of agriculture. This change, however, will be more the *outcome* of urbanization than its cause. More generally, rather than economic growth (and accompanying changes in the structure of employment) being responsible for urban growth and urbanization, the dominant direction of causation may well be the other way around. The argument that urban conditions benefit economic growth dates back at least to the time of Adam Smith. In *Wealth of Nations*, published in 1776, Smith saw that urban growth would be conducive to an increase in the division of labour, and therefore a rise in economic productivity. His reasoning was that the bigger and more concentrated the market, the greater are the economic benefits to be had from increased specialization. Many economists, notably Alfred Marshall (1920), have found other reasons for believing that urban growth is beneficial to economic growth – for example, by helping to spread new ideas, and by facilitating a better match of supply and demand within the labour market.

The idea that there must be rises in agricultural productivity before there is urban growth has also been questioned. For example, there may be existing 'slack' in agriculture that can be used to sustain urban growth during its initial stages. It is worth noting too that levels of physical activity are usually lower in urban areas. Therefore less food energy (i.e. calorie) intake is required per person for people who reside in towns. In addition, provided urban populations are small (e.g. around five thousand people) then, in certain circumstances, it may be feasible for urban residents to provide much of their own food through the cultivation of suburban fields. That said, this is certainly not possible in the case of large urban units (Reader 2005: 166–72; Smil 2000).

There is little doubt that the rises in agricultural productivity that have underpinned the modern process of urbanization have happened mainly because of events that have taken place in the urban sector.[9] Thus Jane Jacobs notes that:

> [m]odern productive agriculture has been reinvented by grace of hundreds of innovations that were exported from the cities to the countryside, transplanted to the countryside or imitated in the countryside [...] To be sure, one can often find fertilizer factories, tractor plants, agricultural research stations, nurseries and electric power plants located in the rural world far from cities. But these activities were not created there. (Jacobs 1972: 18)

The origins of modern productive agriculture rest in precisely the same changes in ways of thinking that made mortality decline possible – in particular, the emergence and rise of science. Again, essentially, this goes back to changes that came out of the Enlightenment. And, whether it was applied to food production, health, manufacturing or anything else, scientific activity was something that was centred mainly in the towns.

*Out-migration from rural areas* As we have observed, rural-to-urban migration is the proximate cause of urbanization. The point is underlined by the fact that in contemporary developing countries the urban rate of natural increase tends to be slightly lower than the rural rate – something that, by itself, would produce de-urbanization. Furthermore, rural-to-urban migration is also a major contributor to urban growth. It is the second-most important contributor (after urban natural increase) in most developing countries if the issue is considered over relatively short time periods, as is often done (see, for example, Preston 1979; Brockerhoff 1999; Cohen 2004). However, if urban growth is considered over longer periods, and the natural increase in the migrants themselves is taken into account, then the contribution of migration to urban growth is much greater.

The demographic explanation for urbanization that is elaborated below is largely independent of the specific reasons why some people – especially young adults – tend to move out of rural areas. Clearly, the immediate reasons for this migration vary between different individuals and situations.

That said, it is evident that rural natural increase can press upon the available agricultural resources, and hence encourage out-migration (e.g. through increased landlessness). Also, rises in farm productivity due to new technologies (e.g. rice-transplanting machines, tractors, etc.) can have a similar effect, inasmuch as there is less work for people to undertake in rural areas. Furthermore, to the extent that economic growth occurs, the employment opportunities and higher wages that it generates in the towns will tend to heighten the flow of people moving from rural to urban areas. Clearly, both 'push' and 'pull' factors are relevant in explaining rural out-migration.

However, although economic considerations are certainly important in accounting for rural-to-urban migration, it is worth noting that there are many other reasons why people migrate – for example, to escape from unhappy family circumstances, for reasons of marriage, and to further their education. At a very general level of explanation, Samuel Preston has remarked that '[w]hen labour requirements in food production are relaxed, people exhibit a preference for a much higher degree of concentration than when agriculture is the dominant activity' (Preston

1994: 4). Ultimately, perhaps, human beings may simply *prefer* to live in larger groups – given the chance. Relatedly, it has long been recognized that towns can generate exciting social events that are almost unknown in purely rural settings (Wirth 1938). Urban areas tend to be more dynamic and interesting places – particularly for young adults. Philip Hauser suggests that the increased rate of social interaction found in urban settings produces 'in the social realm a major transformation the equivalent of genetic mutation in the biological realm' (Hauser 1965: 12).

Of course, the explanation for urbanization that is outlined below requires that there *is* rural out-migration. Therefore, it requires that some individuals decide to migrate to the towns. Such decisions often have an economic dimension. As will become clear, however, net rural-to-urban migration has been happening ever since there were towns for people to migrate to. Indeed, such migration occurred in virtually all pre-transitional populations – i.e. long before the phenomenon of modern economic growth.

In conclusion, structural changes in employment – in particular, the movement out of agriculture – can be seen as more the outcome of urbanization than its cause. Moreover, much the same applies to modern economic growth. There are strong grounds to think that the concentration of people in towns is of considerable benefit to the economy. Indeed, modern economic growth in Europe and its offshoots during the nineteenth century might not have been sustained without a substantial and growing urban sector. At the very least, two interactive processes were at work, and their individual effects are hard to disentangle. This is not to deny that the occurrence of economic growth accelerates urban growth and urbanization – by stimulating greater rural-to-urban migration. Nor is it to deny that – provided infectious diseases are under some control – the occurrence of sustained economic growth can bring about urban growth and urbanization. However, urbanization has also occurred in circumstances of little or no economic growth. Therefore we now consider how the demographic transition from high to low vital rates is ultimately responsible for urban growth and the process of urbanization.

## Demographic aspects of urbanization

A lot of research has addressed the issue of why death and birth rates tend to be lower in urban areas of contemporary developing countries. Such research considers how urban living conditions influence levels of mortality and fertility. In what follows, however, we are chiefly concerned with the *opposite* direction of causation, i.e. how mortality and fertility levels influence urban growth and urbanization.

*Explaining urbanization within the transition* Perhaps the most direct account of how urbanization results from the trajectory of death rates and birth rates within the demographic transition is that provided by Jan de Vries with reference to the experience of Europe (see de Vries 1990: 53–60). This serves as our point of departure here. And it will soon be clear that the explanation almost certainly applies to urbanization in most of the rest of the world.[10] The basic facts of the case are fairly well established (see, for example, Bairoch 1988; Wrigley 1987c). Indeed, several parts of the explanation are contained in John Graunt's famous study *Natural and Political Observations Made upon the Bills of Mortality*, which, using data for London, was published in 1662 (see Graunt 1662 [1964]). However, the role of mortality decline in urbanization is often unrecognized – perhaps partly because the genesis of urbanization itself has not ranked high on the intellectual agenda (Woods 2003: 215).[11]

De Vries begins by noting that the demographic transition is usually presented in relation to populations as a whole (much as was done here in Chapter 4). However, he proceeds to provide a stylized version of the transition – one that differentiates between vital rates in the urban and rural sectors. There is evidence that fertility was often slightly lower in urban areas of pre-transitional Europe; and there are signs that fertility began to decline somewhat earlier in urban than in rural areas. However, De Vries considers that the evidence on urban–rural fertility differences is insufficient to make far-reaching claims. Therefore he directs most of his attention to urban–rural differences in mortality.

Before mortality decline began in Europe, death rates tended to be appreciably higher in urban areas. The reason was that infectious diseases were the main causes of death. And these diseases tend to flourish in towns – where people live in close proximity. However, as we have seen, to a large degree the process of mortality decline consists of the progressive reduction of deaths from infectious diseases. Therefore, mortality decline in Europe involved a greater reduction of death rates in urban than in rural areas. Indeed, by the early decades of the twentieth century mortality levels in urban and rural areas of Europe were often roughly equal. In formal terms, before the start of mortality decline death rates varied directly with population density, i.e. they were appreciably higher in the towns than in the countryside. But as mortality decline proceeded, so death rates became largely independent of density – indeed, for various reasons they often became slightly lower in the towns than in the countryside (de Vries 1990: 53–60; see also Bairoch 1988: 505).

A crucial part of the demographic explanation of urbanization lies in the fact that in pre-transitional circumstances the urban death rate tended to be higher than the urban birth rate. Therefore the urban sector was a demographic 'sink' – i.e. there were more deaths than births. As a result, in the long run, the towns were dependent upon rural-to-urban migration for their very existence. In these circumstances urban growth was restricted and, to the extent that it did occur, it was because of migration. However, there was effectively a limit – i.e. a ceiling – on how 'urban' any population could become. We saw that in 1800 the Netherlands may have been roughly 29 per cent urban. This was a high percentage – which cannot have been too far from the ceiling on urbanization that then applied in the circumstances of north-western Europe (Friedlander 1969; Keyfitz 1980; Wrigley 1987c; de Vries 1984, 1990).[12]

A key stage in the demographic transition occurs when the urban death rate falls below the urban birth rate (de Vries 1990: 53–60). At this point, urban natural increase occurs for the first time. Henceforth the urban population has two sources of growth – namely its own natural increase, and continuing rural-to-urban migration (which also lowers the rural rate of population growth). The ceiling on urbanization is removed. In the resulting period of sustained urban growth, rural-to-urban migration is initially the main contributor to urban growth. However, as the overall level of urbanization in the population rises, so urban natural increase becomes the main contributor to urban growth. So in the early stages of the demographic transition – when the urban sector is relatively small – rural-to-urban migration is the principal source of urban growth. As the transition and urbanization proceed, however – and the urban sector becomes larger and larger – so urban natural increase tends to become the principal source. Indeed, urban natural increase is likely to become the main driver of urban growth well before the total population is half urban (Keyfitz 1980: 149–56).[13]

Mortality decline and rising natural increase in rural areas will mean that some settlements grow to such a size that they are reclassified as urban. And natural increase in rural areas also works to augment the flow of people who move to live in the towns. Indeed, there are reasons to think that the net rural out-migration rate tends to rise as the transition itself proceeds.[14] Furthermore, towards the end of the demographic transition – i.e. when death rates and birth rates are low and approximately equal everywhere – migration is likely to re-emerge as the main factor influencing urban population size. Thus in an increasing number of developing countries that are relatively advanced in terms of the transition, falling rates of urban natural increase mean that rural-to-urban migration is accounting for a rising share of urban growth. Similarly, in parts of Europe international migration has become a major contributor to urban growth during recent decades (see, for example, Chen et al. 1998; UNPD 2008).

Naturally, this demographic account of urbanization provides only the bare bones of what happens. In reality, there are many different versions – depending upon economic, political and other considerations. For instance, there can be substantial variation in the extent to which rural-to-urban migration and urban natural increase contribute to urban growth (Bairoch 1988). Also, the speed of the process can vary greatly. Thus the rapid pace of urbanization in England in the nineteenth century was certainly influenced by the employment opportunities that were being created by the Industrial Revolution which was under way in the towns. And the fact that people were able to find work in the towns helps to explain why fertility decline in rural England took rather a long time to occur – practically all of the 'surplus' rural population were able to move to jobs in urban areas. In contrast, the pace of urbanization in Sweden was much slower. In 1900 only about 22 per cent of the population lived in urban areas. Economic growth was slower in Sweden. Accordingly, it was more difficult for people to migrate from rural areas. In turn, this helps to explain why fertility decline happened earlier in rural Sweden, compared to rural England (Friedlander 1969). So while England and Sweden experienced fairly similar demographic transitions, the timing of their urbanization was rather different – partly because of different economic growth paths.

*Evidence on urban–rural mortality differentials* This demographic account of urbanization is dependent upon the level and trend of mortality in urban areas. Estimates of urban mortality in pre-transitional circumstances tend to be based on fragmentary data. They often pertain only to the deaths of infants and young children. And their interpretation can be complicated – for example, by considerations relating to migration (see Woods 2003). Nevertheless, there is much historical evidence for developed countries that is consistent with the preceding explanation. Even as late as the first decades of the twentieth century, infant mortality rates were sometimes higher in urban than in rural areas of Europe. Moreover, the further one goes back into the nineteenth century the greater the indications of this excess urban mortality (compared to rural mortality) tend to become. Death rates were generally highest in the biggest towns; they tended to decrease with decreasing sizes of town; and they were lowest in the rural areas.

It is worth providing a few illustrations, drawing mainly on the estimates compiled by Bairoch (1988: 229–36). Thus in Sweden in 1851–60 the infant mortality rate was 219 infant deaths per thousand births in urban areas, compared to 137 per thousand in rural areas. The infant mortality rate in Russia in 1880–84 is estimated at about 266 per thousand, but the figures for St Petersburg and Moscow are put at 303 and 351 respectively. In the north-eastern states of the United States in 1890, infant mortality in urban areas is estimated to have exceeded that in rural areas by 63 per cent; and, if children aged 1–4 are considered, then the urban child death rate exceeded the rural rate by 107 per cent. In England, as late as 1906, urban districts had higher infant mortality than rural districts. And in Japan in the early 1920s infant mortality in the larger towns is estimated to have surpassed that in the countryside by 24 per cent. Urban–rural estimates of adult mortality also exist for some countries in the late nineteenth and early twentieth centuries. Bairoch presents figures for Sweden, France, Germany, Japan and the United States – all of which support a picture of significantly higher adult death rates in urban areas.

Turning to estimates of urban–rural mortality differentials in developing countries in the past, the database is much weaker. In particular, it is rarely possible to go very far back in time. Nevertheless, again the estimates that are available are broadly consistent with the same basic picture. For example, Bairoch concludes that in the 1890s infant mortality rates in the larger cities of Latin America generally fell in the range of 210–260 per thousand, compared to 180–200 in rural areas. The figures provided for Cairo and Alexandria are also suggestive of particularly high death rates in major urban centres of the Middle East. For Asia, infant mortality rates in the larger towns fell in the range 350–450 per thousand, compared to 210–250 per thousand in rural areas (Bairoch 1988: 448–52).

An extreme example in Asia is provided by Mumbai (then known as Bombay). In 1901 the city's infant mortality rate was approximately 500 per thousand. This meant that half of all children born in Mumbai died before reaching their first birthday. In households living in the most crowded conditions, the infant mortality rate was about 800 per thousand (i.e. 80 per cent). These facts led to research that identified pneumonia, meningitis and various kinds of diarrhoeal disease as being major causes of infant deaths (Dyson 1997; Mulholland 2006). Given these extremely high death rates, it is unsurprising that most of the city's population consisted of migrants who had come from rural areas. Mumbai simply could not have existed without this migration.

It is possible that some of the comparisons mentioned above overstate the degree to which urban mortality exceeded rural mortality in pre-transitional circumstances. Certainly, the dreadful slum conditions that accompanied industrialization and urban growth in Europe in the nineteenth century sometimes meant that urban death rates increased for a time. However, it is probably more likely that – because they do not extend far back in time – most of the comparisons *understate* the degree to which there was excess urban mortality (compared to rural mortality) in pre-transitional conditions. That said, the really critical issue is the extent to which urban death rates exceeded urban birth rates, i.e. the extent to which pre-transitional urban populations were sinks, and how this situation changed as a result of the demographic transition.

*Urban sinks and their disappearance* It is occasionally possible to compare urban death rates and urban birth rates in circumstances that may have approximated pre-transitional conditions. For example, Bairoch uses vital registration data for Mumbai to show that during the period 1881–1911 there was an excess of deaths over births in the city (i.e. natural decrease) of about 590,000. However, the population grew from 822,000 to about 979,000. Therefore Bairoch estimates roughly that there was net migration into Mumbai of around 750,000. He also suggests that between 1895 and 1904 Singapore's population would have shrunk by about a third had it not been for migration (Bairoch 1988: 449–52).

Such circumstances are strongly reminiscent of those that appear to have prevailed in Europe's major cities in the seventeenth century and before. The towns were incredibly unhealthy places. They would not have existed without a continual stream of young adult migrants. The scale of the problem is indicated, for example, by the fact that life expectancy in London in 1700 was only about 18 years, compared to 39 years in England as a whole (Woods 2000: 365). London's death rate was extraordinarily high – and much higher than the birth rate. Between 1550 and 1824 recorded burials usually exceeded baptisms by at least 35–40 per cent (Wrigley and Schofield 1981). It was only because of an enormous number of migrants coming from the rest of the country that London's population was able to expand in the centuries before 1750 (see Wrigley 1987c; also Graunt 1662 [1964]: 35). Similarly, for the Netherlands, de Vries has shown that cities like Amsterdam experienced natural decrease on such a scale that they were maintained only by migration. Moreover, the country's urban sector eventually reached a point where – given the existing levels of urban mortality and rural out-migration – it was unable to expand any further (see de Vries 1974: 115–17; 1984).

These estimates of the extent to which urban areas were once 'sinks' pertain to pre-transitional circumstances. And they usually relate to major towns, rather than to whole countries. To assess how urbanization results from the demographic transition, however, it would be helpful to examine changes in vital rates in the urban and rural sectors of a whole country as it proceeds through the transition. Yet, as we saw in Chapter 4, it is extremely difficult to find a full illustration of the transition. And it is even more difficult to find sector-specific time series of death rates and birth rates during the transition. Even in Europe, vital rates were seldom published separately for urban and rural areas until the second half of the nineteenth century.

Nevertheless, Figure 5.1 shows sector-specific death and birth rates during the transition for Sweden and Sri Lanka. These may be the only countries for which such an exercise can be attempted on the basis of published vital rates. Partly for ease of exposition, both illustrations are based on average figures (rather than annual rates).[15] Notice that in both cases only a part of the full transition can be addressed. The vital rates for Sweden are probably more reliable than those for Sri Lanka. Some real differences of experience are suggested. Nevertheless, in broad terms the experience of both countries confirms the preceding demographic account of urbanization. Referring to the letters (A–E) in Figure 5.1, we now summarize what is shown.

In Sweden until about the 1840s, and in Sri Lanka until about 1925, the urban death rate was higher than the urban birth rate (see the shaded areas indicated by the letter A in both cases). In other words, the urban areas were indeed demographic sinks for the periods before these years. Therefore, in Sweden until the 1840s, and in Sri Lanka until about 1925, the urban rate of natural increase was consistently negative (see the letter B). Indeed, for these periods the urban birth rate was lower than the urban death rate by about 6 per thousand in Sweden, and by about 4 per thousand in Sri Lanka. This means that there was appreciable urban natural decrease in both countries. The rate of natural increase in the rural areas of both countries, however, remained distinctly positive throughout (see the letter C). Therefore it was rural natural increase which, through rural-to-urban migration, maintained the urban populations and provided the basis for most of

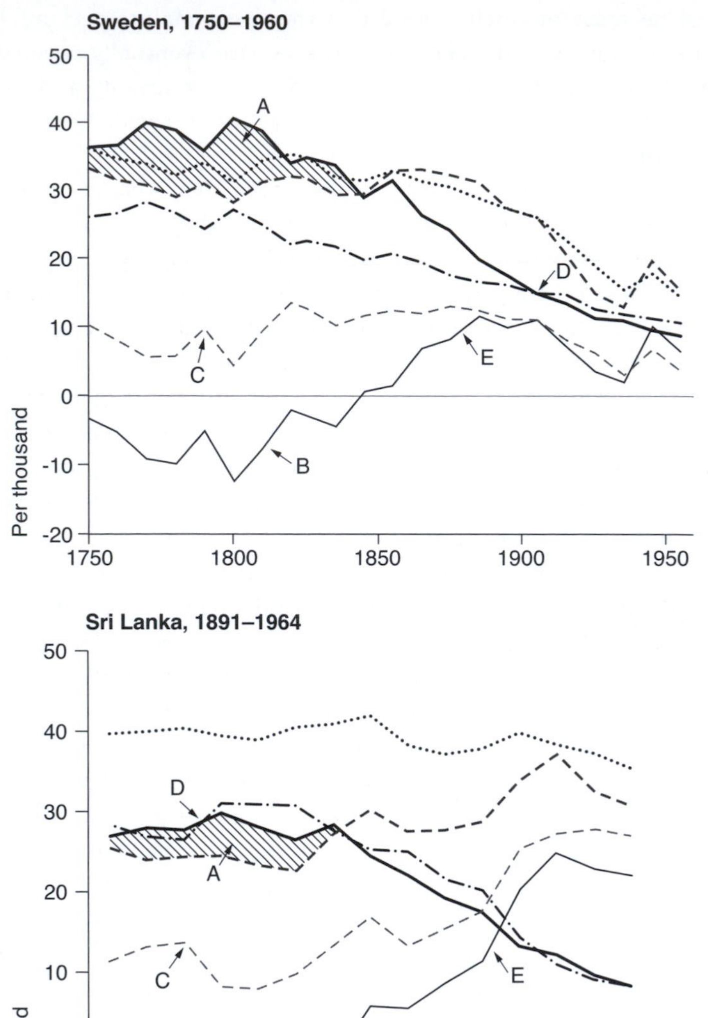


*Principal sources*: Sweden 1750–1820 (Friedlander 1969), 1820–1960 (Sweden, various years); Sri Lanka (Ceylon, various years). See also Dyson (2009) and Dyson (forthcoming).

**Figure 5.1 Crude death and birth rates for urban and rural areas of Sweden and Sri Lanka**

what limited urban growth there was during these early periods.[16] Note too that during these early periods the urban birth rate was lower than the rural birth rate (particularly in Sri Lanka). This suggests that lower urban fertility was also significant in explaining why the urban sector was a sink (see Dyson 2009).

In Sweden the urban death rate behaved exactly as we would expect (see Figure 5.1). Thus in the eighteenth century the urban death rate was extremely high, and much higher than the rural death rate. During the nineteenth century the urban death rate fell faster than the rural death rate. Indeed, it was only at the start of the twentieth century that the urban death rate in Sweden became slightly lower than the rural death rate (see the point indicated by the letter D). In Sri Lanka, the urban death rate appears to have been slightly higher than the rural death rate for most of the time before about 1907 (again, see the letter D). However, in this context it is important to note that the urban death rate shown for Sri Lanka in Figure 5.1 is almost certainly an underestimate. It was calculated excluding the deaths of rural residents that occurred in urban hospitals. However, no corresponding (upward) adjustment could be made to the urban death rate for the deaths of urban residents that occurred in rural areas.[17] Finally, notice that in Sweden from roughly the 1880s, and in Sri Lanka after around 1945, the urban and rural rates of natural increase became much more equal, and they fluctuated in a similar way (see the letter E). Interestingly, because the urban birth rate remained lower than the rural birth rate in Sri Lanka, the urban rate of natural increase remained below the rural rate of natural increase during the 1950s and early 1960s. This is consistent with the idea that in contemporary developing countries lower fertility in urban areas tends to produce slightly lower rates of natural increase – despite considerations of age structure. Anyhow, it is clear that – from around the 1880s in Sweden, and from around the year 1945 in Sri Lanka – urbanization was happening because of rural out-migration (since the rural rate of natural increase tended to be equal to, or slightly higher than, the urban rate).

Many caveats can be made regarding the vital rates plotted in Figure 5.1 – especially in relation to Sri Lanka (see Dyson 2009 and forthcoming). It will suffice to say here that – given the very different contexts provided by these two countries – we would expect to find some real differences in their experiences of the transition between the urban and rural sectors.[18] It is also worth emphasizing that, for the reason mentioned, the urban death rates shown for Sri Lanka in the early years are almost certainly too low.[19] In other words, Sri Lanka's urban sector was probably even more of a sink than is suggested by Figure 5.1.

These considerations notwithstanding, however, it is the fundamental *similarity* of experience between the two populations which is most striking. Thus in both cases the urban death rate exceeded the urban birth rate during the early periods, and therefore the urban sector was a sink. In both cases the urban death rate was higher than the rural death rate during the early periods. And in both cases the urban birth rate was lower than the rural birth rate during the early periods – suggesting that lower urban fertility may have contributed to the towns collectively being a sink. Figure 5.1 shows that in both countries the urban sector eventually ceased to be a sink as the urban death rate declined within the demographic transition. It was this change which made sustained urbanization possible. According to official estimates, the level of urbanization in Sweden rose from about 10 per cent in 1820 to 47 per cent in 1950 (see Sweden 1955). In Sri Lanka the increase was from 10 per cent in 1891 to about 19 per cent in 1963 (see Ceylon 1967). However, in both cases these figures almost certainly understate the degree to which urbanization actually occurred.[20] In Sri Lanka, in particular, many of the settlements designated as 'urban' in 1891 were little more than villages; if the criteria used to define places as 'urban' had remained unchanged then in 1963 more than half of the country's population would probably have been classified as urban.

*The speed of contemporary urbanization* It is sometimes said that the speed of urbanization in contemporary developing countries is unexceptional by historical standards (see, for example, Preston 1979: 196–8; Brockerhoff and Brennan 1998: 78–9; White et al. 2004: 92). This claim rests largely on estimates of urbanization made within the United Nations (see, for example, Grauman 1977; United Nations 2008). These estimates suggest that between 1880 and 1940 the average level of urbanization in developed countries rose from about 19.0 to 47.8 per cent, whereas between 1950 and 2010 the level of urbanization in less developed countries rose from about 18.0 to 45.3 per cent.[21] Therefore very similar increases are implied over the same range of urbanization, and over the same length of time (i.e. sixty years). It is unclear, however, why there should be such similarity; and the comparison itself can be questioned.

The assertion that the pace of urbanization experienced by contemporary developing countries is similar to that experienced by developed countries in the past depends partly upon the particular comparison that is made. For example, the same estimates used in the comparison in the previous paragraph also form the basis for the following comparison. Thus between 1830 and 1920 the level of urbanization in developed countries increased from 8.8 to 37.1 per cent. In contrast, between 1920 and 2010 the average level of urbanization in developing countries increased from 8.7 to 45.3 per cent. This comparison, made over a period of ninety years, is indicative of a *faster* rate of urbanization in contemporary developing countries.

A similar conclusion is supported by the comparisons made in Figure 5.2. Using the same sources, the bold line shows how the average level of urbanization in more developed countries is estimated to have risen between 1800 and 2010. The 'S'-shaped (logistic) form of the overall process – accelerating in the early stages, and decelerating in the later stages – is evident. The estimated trends in urbanization for the period 1950–2010 for the world's developing regions are then compared with this – in each case starting the comparison at the same *level* of urbanization with respect to the reference standard curve (in bold). The speed of urbanization in South-Central Asia appears to have been distinctly slower than that which applied in developed countries in the past.[22] And in the case of the Middle East the overall increase in the level of urbanization between 1950 and 2010 is similar to that experienced by the developed countries between 1900 and 1960. Holding the initial level of urbanization constant, however, in each of the remaining regions the pace of urbanization seems to have been significantly faster than applied historically in the developed countries. This is true for sub-Saharan Africa at the lower end of the scale, and it is true for Latin America at the upper end. In the centre, both East Asia and South-East Asia experienced almost the same increase in urbanization from about 16 to 48 per cent between 1950 and 2010 – an increase that was well above (i.e. faster than) the historical trend (see Figure 5.2).

As we have noted, there are difficulties involved in gauging levels and trends of urbanization. And because the process involves a change in population composition, it tends to occur fairly slowly, and it is inevitably somewhat lagged on other demographic changes. Moreover, as we have stressed, the speed of the process is undoubtedly affected by economic, political and other considerations. Therefore one should be cautious in relation to the present suggestion that contemporary urbanization is occurring at a somewhat quicker rate than applied in developed countries in the past. Nevertheless, it is worth recalling from Chapter 4 that the pace of mortality decline has tended to speed up over time. And modern rates of natural increase have generally been much higher. There are also signs that more recent demographic transitions may be somewhat shorter (i.e. more compressed) than was often the case

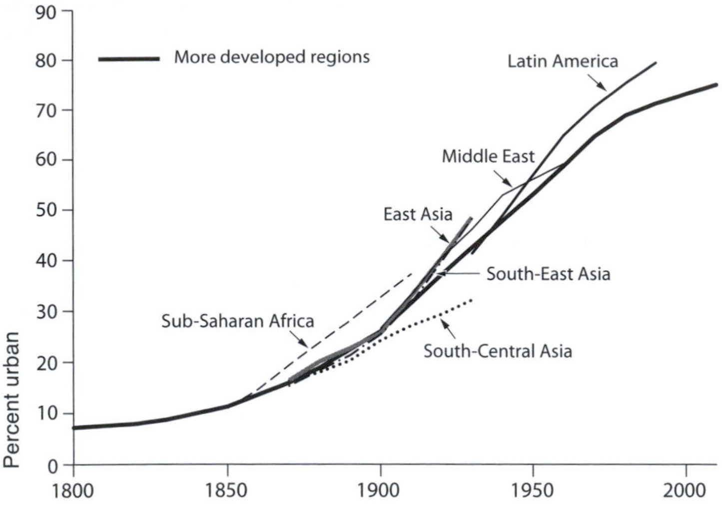


*Note*: The bold line relates to urbanization in the more developed regions. Here it acts as a reference standard. Thus although the trends for the individual developing regions all relate to the period 1950–2010, they have been plotted at the same starting (i.e. 1950) level of urbanization as applied in the more developed regions. Consequently the speed of urbanization can be compared.

*Sources*: Grauman (1977), United Nations (2008). See also Dyson (2009) and Dyson (forthcoming).

**Figure 5.2 Estimates of urbanization, more developed regions, 1800–2010, and individual less developed regions, 1950–2010**

historically. Accordingly, we might expect that the pace of contemporary urbanization in developing countries might also be somewhat faster than in the past.[23]

*The speed of contemporary urban growth* The urban growth rates experienced by developing countries in recent decades are certainly rapid by historical standards. This is true irrespective of the particular time periods that are used for comparison. The point can be illustrated employing the sources and periods used above. Thus between 1880 and 1940 the urban population of the developed countries is estimated to have increased from about 86 to 380 million; this implies urban growth by a factor of 4.4, i.e. at an average annual rate of about 2.5 per cent. However, between 1950 and 2010 the urban population of the less developed countries is estimated to have risen from about 310 to 2,569 million; this implies urban growth by a factor of 8.3, i.e. at an average annual rate of around 3.5 per cent. That said, the urban growth rate for the developing world as a whole is now declining – by 2000–10 it had fallen to around 2.6 per cent per year (United Nations 2008).

We noted that urban natural increase may become the main driver of urban growth well before half of a country's total population is urban. Available estimates are generally consistent with this – although given the nature of the data needed to assess the issue, they tend to be somewhat incomplete and dated. Using information for the 1960s, however, Preston attributed 61 per cent of urban growth in developing countries as being due to urban natural increase (Preston 1979: 198). Estimates cited for the 1980s suggest that urban natural increase accounted for about 75 per cent of urban growth in Africa, 66 per cent in Latin America and 51 per cent in Asia (excluding China) (Brockerhoff and Brennan 1998: 110). Estimates for the 1990s for countries with data that can be used to assess the issue indicate that urban natural increase accounted for more than half of urban growth in six out eight countries in Africa, seven out of eleven countries in Asia, and twelve out of fifteen countries in Latin America (UNPD 2008: 17). Notice, however, that all of these figures imply that there *are* populations where rural-to-urban migration is a more important contributor to urban growth than urban natural increase. As we have noted, such cases often need to be interpreted with respect to a country's position in relation to the demographic transition.

However, irrespective of whether urban natural increase or out-migration from rural areas is the main source of urban population growth in a country, the size of *both* of these determinants of urban growth is likely to be heavily related to, and influenced by, the country's overall rate of population growth (see Preston 1979; Bairoch 1988). In this context, Figure 5.3 depicts how mortality decline is ultimately responsible for both the rise in urban natural increase and the rise in rural natural increase (which leads to a rise in rural out-migration). Relatedly, the rapid urban growth that has occurred in developing countries in recent decades is ultimately a reflection of the rapid natural increase that has happened as a result of the demographic transition. And the fact that urban growth rates are now generally falling in developing countries reflects the basic fact that population growth rates are generally falling as well.

This key point has already been touched on several times. For instance, it is illustrated by Figure 2.4, which shows that the higher the rate of natural increase in a country, the higher the urban growth rate tends to be. Moreover, a given increase in the rate of natural increase is associated with a larger increase in the rate of urban growth. The relationship shown in Figure 2.4 is very strong. Moreover, analysis that

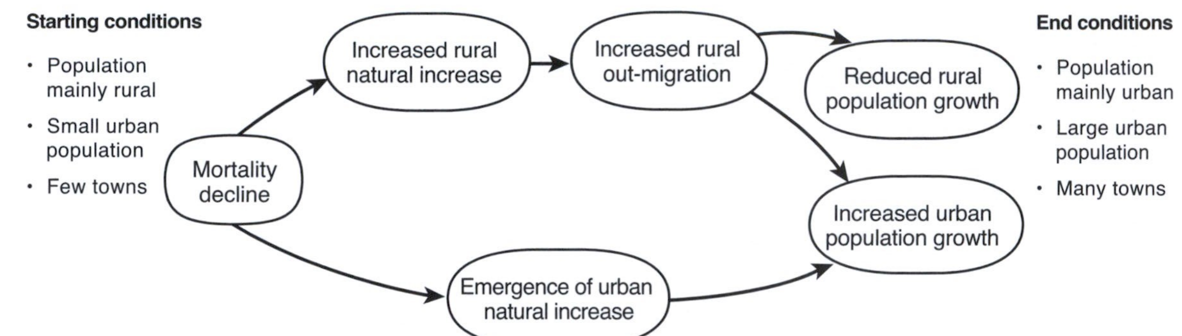


*Notes*: The diagram is highly simplified. In particular, it does not refer to fertility decline – the process that eventually brings about a reduction in urban population growth and (with continuing rural out-migration) a decline in the absolute size of the rural population. Nevertheless, it serves to underline that mortality decline within the transition produces an extended period during which the urban population grows from two sources, while growth of the rural population is reduced by out-migration.

**Figure 5.3 A stylized sketch of the processes behind urban growth and urbanization**

assesses the influence of other factors on the rate of urban growth – e.g. economic, political, regional, etc. – shows that the national rate of population growth is the dominant factor (see, for example, Preston 1979).

Governments in developing countries frequently express concern about the rapid expansion of their urban populations. In this context, Preston has tellingly remarked on the curious fact that 'family planning services are rarely seen as a candidate for slowing urban growth, which probably reflects an artificial but well-entrenched distinction between population growth and population distribution policies' (Preston 1979: 210–11).



## Conclusions and discussion

In summary, and standing back, urbanization is brought about by a particular demographic sequence. In pre-transitional circumstances, the level of urbanization is restricted by the fact that the urban death rate is higher than the urban birth rate. The higher urban death rate results from the predominance of infectious diseases – which thrive in the towns. The urban birth rate is likely to be lower than the rural birth rate. This may partly reflect the higher load of infectious diseases in urban areas.[24] More generally, however, the ratio of men to women in the marriageable ages is often unbalanced in the towns. In pre-transitional conditions the urban sector requires a flow of rural outmigrants in order to be maintained.

As mortality decline occurs because of the control of infectious diseases, however, there comes a point where the urban death rate falls below the urban birth rate. This crossover point may be delayed if early urban growth causes a deterioration in urban living conditions, and therefore some delay in urban mortality decline. Eventually, however, the urban areas cease to be a 'sink' and urban natural increase occurs. As urban growth gets under way, when the urban sector is still relatively small, rural out-migration is likely to be the main cause of urban growth. Later, as the level of urbanization rises, so urban natural increase is likely to become the main cause of this growth. There is net migration from rural to urban areas both before and throughout the demographic transition. Although the urban rate of natural increase rises as the urban death rate falls, it usually remains lower than the rural rate of natural increase. Therefore, rural-to-urban migration is required for urbanization to occur. The volume of this migration will be augmented by rural natural increase as the demographic transition proceeds. Such migration reduces the rural rate of population growth and raises the urban rate (see Figure 5.3). At a later stage, when the rural rate of natural increase has become relatively low, the continuation of rural out-migration produces a fall in the total size of the rural population. Also, when urban natural increase has become low, then migration will again be the main determinant of urban population change. In the end, the population has moved from being mainly rural to being mainly urban, and there has been very considerable urban growth.

Clearly, there can be a huge amount of variation as regards this stylized explanation. And it is impossible to address this variation here. It must also be emphasized that mortality decline contributes to urban growth and urbanization by increasing the size of rural settlements so that they come to be reclassified as urban areas.[25]

Certainly, economic growth in a country's urban sector often accelerates migration out of rural areas. And it is important to underscore the fact that the present account requires that there is net rural-to-urban migration throughout.[26] There are many reasons why this migration occurs. In the modern era, net out-migration from rural areas has often taken place in improving economic circumstances. Clearly, however, this has not always been so. People may also decide that they will be better off if they migrate to the towns during worsening economic times. There is evidence consistent with this – for example, that individuals frequently migrate to urban areas during times of dearth and famine. Whether economic circumstances are improving or deteriorating, what is required is for people to assess that their *own* particular circumstances will be improved if they move to the towns. In the past, economic development and urbanization have accompanied each other closely enough to encourage the idea that the former process causes the latter. But that is somewhat misleading.

As we have stressed, urban areas must be provisioned – particularly in terms of food and energy (e.g. for cooking, and perhaps for heating). Yet while difficulties relating to supplies of food and other basic necessities may have occurred with respect to the growth of specific towns in the past – especially if they had large populations – there is no reason to believe that the overall process of urbanization has ever been much constrained by these sorts of difficulties. This is true both with respect to developed countries in the past, and in relation to developing countries more recently. Moreover, since levels of physical activity are reduced in urban areas, and nowadays health conditions are usually better there as well, food energy requirements tend to be lower for urban dwellers.

The expansion of the urban sector has itself tended to assist the process of mortality decline. In general, the towns have been the crucible for the rise of modern scientific activity – which has greatly benefited mortality, health, agriculture and so much else besides. In modern circumstances, however, the towns also offer important economies of concentration when it comes to improving health. Thus the diffusion of public health education, or childhood immunizations, is easier in towns (compared to rural areas). Such considerations help to explain why death rates in contemporary developing countries are usually lower in urban areas. And urban dwellers also tend to lead in the process of fertility decline.

Therefore, other things equal, the faster the process of urbanization in a country, the faster should be its progress with respect to both mortality and fertility decline. In this context, recall that we have also suggested that more recent cases of the demographic transition may be occurring over somewhat shorter durations of time (i.e. there are signs of compression).[27] To the extent that this is so, and mortality decline and natural increase are also faster, there are reasons to think that the process of urbanization may also be experiencing some compression. And, indeed, we have detected signs that contemporary urbanization may be happening at a more rapid rate than was generally the case in the past.

The present account of urbanization also helps in understanding how basic patterns of migration change over time. Wilbur Zelinsky (1971) famously proposed the existence of a 'mobility transition' that was envisaged as closely paralleling the occurrence of the demographic transition. His mobility transition involves a society experiencing successive temporal phases of migration. For example, it was proposed that there was a change in the nature of migration from being mainly rural–rural to being mainly urban–urban. And it was suggested that the mobility transition involves a tendency for the level of rural-to-urban migration first to rise, and later to fall. Zelinsky, however, regarded the mobility and the demographic transitions as being largely independent outcomes of 'modernization' (i.e. development). And urbanization was seen as resulting mainly from the mobility transition (i.e. from migration).

The present explanation, however, provides an integrated account of how the processes of the demographic transition, and rural-to-urban migration, both contribute to urbanization. The fact that rural–rural migration is gradually supplanted by urban–urban migration – for which there is much evidence – emerges here as the inevitable outcome of these demographic processes.[28] After all, in a largely rural population it is likely that most migration will be rural–rural; and in a largely urban population it is likely that most migration will be urban–urban. The initial rise in rural-to-urban migration is chiefly a reflection of the rise in rural natural increase which occurs as part of the demographic transition. And the later fall in rural-to-urban migration reflects the fact that, eventually, there are fewer people left in rural areas who can out-migrate.

In general, the demographic transition probably stimulates the propensity to migrate – particularly through the many pressures that are created as a result of mortality decline.[29] In addition, the natural increase produced by the transition certainly raises the *number* of people who are involved in most types of migration flow – both internal and international. It may also be that urbanization has the effect of increasing human movement. For example, it has been claimed that towns awaken a basic urge in people to be somewhere else (Reader 2005: 233–47). Nevertheless, it is worth noting that there are aspects of the demographic transition which may reduce migration, other things equal. Thus population ageing may eventually lead to a decline in the level of mobility. And, during the transition's intermediate stages, it is possible that the movement of women, in particular, is reduced by the fact of larger numbers of surviving children. That said, the subsequent attainment of low fertility probably enhances women's mobility.

The present explanation for urbanization also sheds light on the changes brought about by HIV/AIDS in recent decades. Baldly put, the present explanation is that urbanization results from mortality decline reflecting a fall in deaths from infectious diseases. The issue therefore arises as to whether this basic relationship can operate *in reverse*. In this context, HIV/AIDS is an infectious disease that has produced large rises in death rates in the countries of eastern and southern Africa. As one might expect, HIV/AIDS tends to be more prevalent in urban areas. Consequently, there are strong reasons to think that in these African countries it has been raising urban death rates by more than rural death rates. Also, infectious diseases, including HIV/AIDS, tend to have a downward influence on fertility. Therefore, there are grounds for considering that in these countries urban birth rates have probably been reduced by more than rural birth rates as a result of the disease. Finally, there are reasons to believe that net rural-to-urban migration may also have been reduced – compared to what would have happened 'in the absence of HIV/AIDS'. For example, there is evidence that families in towns often move back to rural areas after the death of an adult member (e.g. to minimize living costs). Thus we would expect there to be a slowing of urban population growth, relative to rural population growth – i.e. a reduction in the pace of urbanization. And, indeed, there are signs that HIV/AIDS has systematically slowed the pace of urbanization in the countries of eastern and southern Africa (see Dyson 2003).[30]

This chapter has dealt with the process of urbanization in a broad way. Essentially it has considered what has been described as the *first* urban transition – i.e. the rise in the level of urbanization from under 10 per cent to around 70 per cent (Skeldon 2008). We have not addressed topics like suburbanization and counter-urbanization – changes that tend to affect societies that are already fairly urban. Indeed, the attainment of a level of urbanization towards the upper end of the present scale means that a population can be considered as entirely urban for many purposes. Thus the distinction between 'urban' and 'rural' probably means much more in a society that is 10 per cent urban, compared to one that is 70 per cent urban. In the latter case, the 30 per cent of people who are 'rural' are likely to lead lives that are similar to those of the majority who are 'urban'. In short, at high levels of urbanization the conventional binary distinction between urban and rural populations loses much of its point.

As we have stressed, the present account does not provide all of the story. It is important to note that in pre-transitional circumstances a lack of surplus supplies of food and energy also worked to restrict urban growth and urbanization. And changes in relation to the availability of food, energy and transport have also been critical in accounting for what has subsequently occurred – especially in relation to the establishment of towns of much size.[31] Each experience of urban growth and urbanization is distinct, and economic considerations are certainly germane in influencing what happens. That said, the chief reason for urban growth in contemporary developing countries is natural increase resulting from the demographic transition. And the explanation for why these societies are urbanizing also lies primarily in the changes brought about by this transition. These basic demographic considerations do much to explain the seemingly inexorable nature of both urban growth and urbanization in the modern world.

The governments of many countries – including those as diverse as communist China and apartheid South Africa – have tried to slow urban growth and urbanization by placing restrictions on movement (Beall and Fox 2009). Unsurprisingly, however, these efforts meet with little success, if viewed in long-run perspective. There is no doubt that rapid urban growth is often problematic. But the provision of family planning services can help in reducing this growth – although this is often unappreciated. Urbanization, however, is a somewhat different – and almost always a beneficial – development. Provided that the demographic transition is under way, then urbanization is inevitable; however, it can be achieved with more, or less, urban growth.

The five main processes of the transition – i.e. mortality decline, population growth, fertility decline, population ageing and urbanization – have now been addressed. Therefore, we can turn to consider their many effects.

PART THREE

# The effects of the demographic transition

# 6 • Social effects of the transition

We now turn to the effects of the demographic transition. This chapter considers effects that can broadly be described as *social*. It begins by discussing the implications of the transition for people's basic attitudes towards life – if you like, the socio-psychological consequences. A key point here is that mortality decline generates higher levels of confidence in society as regards the worldly future. As the environment in which people are born and raised becomes increasingly secure, so individuals think more about their long-term prospects and make practical plans accordingly. These changes in attitudes and expectations tend to occur gradually, and they usually go unnoticed. The chapter then discusses the transition's repercussions for families and households. These effects vary as the phenomenon itself proceeds. In general, however, the transition results in societies in which smaller households tend to prevail.

The demographic transition also produces a decline in the importance that is attached to marriage in society – a development with particular implications for women. Especially, but not only, because of fertility decline, women experience an increase in autonomy, and their lives become more like those of men, i.e. there is a reduction in gender differentiation.

The final group of effects discussed here are the many social consequences of urban growth and urbanization. It is argued that – in bringing urban growth and urbanization about – the demographic transition has a massive impact on the overall level of societal complexity.

The general direction of the discussion is to start at the individual level, and then move towards higher levels of aggregation. The present consideration of the transition's social effects provides a basis for discussing its economic and political consequences in the next chapter. Irrespective of the kind of effect that is being considered, however, some preliminary remarks are required.

## Preliminary remarks

There has been remarkably little work on the consequences of the demographic transition. Of course, most of the effects addressed below have been the subject of research and writing. However, rarely, if ever, have they been considered in an integrated way and from the perspective of the transition.

Several decades ago, Paul Demeny commented on this extraordinary neglect of the 'multifarious' effects of the transition, with particular reference to the work of historians (Demeny 1972: 154). However, in general there has been relatively little progress in the subsequent years. That said, there are two areas of research where it is possible to draw from a literature that is relevant and reasonably consolidated. Thus, although it is seldom framed with respect to the demographic transition, there is a lot of writing on the consequences of urban growth and urbanization – and this literature will be referred to here. In addition, there has been a welcome tendency among economists to consider the economic effects of each of the transition's main processes.

A consideration of the transition's effects can tackle the subject in broadly two different ways. One way is to organize the discussion in terms of each of the transition's processes. For example, we might first take mortality decline, and consider its various effects. And we might then do the same for each of the other processes in turn. Another approach, however, is to organize the discussion in terms of the effects of the transition as they unfold with respect to different aspects of life – for example, the social, the economic and the political. Both of these approaches are reasonable. They both permit consideration of how the transition's influence can change as the phenomenon itself proceeds. And there are elements of both in what follows. That said, and largely for reasons of efficiency (i.e. space), it is the second approach which has chiefly been used to organize the discussion here.

It is important to emphasize that the following review of the transition's consequences is little more than a sketch. And, necessarily, it is selective. The value of the exercise, such as it is, derives chiefly from the fact that it is framed in terms of the demographic transition and its major processes. Clearly, it is difficult to be precise about the phenomenon's contribution to the various societal changes – social, economic and political – that are examined. Other forces have also influenced world development during the last two or three centuries – not least, modern economic growth and technological change (both of which have been dependent upon the increased use of fossil fuels). However, there is little reason to think that these other forces have had a larger impact on world development than has the demographic transition. And any account that fails to put this transition centre-stage is seriously deficient. *That* is the point of the following discussion.

## Socio-psychological effects

Although they unfold at several levels, the socio-psychological consequences of the demographic transition are particularly salient for individuals and households. However, research on this subject is inevitably limited by the fact that data on the socio-psychological characteristics of pre-transitional populations are scarce. Nevertheless, the implications of mortality decline for people's attitudes, values and behaviour have received some attention. And plausible suggestions as to the socio-psychological implications of the transition's other main processes can at least be proposed.

No reader of this book will have grown up in truly pre-transitional mortality conditions – i.e. circumstances where the death rate has undergone no decline at all, is punctuated with major peaks, and where the demise of a child, relative, neighbour or friend is very common.[1] People living in developed countries are now very far removed in time from such circumstances. Indeed, for most of them, experiencing the death of a member of their immediate social network is rare; and death is also distant in that it is restricted almost entirely to the passing of elderly people.[2] So far as the residents of developing countries are concerned, we have seen that life expectancy has improved very substantially in most of these countries. Therefore, admittedly at different speeds, these populations are also moving in the same general direction – i.e. towards a situation in which death is increasingly a relatively rare and distant event for most people.

However, in pre-transitional societies, death was never very far away for people of all ages. And an important feature of this was that it was common for parents to experience the loss of most, or indeed all, of their children. Influenced especially by the book *L'Enfant et la Vie Familiale sous L'Ancien Régime*, written by Philippe Ariès (1960), there is a substantial body of scholarship which argues that, in Europe in the past, parents tended to exhibit a significant degree of emotional detachment from their offspring – compared to the situation that generally prevails today. That is not to say that men and women failed to experience any grief at the loss of a child, but rather that the sentiment was often relatively muted – for understandable reasons.

In circumstances of high mortality, and great hardship, practices that we would regard as extremely neglectful, hard hearted, indeed even criminal, were sometimes socially acceptable and quite common. Infanticide has probably been practised in all societies to some degree. But in pre-transitional populations the use of infanticide to influence family composition was often widespread. For example, in much of north-western India the killing of some female infants at birth was fairly routine until the nineteenth century (Miller 1981). Similarly, research on eighteenth-century China suggests that around 10 per cent of all females (and some males) were killed at birth; indeed, among the imperial lineage the figure for female infants is put at roughly 40 per cent (Lee et al. 1994).

In Europe, and elsewhere, infanticide was also practised partly because of the shame associated with having an illegitimate birth (van de Walle 2003). In addition, especially in urban areas, parents frequently sent their babies away to be wet-nursed by women who lived in the countryside – and in such cases the chance of the infant dying was extremely high. The abandonment of infants and young children by parents, which also resulted in exceedingly high mortality, was extensive in much of Europe. The frequency of abandonment may have increased in the nineteenth century – perhaps partly because, with the occurrence of mortality decline, there were rising numbers of children around to be supported (Shorter 1976; Stone 1977; Tilly et al. 1992; Kertzer 1997). In considering these and other seemingly harsh practices, it should be recalled that in pre-transitional conditions not only were infant and child death rates high, but adults engaging in sexual intercourse had few means of controlling their own fertility.

So there are strong reasons for believing that, before the demographic transition, people generally took a harder and more dispassionate attitude towards the fate of their children (and indeed other members of society). It did not make sense to make large emotional investments in young children – especially the weaker and less wanted ones. Many babies would not survive for long. And death was often interpreted in a context that had a strong religious dimension – something that itself was probably influenced by the harsh demographic realities. Susan Scrimshaw (1978) has shown that the resulting patterns of child neglect were often subtle, and that they were usually *unconscious* rather than conscious. She refers to the 'angelito' theme, which was prevalent in much of Latin America as late as the 1960s. The death of an infant created little social upset in a household or community. She quotes Moritz Thomsen, an observer of people in rural Ecuador, many of whom held:

> the unshakable belief that when a baby dies, it dies in a state of grace and flies directly to heaven. Within this framework, then, death is something to celebrate; he has been released without sin from a life of poverty and suffering to become one of God's little angels [...] I would talk to farmers, who, when I asked them how many children they had, would

> say sadly and as though cursed 'Oh, ten, I think. I've had bad luck; not even one *angelito*.' (Thomsen 1969: 35)

In Chapter 4 we concluded that the origins of the demographic transition ultimately lie in the new ways of thinking that emerged as part of the Enlightenment. The first glimmerings of these intellectual changes may have occurred before the eighteenth century. Nevertheless, it is clear that from roughly that time there was a growing appreciation that it was possible to influence the forces of nature – including those that affect mortality.

However, with respect to both historical and contemporary cases of mortality decline, there has probably been a synergistic relationship between the introduction of measures that help to reduce death rates on the one hand, and the extension of more secular attitudes and behaviour towards health and disease on the other. To give a simple illustration, Jenner's development of vaccination at the end of the eighteenth century reflected a gradual change in attitudes towards dealing with disease. But it also had a major impact in demonstrating that practical measures to prevent disease were possible. Again, looking at mortality decline in rural south India in the 1950s, 1960s and 1970s, Caldwell and colleagues refer to a secularization of attitudes towards health and disease (Caldwell et al. 1988: 132–60). This process was gradual, multifarious, often subtle, and two-way. For example, its components included the growing realization that certain troubling physical conditions which affected old people were not inevitable, but could instead be treated. Also, people gradually became aware that changes in behaviour – such as taking a sick child to see a doctor at a health centre – could influence outcomes. The point being made is that an increased degree of agency helps to bring about mortality decline, but it also *results* from the process as well.

Naturally, it takes time for a society's socio-psychological characteristics to be influenced by mortality decline.[3] Lags are inevitably involved in what is largely an adaptive process. Usually people do not recognize that death rates are improving. Nevertheless, as mortality decline proceeds, so women and men inevitably become more confident as regards both their own survival chances and those of their children. The changing demographic realities produce a gradual shift in expectations, attitudes and values. This development is unconscious – but it greatly alters how the future comes to be viewed.

Before the demographic transition it was normal for parents to lose most of their children. The attainment of low mortality, however, means that a new chronological normality becomes established (see Livi Bacci 2000: 183–9). There is now a strong expectation that parents will die *before* their children (rather than the reverse). In conditions of low mortality, the death of a child is seen by everyone as a particularly great tragedy – whereas in conditions of high mortality such a happening was routine. Comparing the start and later stages of mortality decline, Massimo Livi Bacci observes that '[t]he thought of death, which once impregnated every living moment, is now relegated to a precise and circumscribed phase of life' (Livi Bacci 2000: 186). Indeed, death's absence at most ages only works to augment the value in which life is held. Therefore, the relationship between parents and individual children tends to become invested with heightened significance and intensity because of mortality decline. And this change is likely to be enhanced as fewer children are born (i.e. as fertility is controlled).

In a more stable and predictable world, greater attention is given to planning for the long-term future. In pre-transitional conditions most people were born into the roles that they would subsequently hold for the rest of their – often short – lives. But greater security and longevity mean that at all levels – i.e. from the individual to the state – increasing importance comes to be attached to education and training. Parents tend to invest more time, effort and resources in each of their offspring. Increased attention is given to raising the 'quality' of the fewer children that are had. This focus on improving child 'quality' is not simply a reason for why people decide to have fewer children – it is actually more an *outcome* of both mortality and fertility decline.[4]

In themselves, these developments are likely to mean that people's life chances become less dependent upon ascription (i.e. who their parents were) and more determined by educational qualifications and personal effort, i.e. achievement. Furthermore, the increasing weight that is attached to formal education is reinforced by changes that take place as a result of urban growth and urbanization (see below).

Mortality decline probably has the profoundest consequences for the socio-psychological characteristics of individuals and society. Yet the transition's other processes probably also have effects of this kind, and deserve brief consideration.

As noted, it seems plausible to suggest that the intensity of the relationship between parents and children is strengthened by the fact of fertility decline – a process which, after all, leads to a smaller number of children being around in families. Thus, in the context of the decline of fertility in Europe, Livi Bacci observes that 'the child has moved from the periphery to the center of family life' (Livi Bacci

2000: 188). Moreover, as will be discussed below, the nature of women's lives is affected greatly by fertility decline. One aspect of this is that women become increasingly independent of men – a development that certainly influences their outlook and values. It is also worth remarking that the spread of birth control provides another example of how secular attitudes come to prevail in more areas of life. Thus adults no longer see the number of children they have as being the result of divine providence (e.g. 'as many as God brings'). And problems of infertility are increasingly dealt with first through medical services, as opposed to approaches like prayer and propitiation.

Notice that the preceding discussion of socio-psychological effects is framed largely from the perspective of *adults* – for example, parents becoming emotionally closer to their children, or men and women thinking more about their own future prospects. It is natural and easy to discuss things in this way. However, framing the discussion from this perspective tends to obscure the reality that, as the transition proceeds, so adults come to form a much larger fraction of society. Thus in some countries today 40–45 per cent of the population is aged under 15 years, while in other countries the figure is only around 15–20 per cent.[5]

The socio-psychological characteristics of any pre-transitional society were inevitably influenced by the fact that a relatively high proportion of the population consisted of children and adolescents. Conversely, the characteristics of a society that is near the end of the demographic transition are influenced by the fact that most of the population are adults – usually about three-quarters of people will be aged 20 years or more. Of course, not all 'adult' characteristics are necessarily good ones. And, at either the individual level or at higher levels of aggregation, adulthood provides no guarantee of sensible and considerate behaviour. Nevertheless, maturity is generally associated with adults, and immaturity with children. Indeed, in both cases the terms are virtually synonymous. Moreover, adults certainly have higher levels of experience (and agency) than children. The fact that some societies are more adult than others in this respect must be significant, although it is very rarely mentioned.

It is sometimes claimed that older people are more conservative (i.e. less flexible) in their views, although the evidence on this is debated (see, for example, Kausler et al. : 51–3). That said, especially at *later* adult ages, people's cognitive abilities tend to decline; and at really advanced ages (e.g. over 90 years) levels of dementia can approach 30 per cent (Lobo et al. 2000). However, even taking these considerations into account, it is almost certainly the case that demographically advanced societies are generally more mature – i.e. more adult – in terms of their socio-psychological characteristics. There is little doubt that population ageing causes a significant change in the socio-psychological make-up of society simply because of the fundamental shift in age composition.[6]

Turning to the socio-psychological effects of urban growth and urbanization, it has long been known that patterns of social interaction, and the nature of the relationships that people experience, tend to differ between rural and urban situations (see, for example, Hauser 1965; Moore 1974). There are strong reasons for believing that in pre-transitional societies – where most people lived in rural communities – comparatively small and localized social networks tended to prevail. A relatively high proportion of the people with whom an individual would interact consisted of relatives (i.e. family members and other kin). Moreover, these kinds of relationship were relatively long lasting. It follows that interests and transactions of several different types were channelled through the same, comparatively small, number of personal relationships – and, in these circumstances, it was very difficult to compartmentalize the subject of one particular interaction from another.

In contrast, in urban areas people generally have much wider social networks – in which relatives and kin comprise a smaller proportion of the members. Social relationships are often *specific* to a particular interest or transaction in towns. Moreover, many of these relationships are fairly instrumental and short lived. Of course, here as elsewhere, the contrast being made is one of degree. For example, kinship relationships remain significant in post-transitional, mainly urban populations. Nevertheless, by changing the residential composition of society, urbanization shifts the balance of the kinds of relationship that tend to prevail.

It may also be that certain socio-psychological phenomena emerge only in urban situations – perhaps especially large towns. The classic paper by Wirth (1938) suggests that the combination of population scale, density and heterogeneity characteristic of towns leads to powerful and exciting social events which are almost inconceivable in smaller settings (e.g. hamlets and villages). Recent research also holds that there is an association between urban life and qualities like imagination and ingenuity (see, for example, Florida 2004). Ultimately, what is being referred to here are changes in social psychology that seem to arise when large numbers of people live together in relatively intense conditions of high density and diversity. However, there is also a tendency to associate certain adverse phenomena – such as depression, alienation, anxiety and feelings of social isolation – with life in large towns. If these negative phenomena are indeed more prevalent in urban areas, then it may partly be because of a relative absence of social support networks (e.g. family members and other kin). That said, it is important to note that we cannot be sure that such phenomena really are more prevalent in urban settings. There has, for example, been little research on the extent to which social support networks and levels of stress vary between large and smaller towns (see Harpham et al. 2004: 267–8).

## Effects on household structure and size

There was enormous variation between the kinship systems and rules of residence that applied in different societies under pre-transitional conditions. Anthropological and historical accounts often convey an impression that most people lived in large, extended households which included family members of several different generations. However, as quantitative data on the subject became available during the twentieth century, and with a growing body of historical research, this view has been revised.[7]

It is likely that large and complex households were seldom the main residential units in pre-transitional populations. Indeed, there appears to have been considerable similarity in both the size and the structure of most household units in most societies – irrespective of the particular kinship systems and ideal rules of residence that existed. Most households were probably fairly small, and it is likely that many people lived in residential units which approximated the nuclear family, or had such a family at its heart (see, for example, Levy 1965; Burch 1967). Recall that, in general, in pre-transitional conditions an average couple had only about two children who would survive into adulthood. And, underpinned ultimately by relatively high fertility, horizontal family relationships – e.g. those between siblings and cousins of the same generation – tended to predominate. Relationships that were vertical – i.e. across the generations – were relatively less dense.[8] The explanation for these basic similarities lies largely in the demographic conditions which prevailed. For example, high death rates restricted the number of relatives from different generations who were able to live together.

However, mortality decline exerts upward pressure on the size of families and households. The most important source of this pressure is the decline of death rates among infants and young children. But, as we saw in Chapter 4, there is evidence that total fertility often increases before it starts to decline – and this too would contribute to the upward pressure.

Because the historical transitions were generally relatively gradual affairs, the resulting upward force was probably comparatively modest in such cases. However, in many developing countries the rapid fall in death rates from the middle of the twentieth century – often combined with rises in fertility – undoubtedly led to upward pressure that was relatively abrupt and significantly greater in scale. Mortality decline in developing countries at this time was conducive to a greater degree of co-residence among extended family members – i.e. the process made it easier for the rules of residence associated with traditional kinship systems to be realized. Illustrative calculations suggest that the forces at work were sufficiently powerful that, in some contexts, the average size of families might double in just a couple of decades. However, the increases in household size that actually occurred were generally rather modest (see, for example, Burch 1970; Bongaarts 2001a). And this suggests that the pressure was dealt with in other ways – for example, through changes in the ways that rules of residence were actually implemented, through an increased tendency to establish new households, and through the migration of family members to live elsewhere (e.g. in the towns). We have also seen that the pressure had particular implications for adult women.[9] And that it was crucial for the eventual adoption of birth control.

Of course, the occurrence of fertility decline within the demographic transition leads to a reduction in average household size. It does this mainly by reducing the number of children per household. For example, in the United States average household size fell from 5.5 to 2.6 persons between 1850 and the end of the twentieth century. The contribution of fertility decline to this fall is reflected in the fact that in 1850 there were 2.3 persons aged under 15 years per household, but by 1998 the figure was just 0.6 (Bongaarts 2001a). In addition, however, over the long run the transition also reduces average household size by decreasing the number of *adults* per household. Notice that the preceding figures for the United States indicate that the number of people aged over 15 years per household fell from 3.2 to 2.0. This fall partly reflects the weakening of marriage in society, i.e. increased separation and divorce, and many more single-parent households (see below). There is also evidence from Europe and North America of an increasing tendency of old people to live alone – a development which, incidentally, may contribute to higher levels of loneliness. This increased tendency of elderly people to live by themselves may partly be a matter of preference (i.e. they may wish to retain their independence). But in circumstances of low fertility – and high geographical mobility – it may also reflect the fact that there are fewer family members living nearby with whom elderly people can live. Anyhow, the overall result is that whereas the average household size in these advanced societies was once about 4–6, today it is usually around 2–3 people.

Turning to developing countries, declines in average household size begin to become apparent in the data from about the 1970s onwards – i.e. with the onset of fertility decline in many societies. The declines in household size that appear to have been experienced so far have sometimes been rather modest (Bongaarts 2001a). Part of the explanation for this may be that, with the age of marriage rising in almost every country, young adults are leaving home to establish their own independent households at later ages. Nevertheless, it is important to stress that the general tendency in developing countries is still one of convergence towards smaller household structures – much as we would expect in circumstances of fertility decline. Furthermore, the tendency is usually more advanced in urban than in rural settings (see Bongaarts 2001a).

In sum, demographic conditions in pre-transitional societies meant that horizontal family relationships tended to be more important. Most households were not large, and they seldom contained members from several different generations. However, with mortality decline, average household size tends to rise. Mortality decline also tends to raise the rate of new household formation. And the joint survival chances of husbands and wives – effectively the number of years that they will both be alive – increase, and families last for longer and longer durations (see, for example, McNicoll 1984; Bongaarts 1987). People also experience key personal events – such as the death of a parent, or becoming a grandparent – at much later ages (Murphy 2009). Therefore, mortality decline leads to circumstances where vertical family relationships become more prominent. The eventual occurrence of fertility decline means that households then become smaller. There are now fewer children around, and increased levels of marital instability lead to more single-parent households, for example. There may also be a heightened tendency for older people to live by themselves. With regard to the fact that the demographic transition makes vertical relationships more dense, and horizontal relationships more sparse, Ron Lee has observed that 'these changes appear to be quite universal so far' (Lee 2003: 185).

So the same basic demographic processes appear to be bringing about broadly similar changes in very different settings. Of course, differences between societies remain. And in some populations these changes are still at a relatively early stage. Nevertheless, there are reasons to believe that there will be a considerable degree of convergence in the long run.

## The decline of marriage

Some form of marriage was a central institution in almost every pre-transitional society.[10] The extent to which marriage was recognized in formal terms varied. But the institution usually formed the basis of the family – wherein children were raised, resources were transferred between generations, and elderly people were cared for. The importance of marriage was seldom questioned.

However, during the second half of the twentieth century the institution weakened considerably in those societies that are most advanced in terms of the demographic transition.[11] Levels of marital disruption increased, new forms of partnership arose, the relationship between marriage and childbearing became much looser, and alternative family and household structures came into being. Furthermore, there are signs that similar changes are occurring in an increasing number of developing countries. The ways in which mortality decline and fertility decline are bringing about this transformation are fairly clear. To understand them, it is useful to consider the circumstances of women in societies at different stages of the demographic transition.

In populations where fertility is relatively high and has not yet begun to decline, women's lives are generally dominated by issues relating to marriage, fertility and the care of young children (see, for example, Collver 1963). Indeed, these are the primary ways in which most women are likely to find a measure of security and fulfilment in life. Naturally, the specifics of the situation would vary greatly between different populations. Nevertheless, in general, a woman would get married while she was still young – usually in her middle or late teens, perhaps her early twenties.[12] She might then experience the birth of her first child, say, a couple of years later – i.e. while she was still in her teens or early twenties. Provided that both she and her husband survived, she would then continue to give birth every few years until she reached the end of her reproductive span. The length of the interval between each of her births would probably be three or four years, although it was sometimes shorter. The length of the interval would depend, among other things, on how long she breastfed her children, and how long she abstained from having sexual intercourse following each experience of childbirth.[13] In these circumstances, a woman might have her final birth while aged in her forties – and by this time her eldest (i.e. firstborn) child might well be married, provided it had survived, and especially if it was a girl.

Of course, in truly pre-transitional circumstances not only was fertility high, but mortality was high as well – and this was crucial in determining what was likely to happen. In such conditions several – quite possibly all – of the children that a woman had were likely to die. That is, it was often a case of repeated childbearing to very little effect in terms of the number of *surviving* children – and in this sense childlessness was fairly common. There was also a high chance that the woman's husband, who would be older than her, would die before she did – and if this happened it would bring her childbearing to an end, unless she remarried.[14] Naturally, there was a significant chance that she would die herself before she reached the end of her reproductive years. And even if she survived into her forties, her firstborn child might well be dead by that time.

While no modern population is subject to pre-transitional conditions with respect to mortality, as we have seen there are still quite a few countries where the level of total fertility per woman remains high – for example, throughout much of sub-Saharan Africa, and parts of the Middle East and South-Central Asia (see Chapter 3). In such places the essential scenario outlined above still generally applies – that is, marriage, childbirth and childcare tend to dominate the course of women's lives. And because there has been some improvement in mortality, the role of childcare – looking after several children simultaneously – may be especially pronounced. In these circumstances marriage is usually important for both partners, but it is especially so for the woman.

Now consider the circumstances of women in a society that is nearing the end of the demographic transition in terms of vital rates – one in which the levels of mortality and fertility are both low (and may have been for some time). The first countries to experience these conditions were those of western Europe and North America.[15] Therefore it is useful to consider the situation in these societies during the 1950s and 1960s – again, through the use of a broad characterization. In fact, there was a limited and short-lived resurgence in fertility in these countries at that time – something often referred to as the 'post-war baby boom'.[16] Total fertility per woman averaged about 2.5 births in western Europe, and about 3.3 in North America.

In these conditions a woman could expect to get married while she was still fairly young – say, in her early twenties. She would have her first birth two or three years later, and a second birth two or three years after that. If she did have a third birth she would probably still only be aged in her late twenties or early thirties (Collver 1963). By the time she reached her fiftieth birthday her children might well have left home – recall that by this time her youngest child might be aged about twenty. Yet because life expectancy in Europe and North America was now at a high level, such a woman would have a very good chance of living on for another thirty years – a period during which she would probably have no children around in the household to care for. As Kingsley Davis and Pietronella van den Oever (1982: 502) pointedly enquire: 'What is she to do during this period, which comprises more than half of her lifetime after marriage?' Her situation would not be helped by the fact that her husband was likely to die several years before she did. This was partly because he would (again) be older than her. But it is also the case that at later adult ages the death rates of men tend to be higher than those of women – a fact which leads to there being many more elderly women alive at later ages in these societies than there are men (Davis and van Oever 1982).[17]

There are reasons to think that the 1950s and 1960s was the time in these societies when men and women spent the greatest proportion of their adult lives living together as married couples, and with children around in the household (see Watkins et al. 1987). But the situation contained the seeds of its own transformation. Thus conditions of low mortality placed increased strain on the traditional conception of marriage as a lifelong partnership. After all, many people make a choice at marriage that they subsequently live to regret. The selection of an unsuitable marriage partner was less of an issue in pre-transitional circumstances – when the joint survival chances of a newly married couple were much lower. However, by the 1950s and 1960s life expectation was high. And the attainment of low fertility also raised the crucial question of what women were to do with so much of their lives, when there were no children around to look after.

Against this background, a dynamic set of processes became established in which marriage has become progressively weaker, and alternative institutions have emerged (see Davis and van den Oever 1982). Social arrangements relating to marriage and family formation have become much more fluid. This is a large and still-developing story, but several key elements can be identified. Thus divorce and separation have increased greatly – partly because people are living longer, and some couples can put up with each other only for so many years (Keyfitz 1987: 8). Susan Cotts Watkins and others remark that '[t]he view from the present forward to a long remaining life with a spouse may provoke a revision of what is owed to that spouse, or of what could be gained by a new contract negotiated under new conditions' (Watkins et al. 1987: 355). The rise in divorce and separation has meant that, instead of being reared by a married couple, an increasing proportion of children are raised by one parent – usually the mother, a fact that has not gone unrecognized by adults of either sex.[18] Of course, people do remarry, but second marriages tend to be even less stable than first ones.

The diminution of childbearing in women's lives means that they come to attach much less significance to their domestic roles, and they think more about their own employment prospects (see Davis and van den Oever 1982). Relatedly, parents attach greater importance to educating their daughters – after all, daughters are increasingly likely to need, and desire, careers of their own. For understandable reasons, married women reduce the extent to which they depend on their husbands. In contemporary North America and western Europe, marriage is now as likely to end in divorce as in widowhood (Pullum 2003). Moreover, men also recognize that marriage is being eroded, and that their roles of father and household head are diminishing (see Clare 2001). In these circumstances 'marriage undergoes attrition in two ways: it is postponed or not undertaken at all, and when it is undertaken, it is increasingly brittle' (Davis and van den Oever 1982: 508).

In many developed countries the average age of women at first marriage is now several years higher than the average age of women at first birth. Many more people now live in consensual (i.e. informal) unions. But consensual unions are less stable, and less conducive to having children – considerations that give women even greater reason to pursue their own careers (Kiernan 2003). These facts do much to explain why fertility is below the replacement level in almost all societies that are advanced in terms of the demographic transition. Higher levels of employment among women have led to lower fertility, and vice versa. Whereas marriage was once intimately associated with childbearing, now the strength of the connection is very much reduced. Some women who marry decide not to have children. And births outside of marriage are frequent.[19] As in pre-transitional circumstances, childlessness is quite common among women, but it is childlessness in a completely different, essentially volitional sense.

These social changes have been dubbed the 'second demographic transition' (see, for example, van de Kaa 1987). But they are much better seen as *lagged* effects of the overall transition itself – in particular, the attainment of low fertility and low mortality. Naturally, the responses of different populations have varied in their details. Different societies have used different combinations of response. Thus while the age of marriage has increased in almost every European country, there remains considerable variation in the prevalence of consensual unions (Kiernan 2003). The immediate explanations provided by researchers to account for similar developments have also varied. Thus in western Europe and North America the rise in divorce has been attributed to the growth of more individualistic attitudes. But in eastern Europe – where there have been similar developments – the explanation has sometimes been framed in terms of the socio-economic difficulties associated with communism and its collapse (Goode 1993). Such variation in explanation is only to be expected – given the different histories and circumstances of different populations. Ultimately, however, various societies are responding in broadly similar ways to the same new demographic realities.

Analogous changes relating to marriage are under way elsewhere in the world. The clearest evidence pertains to societies that are relatively advanced in terms of the transition. There is little doubt that similar developments have been occurring in Japan (see, for example, Ogawa and Ermisch 1994). There are signs too that young adults in countries in East and South-East Asia are asking whether marriage and parenthood have much to offer them. For example, it has been said that Chinese populations – such as those of Singapore, Taiwan and Hong Kong – are engaged in a 'flight from marriage' (Leete 1994). Also, in places like South Korea, Thailand and Malaysia, increasing numbers of young women are reported to be 'staying away from marriage in droves' (Jones 1997a: 74). Even in the few societies where the divorce rate seems to have been falling – such as certain Islamic societies in South-East Asia – the trend may not be all that it seems. Thus the fall in divorce may partly reflect a decline in arranged marriages. So-called 'love marriages' may be more stable. Moreover, even in these Islamic societies there is evidence of increased levels of pre-marital sex and informal consensual unions. Therefore the fall in divorce may partly reflect a declining tendency to get formally married in the first place (see Jones 1997b).

Divorce rates in developing countries are generally rising. Thus the United Nations reports that, for developing countries with available data, between the 1970s and the 1990s the median divorce rate rose from about 7 to 12 divorces per 100 married men, and from 5 to 15 divorces per 100 married women. The overall conclusion is that 'not only has there been a tendency for people to marry later, but the instability of marital unions has been rising' (United Nations 2003: xiii).

As we noted in Chapter 4, the age of women at marriage is increasing in almost every developing country. In part, this probably reflects the greater tendency of young women to remain in education while in their teens. However, it also reflects the fact that the ratio of women to men in the age ranges at which people usually get married has been rising as a result of mortality decline (i.e. a so-called 'marriage squeeze' effect). Census data for developing countries almost always reveal declines in the proportion of women who are recorded as 'ever married' over time. These declines are most pronounced in the 15–19 and 20–24 age groups – reflecting the rising age of female marriage. However, in many countries, declines are also evident for women in higher age groups (e.g. 30–34 and 35–39). These trends reflect circumstances in which, for women, rises in the age at marriage, increases in education and employment, and lower levels of fertility are all interacting in mutually reinforcing ways.

Several points should be emphasized in concluding. The effects of sustained low levels of mortality and fertility on marital and related social arrangements are lagged. The influence of these new demographic conditions on social processes is remote – and almost always unseen. Although we would expect the attainment of low mortality and low fertility to eventually bring about broadly similar changes everywhere, we would not expect to see exactly the same responses in different populations. Relatedly, it is must be acknowledged that other factors have contributed to what we have termed the 'decline of marriage'. For example, in many developing countries attitudes towards marriage have been influenced through the media. And the spread of education and urbanization also affects marriage. That said, some of these 'other factors' themselves arise partly from the demographic transition.[20] And it is difficult to envisage the establishment of these new social arrangements with respect to cohabitation and childbearing in the absence of low mortality and low fertility. A corollary of the decline in marriage is that women come to experience increased levels of independence, and it is to this that we now turn.

## Reductions in gender differentiation

Pre-transitional societies differed considerably in the extent to which they afforded women a degree of personal autonomy. But it is fair to say that women's roles were usually very constrained (as they often still are). There were always the restrictions arising from marriage and repeated childbirth. These constraints meant that most women's lives revolved around concerns of the domestic domain (i.e. the home).

The continuing demographic transition, however, has changed – and is changing – this situation in developed countries; and, increasingly, it is benefiting the circumstances of women in many developing countries as well. The central point is that, especially during the *latter* stages of the transition, lower fertility and the attendant weakening of marriage bring about a reduction in gender differentiation in society. This reduction may not be happening either as much, or as fast, as many observers would like. But the factors that condition the extent and speed of the process in different situations are not our prime concern here.

For countries with available estimates, Figure 6.1 illustrates the

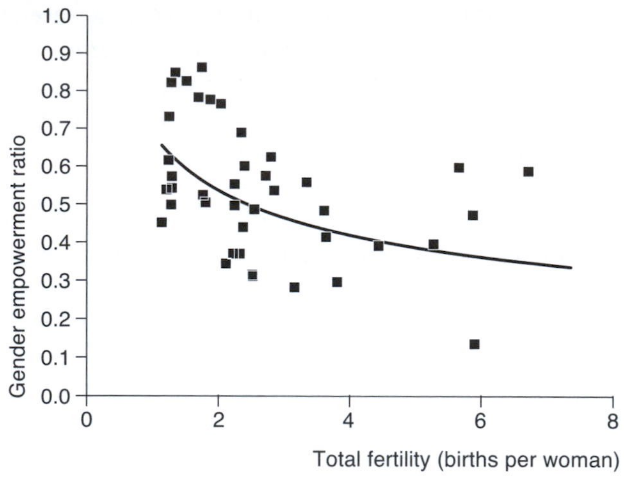


*Sources*: UNDP (2008), United Nations (2009)

**Figure 6.1 The relationship between total fertility and the UN gender empowerment measure, forty-one countries, around 2007**

relationship between the level of total fertility and the Gender Empowerment Measure (GEM) of the United Nations.[21] The GEM reflects a country's level of gender equality in terms of women's involvement in relatively high-level economic and political affairs – such as their representation among legislators and professional workers. Therefore it is far from being an ideal indicator of the degree of gender equality that is characteristic of a society as a whole. Moreover, the relationship shown in Figure 6.1 would almost certainly be improved if estimates of the GEM were available for more countries with high levels of fertility.[22] Nevertheless, there are signs that countries with low fertility tend to have higher levels of gender equality. This may partly reflect the fact that higher levels of gender equality help to facilitate the occurrence of fertility decline. But it is probably significant that all of the countries that have achieved exceptionally high levels of gender equality (i.e. values above 0.7) have low levels of fertility. There are good grounds for thinking that the attainment of low fertility helps in the long run to raise the level of gender equality in society.[23]

So far as developed countries are concerned, there are reasons to believe that progress through the demographic transition has underlain much of the increase in women's independence that has occurred since the middle of the twentieth century. We have already remarked that, because of the weakening of marriage, parents of girls – and girls and young women themselves – have come to attach greater importance to the acquisition of education. It has also been argued that in circumstances of low fertility the fact that there are only a small number of children around in households tends to reduce differences in the ways in which boys and girls are socialized (see Lloyd 1994). For example, where there are only a small number of children, a girl is more likely to have to undertake household tasks that are traditionally associated with boys, and vice versa. In other words, low fertility *by itself* may work to reduce the degree of gender differentiation within families – including, of course, with respect to the education of children.

There have been significant increases in the educational levels of girls and women in most developed countries in recent decades.[24] Indeed, in Europe and North America girls tend to outperform boys in both primary and secondary schools. As many women graduate from university as men, and on leaving school or university their immediate employment prospects are said to be equal to those of men (Clare 2001: 4). As a result of these changes, women have become represented in the formal labour force to a much greater degree; and, almost certainly, they derive increased independence from earning their own wages. While it is true that many women work in low-paid and part-time jobs, it is also true that women have gradually become more represented in types of employment that are better remunerated (e.g. in the professions, and government service). Of course, the amount of progress varies, and it can be piecemeal. Discrimination in pay and promotion persists; and many women find themselves juggling paid work with responsibilities for the care of children and other dependants (e.g. old people). Nevertheless, the broad direction of change is unmistakable.

So in demographically advanced societies the lives of women have tended to become more like those of men. And there are reasons to believe that this may be true with respect to aspects of life other than education and employment. Similar arguments can be made with respect to patterns of dress and smoking, for example. The female voice has also become progressively deeper in recent decades – a trend that has been interpreted as resulting from the wider changes in women's lives. In this context Anne Karpf comments that '[i]n the voices of men and women we can hear their evolving roles and relative power' (Karpf 2007: 181). Likewise, in discussing the increased use of androgynous names in the United States – i.e. names that can be given to a child of either sex – Lieberson and colleagues remark that it is usually women 'who adopt tastes initially associated with males rather than vice versa' (Lieberson et al. 2000: 1285). In short, reductions in gender differentiation have been asymmetrical. Women are becoming more like men to a greater degree than the reverse is happening.

Turning to circumstances in developing countries, again it seems that the implications of the demographic transition for the lives of girls and women are generally positive – although it is important to acknowledge that the resulting gains are not necessarily generated in straightforward or clear-cut ways (see, for example, McNay 2005). There is a lot of evidence that conditions of high fertility tend to have adverse implications for women's health, and that the position of women in society is frequently restricted greatly by the demands of childbirth and childcare (see, for example, Oppong and Wéry 1994; K. Mason 1997b). In general, high fertility helps to maintain traditional sex roles, and thereby reinforces gender differentiation (Lloyd 1994; Lloyd and Gage-Brandon 1994). A key part of the limiting effect of high fertility on girls derives from the fact that, as they get older, they are frequently required to take care of younger brothers and sisters.

However, in recent decades government programmes to provide universal education for children of both sexes have been associated with increased levels of female education in many countries. There is little doubt that if such programmes are implemented with sufficient vigour then they can produce a rise in the educational level of girls, largely irrespective of the prevailing demographic conditions. Nevertheless, there is also little doubt that the occurrence of fertility decline in a country makes the implementation of a programme of mass schooling easier – for the simple reason that educational facilities (e.g. teachers, school buildings, books, etc.) are required for smaller numbers of children. Therefore, at the aggregate level, it is reasonable to think that fertility decline tends to benefit the schooling of girls – because it facilitates the introduction of mass schooling in general. Research also suggests that lower fertility within households helps the education of girls – among other things, by reducing the childcare duties in relation to younger siblings that they are expected to undertake (see, for example, Adnan 1993; Kabeer 2000; Bhat 2002).

The attainment of low fertility and the concentration of childbearing into a relatively short period of life have almost certainly assisted the entry of women into the labour force in many developing countries. For example, McNay (2005) maintains that in parts of East and South-East Asia there have been significant rises in female labour force participation, and these rises have tended to happen alongside the occurrence of fertility decline (causal influences probably working in both directions). Similarly, Bauer's research on East Asia suggests that fertility decline has heightened women's non-domestic economic roles. And mortality decline is said to have raised the incentives of women to find work outside of the home – owing to the increased length of the post-child-rearing phase of life (Bauer 2001). Even in India, a country where patriarchal tendencies are often strong, there are signs that fertility decline has helped to open up educational and employment prospects for young women. These developments are most apparent for middle-class women in urban areas. However, even in rural areas there has been a rise in women's share of agricultural employment, and a reduction in wage differentials between women and men (McNay, Unni and Cassen 2004). Of course, economic changes, educational policies and the mass media have also contributed to these gains (Rishyaringa 2000; Dyson 2002). But progress would probably have been very much less in the absence of fertility decline (Bhat 2005).

It is important not to get carried away and exaggerate the scale of the changes that are occurring. And, to reiterate, not all of the changes can be attributed to falling levels of mortality and fertility. Nevertheless, it would be surprising if the attainment of low fertility in an increasing number of developing countries was not having the underlying effect of reducing levels of gender differentiation, and in an asymmetrical way. Key parts of the story are the rising age of women at marriage, the weakening of marriage, and rising levels of female education and employment. The growing independence of women from men can be downplayed or even missed by observers. But then experience suggests that data are often late in revealing, and researchers still later in noticing, the emergence of major new trends.[25] In this context, it is worth pointing out that while much research has been undertaken on how measures of women's status affect levels of child mortality and fertility, there has been very little research on the opposite direction of causation – i.e. how progress through the demographic transition itself affects the position of women in society (see Mason 1997b; Dyson 2001; McNay 2005).

### Urbanization and societal complexity

The expansion of the urban sector has been crucial for almost all aspects of societal change, in both developed and developing countries. Indeed, it is difficult to think of any major dimension of development that can be attributed to the rural sector – in the sense of both arising in that sector and being sustained by events there.

In Europe and North America in the nineteenth and twentieth centuries progress of most kinds occurred in the expanding towns. This is generally recognized with respect to the growth of industry and

TABLE 6.1 Selected dimensions of the rise in societal complexity resulting from urban growth and urbanization

1. Increased division of labour in society – i.e. greater occupational specialization
2. Greater use of systems of exchange – i.e. money, markets, trade, accounting
3. Issues arising from population concentration – e.g. sewage, water, fire, social order
4. General expansion of systems of administration and government
5. Increased requirements for skills, training and education
6. The growth of the institutions of 'civil society' – e.g. charitable trusts, trade unions, law, the press

commerce. But it was equally true with respect to advances in fields such as education, science, law, medicine, the arts, journalism, publishing and the many institutions of civil society (e.g. charitable trusts, community groups, trade unions, etc.). In contemporary developing countries as well, undertakings in all of these fields are centred predominantly in the towns. Of course, progress does occur in rural areas – for example, as regards the spread of education and increases in agricultural productivity. However, ultimately this progress usually gets its principal drive, coordination and purpose from people and organizations in the towns.[26]

Here we consider some of the broad social effects that arise from the expansion of the urban sector. These effects interact with various economic and political consequences that are addressed in the next chapter. However, the social effects considered here can be regarded as at least analytically distinct from the economic and political effects.[27] Parts of the following discussion are framed in terms of 'urban growth'. This is because some of the social effects considered arise chiefly from the creation of larger and larger towns, rather than from an increase in the level of urbanization per se. However, as we saw in Chapter 5, in contemporary circumstances urban growth and urbanization almost always occur together. And it is obvious that the higher is the level of urbanization in a society, the greater will be the influence of developments in the urban sector on the society's overall characteristics.

As we have seen, before the demographic transition the urban sector – insofar as it existed – was almost always very small.[28] Nevertheless, to the extent that there was social diversity within a population, this diversity tended to be significantly greater in the towns compared to the rural areas. And the towns were the centres of power, wealth, trade, administration, learning and culture. Therefore, in important respects, pre-transitional towns contained several broad types of activity that would subsequently experience considerable growth and differentiation as a result of urban growth (and urbanization).

As Table 6.1 suggests, the occurrence of sustained urban growth as a result of the transition has produced major increases in the complexity of the activities that are undertaken in urban areas, and it has also led to an expansion of the range of the activities that are undertaken.

The fact that an increase in population size tends to cause an increase in the degree of differentiation in society has long been known. As we saw in Chapter 5, Adam Smith was well aware that major towns tended to contain much higher levels of diversity in terms of employment. He maintained that occupational specialization is stimulated by the economies of scale associated with the production of goods for large and concentrated markets. In the nineteenth century, the social theorist Herbert Spencer observed that 'along with increase of size in societies goes increase of structure [...] the social aggregate, homogenous when minute, habitually gains in heterogeneity along with each increment of growth' (quoted in Schnore 1965: 6). Towards the end of the nineteenth century, Emile Durkheim addressed the mechanisms through which a rise in population density might produce growth in the division of labour. He emphasized the resulting increase in the rate of social interaction – an increase that might be heightened by improvements in transport and communication. Durkheim argued that the higher rates of social interaction found in urban areas produce raised levels of *competition* between people and that, in turn, this leads to higher levels of occupational differentiation. He also considered that greater specialization makes it somewhat easier for people to live alongside one another in towns. In short, urban growth spurs greater differentiation in society, and greater differentiation also helps to facilitate urban growth – at least in some respects (see Schnore 1965: 3–9).

The precise ways in which urban growth produces increased differentiation are not of great concern to us here. It is clear, however, that a full explanation would require reference to structural changes in the urban economy (Syrquin 2006). As we noted in Chapter 5, the process of urbanization is associated with a basic transformation in the structure of employment – that is, out of agriculture and into the manufacturing and service sectors.

Almost inevitably, then, sustained expansion of the urban population within the demographic transition generates growth and differentiation in terms of employment. For example, food and other supplies have to be purchased in rural areas, and then transported to the expanding towns. These supplies must then be stored in the towns, and subsequently distributed to their inhabitants – almost always through the development of the retail sector. All of these activities – i.e. purchasing, transportation, storage and selling – are likely to involve the creation of more, and more varied, forms of employment. Still further growth and diversity in employment will be generated by the transport to rural areas of the increasing number of products of the urban economy. After all, food and other supplies have to be paid for in some way. A well-known statement of Karl Marx reflects this well: 'The foundation of every division of labour that is well developed, and brought about by the exchange of commodities, is the separation between town and country. It may be said that the whole economic history of society is summed up in the movement of this antithesis' (Marx 1887 [1954]: 352). Therefore, urban growth and urbanization stimulate a rise in trade between rural and urban areas. And, as individual towns expand, so there is greater exchange of goods and services within each town. Moreover, as the level of urbanization rises, so there tends to be an increase in the number of urban units, and consequently an increase in the volume of trade between different units. All of these developments underpin the expansion of markets and the increased use of monetary exchange and related systems of accounting (see Table 6.1).

The formation of larger and larger towns also raises quite new challenges that eventually must be addressed. For example, there are matters of urban planning – e.g. as to where, when and how new structures are to be built. The disposal of urban waste, including human waste, raises major issues. Everyday solutions, like tipping refuse and turds into the streets, present difficulties of their own – for example, in relation to water supplies. The collection and transport of human waste for use as manure has long been part of the 'exchange of commodities' between urban and rural areas in many societies – perhaps most notably China (see, for example, Ponting 2007: 346–52). However, even in contemporary Europe and North America, treated sewage and effluent is still sometimes spread across fields as manure (CGER 1996). Urban growth also generates new challenges in relation to urban transport, the control of fires, and the maintenance of public order (see Table 6.1). The appalling living conditions found in many towns, past and present, has also spurred the growth of activities aimed at social improvement – like slum clearance, self-help groups and the provision of social housing. And from the nineteenth century onwards, issues of public health and pollution in urban areas have become increasingly important.

For these and other reasons, it is to be expected that urban growth stimulates the development of multiple units and layers of administration and government. The expansion of the urban sector is also likely to be accompanied by an increase in rules, regulations and laws. And urban problems (e.g. relating to fire control and water supply) are likely to be addressed in ways that become progressively more specific and technical (Montgomery et al. 2004: 70). Importantly, the increase in occupational specialization that accompanies urban growth will almost certainly lead to heightened requirements for education, training and skills (see Table 6.1). In sum, the enlargement of the urban sector produces increasing differentiation with respect to a growing range of human activities. These changes are likely to be greatest in the urban sector itself, but they will also be reflected within the rural sector, and with respect to the host of intermediary activities that link people living in urban and rural areas.

The mechanisms through which urban growth stimulates greater differentiation in the structure of employment are likely to operate across the whole range of human affairs – for example, in relation to artistic, cultural, religious and sporting activities. And, just as increased specialization consequent on urban growth is thought to benefit economic productivity, so analogous productivity gains almost certainly arise with respect to these other types of activity. Part of the 'major transformation' in the social realm which Hauser saw as arising from the conditions of urban life may well derive from such heightened specialization (Hauser 1965: 12). And urban growth and urbanization almost certainly work to broaden people's horizons and ways of thinking. In pre-transitional rural circumstances it seems likely that most people's interests and concerns extended little beyond their own immediate locality. However, whether we consider urbanization in the past or in developing countries today, the experience of living in a town tends to connect people more with the wider world. And the fact that personal relationships in urban areas are often relatively short-lived and specific has its roots in the fact that towns contain much greater amounts of differentiation (Hauser 1965).

As we saw in Chapter 5, urban growth and economic growth tend to reinforce each other. Nevertheless, it is worth emphasizing that provided the urban sector is sustained in terms of its essential supplies (i.e. of food and energy) then much of the increase in occupational specialization that its growth generates could be expected to happen independently of the occurrence of economic growth. Thus there could be increased differentiation with respect to many different kinds of activity – e.g. administration, provisioning, charity, the disposal of waste – without much economic growth. Often against a background of very rapid urban growth, many of the activities undertaken by people working in the informal sector of numerous towns in poor developing countries today – e.g. street hawking, casual labour, scavenging, etc. – are of little absolute value in economic terms, although they do help individuals to eke out some form of living. In such circumstances, the increasing differentiation of employment may happen more because of the fragmentation of existing work, rather than because of the creation of new economic activity (Davis 2006; Seabrook 2007).

Parallels are sometimes drawn between the dreadful work and living conditions found in the towns of some contemporary developing countries, and the conditions that existed in the towns of developed countries in the nineteenth century. By the start of the twentieth century, most societies in Europe and North America had been transformed by the combination of urban growth and economic growth (Ponting 2007). And both of these types of growth contributed to the massive increase in the general complexity of these societies. However, in Europe and North America, economic growth was based on the increased use of fossil-fuel energy. So far as developing countries are concerned, almost all of them are likely to experience a rise in societal complexity as a result of urban growth and urbanization during the coming decades. However, the extent to which they also experience a rise in their complexity due to economic growth is likely to be variable. Among other things, it will depend upon the degree to which they are able to get access to supplies of energy.

In concluding, it is important to stress that this discussion of the social effects of urban growth and urbanization only scratches the surface. Thus there has been no discussion of changes in vertical differentiation that can arise with urban growth (e.g. the creation of social classes); no consideration of how informal social control mechanisms are increasingly joined by more formal mechanisms of control (e.g. the police, courts, prisons, etc.); and no discussion of phenomena like street gangs, commercial sex, and drug addiction – all of which probably become more prevalent with urban expansion. In short, it should be clear that the cumulative increase in societal complexity that results from urban growth and urbanization can be discussed in many more ways and, of course, with respect to both historical and contemporary circumstances.[29] Overall, however, international comparisons suggest a positive link between the level of urbanization and the level of human development (see, for example, UNCHS 2001).

## Conclusions and discussion

While everything interacts with everything else, and while it is impossible to distinguish all of them neatly, it should be clear that what we have termed the 'social' effects of the demographic transition are incredibly important.

In brief, the argument here has been that people's attitudes, values and emotions, the nature of the relationships they form, their feelings about marriage and having children, and – perhaps particularly for women – their experience of personal autonomy, are all influenced hugely by the processes of the transition. Moreover, the size and structure of the households people live in, and the complexity of the societies in which they dwell, are affected greatly too. In addition, the transition plays a crucial role in leading people to think more about their future prospects. It heightens the degree of control that individuals have with respect to the course of their own lives. In this way, and by contributing to the growth of specialization and competitiveness, it underpins the increased importance that comes to be attached to education. In post-transitional societies people are more mature and experienced. Many of these consequences unfold gradually; they happen to people unawares; and they are unseen, even to many observers. Nevertheless, in the end, the demographic transition contributes to a fundamental change in the nature of human society – one which, it might be suggested, involves greater emphasis on competition and personal achievement.

Mainly for reasons of space, several issues have not been addressed in detail here, although they deserve brief discussion in concluding.

The preceding discussion of the transition's implications for households, marriage and women has been framed with reference to societies in which monogamous unions prevail. This covers most of the world. But in sub-Saharan Africa polygynous marriage (i.e. where men have more than one wife) was, and to varying degrees still is, the baseline for change.[30] It might be asked whether the eventual implications of the demographic transition for individuals and households are likely to be different in such circumstances. Addressing this matter is complicated – partly because political and economic forces have also caused changes in the nature of family arrangements (especially in southern Africa). Having said that, however, there is little reason to think that the transition's influence will be much different in this area of the world, in the long run. In short, the transition might be expected to contribute to a decline in household size, a weakening of marriage (whether polygynous or not) and greater autonomy for women. Widespread polygyny is made possible only because there is a large age gap between married men and married women. But the age of women at marriage is rising in sub-Saharan Africa (as elsewhere), and there are reasons to think that this development may already be contributing to a decline in polygynous marriage (Hayase and

Liaw 1997). Moreover, urbanization is probably having a similar effect – it being harder for men to maintain polygynous households in urban areas. Extensive polygyny is also facilitated by young age distributions (which raise the ratio of younger marriageable women, with respect to older men). But fertility decline will produce older age distributions in the future. Finally, and perhaps most importantly, as birth control spreads – albeit very slowly in some countries – it should work to the benefit of women. Especially in southern Africa, the sustained absence of men due to labour migration badly disrupted marriage patterns and gender relations long ago. In South Africa, for example, large numbers of women live in female-headed households and are said to regard men as 'superfluous' in many respects.[31] These circumstances have stimulated an interest in contraception among women. But contraception has also helped women to maintain some independence in the face of opposition from men (Timaeus and Moultrie 2008).

This sketch of how the transition's processes can be expected to bring about broadly similar changes (e.g. a weakening of marriage, greater independence for women, increasing prominence of vertical kin ties) in the different circumstances of sub-Saharan Africa underscores that other forces are involved in bringing about social change. But it also illustrates how the transition's processes can work to reinforce each other. Thus, in all parts of the world, if mortality decline and fertility decline lead to greater pressures being placed upon the institution of marriage, and therefore smaller households, there are reasons to believe that the increased propensity of people to live in urban areas may have a similar effect. Likewise, elderly people may suffer increased levels of loneliness because of fertility decline, but urbanization may contribute to increased loneliness as well.

There is also the matter of where we should draw the line in discussing the transition's effects – which can cascade over several generations. For example, if one effect of the demographic transition is to make women's lives more like those of men, it may eventually be the case that there is a movement in the *opposite* direction, partly by way of compensation. Indeed, in the most demographically advanced societies today, there are signs that fathers are becoming more involved in the care of young children (Clare 2001: 129–93). Or, to give another example, the attainment of low fertility eventually has a multitude of effects. Thus the practices of caring for children are no longer routine and observed regularly by children and teenagers within families. As a result, it has been suggested that young adults may lose confidence in their ability to have and rear children themselves – leading, among other things, to the need for 'how-to-do-it' books for parents (Keyfitz 1987).[32] Clearly, we cannot mention all such possible chains of cause and effect here, let alone discuss them. Nevertheless, ultimately it is important to locate such developments within the context of the demographic transition.

A related issue is the length of the time-lags that are involved between the occurrence of the transition's main processes and the occurrence of its various social effects. We have seen that some very long lags can be involved within the transition itself – for example, between mortality decline, fertility decline and changes in population composition. But some very long lags are also likely to be involved with respect to the social consequences of the transition. This can be illustrated fairly clearly with respect to certain formal effects, such as the availability of family members within kinship networks. Thus, in the most demographically advanced societies today, the number of living siblings a person in their nineties may have depends partly upon the fertility of people who themselves were born well over a century ago (Murphy 2009). However, it is more difficult to ascertain just how long the lags are likely to be between, for example, mortality decline and changes in people's attitudes, values and emotional responses towards death.

In turn, this raises yet another matter – namely, how sure we can be that the various social effects that have been discussed above will actually occur. The short answer is that they are all regarded as inevitable, in the very long run, and provided that no major extraneous factor intervenes. That said, variation in circumstances between different societies will clearly condition the extent of some of the effects. Thus it seems certain that urban growth and urbanization will produce an increase in societal complexity everywhere. However, as we have implied, the degree of complexity that is actually attained will be conditioned by the extent of economic growth, for example. Likewise, fertility decline and mortality decline can be expected to produce a fall in gender differentiation everywhere, eventually. But in some circumstances this may take a very long time. And complete gender equality – whatever that entails – may never be achieved. On the other hand, through the international transference of ideas, some of the transition's social influences (e.g. relating to gender equality) may be transported to other societies somewhat in advance of the occurrence of the demographic transition itself. That is, it seems likely that relationships between demographic processes and their social effects will sometimes be short-circuited.

Similar considerations apply to the political and economic effects of the transition, to which we now turn.

# 7 • Economic and political effects

Several consequences of the demographic transition that are related to its economic and political effects were mentioned in Chapter 6. For example, we saw that mortality decline means that greater emphasis is given to planning for the future. We noted that urban growth increases the division of labour in society. And we saw that urban growth leads to the expansion of systems of administration and government. In general, growing societal complexity implies a higher degree of interdependence between the different parts of a population, and therefore a greater need for systems of coordination and control.

However, there is much more to say about the economic and political effects of the transition – even though, as others have observed, economists and political scientists have often neglected the influence of fundamental demographic processes (see Bloom and Canning 2001; Doces 2007). Again, what follows is merely a sketch. And while it is important to acknowledge that economic and political factors condition demographic processes, the focus here is on what is seen as being the dominant direction of causation, i.e. from the demographic processes to their economic and political effects.

With respect to development in both the economic and the political realms, the transition's processes have tended to be positive hitherto. In particular, there are reasons to believe that these processes have contributed to both the occurrence of modern economic growth and the emergence of modern systems of representative democracy. However, the sustained rapid population growth experienced by some poor countries in recent decades has probably had negative effects. And concerns also arise with respect to the environmental consequences of population growth.

## Economic effects

We will consider the economic effects of the transition's processes in roughly the order in which these processes occur – starting, of course, with mortality decline. The discussion is fairly abstract. In reality, societies experience the processes in different contexts and at different speeds. And, in any particular case, the transition's overall impact – positive or negative – will be the sum of the effects from its individual processes.

*Mortality decline* Mortality decline is probably the single most important dimension of development. Indeed, it seems likely that, were they to be fully informed, then most people living in countries with reasonably high life expectancy today would value the decline in mortality at least as highly as any improvement that may have occurred with respect to the standard of living.[1] Furthermore, as we saw in Chapter 4, for much of the twentieth century economic growth appears to have made only a modest contribution to mortality decline. Although the attainment of a basic level of material welfare is clearly of significant benefit, McKeown's thesis that mortality decline is caused chiefly by an improvement in the standard of living has been found to be rather wanting.

It may be that modern economic growth can occur independently of mortality decline – at least for a time, although probably only to a limited degree. Richard Easterlin maintains that in parts of north-western Europe, perhaps especially England, there was sustained economic growth during the late eighteenth century, possibly before the onset of sustained mortality decline.[2] Certainly, the awful living conditions that accompanied industrialization and economic growth in urban areas of Europe during the nineteenth century sometimes led to rises in death rates (see Easterlin 1996: 69–75; also Schofield and Reher 1991). And, in more recent times, increasing incomes have often gone hand in hand with greater consumption of tobacco, alcohol, processed foods, and higher levels of physical inactivity – none of which is of much benefit to people's health.

On the other hand, it is almost certainly the case that, in itself, mortality decline assists economic growth and thereby contributes to an improvement in the standard of living. As we have observed, an increase in life expectancy from low to high levels leads people to think more about the future. Mortality decline raises the level of confidence among adults, and it may also help to create an environment that is more conducive to risk-taking and innovation. There is evidence for contemporary developing countries that mortality decline tends to increase rates of savings and education – thereby raising levels of investment in physical and human capital (see, for example, Bloom and Canning 2001; Kalemli-Ozcan 2002).

Also, people's economic productivity is probably enhanced because of the health gains that accompany mortality decline. In this context it is important to recall that, in large measure, mortality decline occurs because of falls in death rates from infectious diseases. These diseases remain a significant cause of the inadequate nutritional status of children in many poor countries today. As infectious diseases are brought under some control, however, there tends to be an improvement in the nutritional status of children and, with a lag, the fitness of the working-age population.[3] There is considerable evidence that healthier workers tend to be more productive workers (see, for example, Strauss and Thomas 1998).

We would also expect to find that in a healthier population with low mortality: children will attend school more often, and be more responsive to what they are taught; fewer days will be lost to work because of sickness; and people will tend to be both physically stronger and mentally more alert while they are at work. It is worth adding that improvements in the capacity to control disease vectors have almost certainly had positive economic effects. For example, in the 1950s and 1960s the use of insecticides to control the mosquitoes responsible for malaria transmission opened up large tracts of land for cultivation in many parts of Asia.

In developing countries in recent decades, it has been much easier to bring about a major rise in life expectancy in a short time than it has been to bring about a major rise in living standards in a short time. And, other things equal, a major improvement in mortality both provides the basis for and assists the occurrence of sustained economic growth.[4]

*Population growth* Whether population growth has a positive or a negative effect on economic growth is one of the oldest concerns of the social sciences. The matter is complicated, in part because concepts like 'per capita income' and the 'standard of living' can be difficult to gauge. A country's rate of population growth is a matter of fact, and nowadays it is generally measured or estimated fairly accurately. But the rate of economic growth – a complicated concept, which ultimately rests upon issues of value – cannot be determined in nearly such a clear-cut way.

Nevertheless, research in economic history suggests that, in pre-transitional circumstances, if a society experienced a sustained period of relatively fast population growth then eventually this would almost always bring about a *fall* in the standard of living.[5] The explanation was that there were fairly severe limits to the technical progress that could be achieved in agriculture. Therefore, populations could increase only very slowly if there was not to be a fall in the standard of living.[6] There tended to be something of a homeostatic relationship between population growth and economic growth. For example, a period of population growth would sooner or later depress living standards – and therefore either the death rate would rise, or the birth rate would fall (e.g. as marriages were postponed), or both of these feedback mechanisms would operate. The result was that the period of population growth would be brought to an end. The main situation in which population growth was *not* curtailed in this sort of way was one in which new supplies of land could be opened up and exploited. Of course, such exceptional 'pioneer' conditions were precisely those enjoyed by European offshoot populations in North America.

The reasons why relatively fast population growth (for pre-transitional conditions) eventually caused a fall in living standards in the usual circumstances where the supply of land was *fixed* were famously addressed in the work of Thomas Robert Malthus (1798; 1830 [1970]). And the various ideas that Malthus explored during his lifetime appear to explain the way in which most societies actually worked in the era before modern economic growth. Thus as Gregory Clark states: '[b]efore 1800 the rate of technological advance in all economies was so low that incomes could not escape the Malthusian equilibrium' (Clark 2007: 30; see also, for example, Bloom and Canning 2001: 167).

There is remarkably good quantitative evidence on this for England, from about the mid-sixteenth century onwards (see Wrigley and Schofield 1981; also Wrigley 1988). If the country's average annual rate of population growth exceeded 0.5 per cent then living standards eventually fell (i.e. people got poorer). However, the situation changed after about 1800 – as the country's economy was increasingly based upon energy obtained from the burning of coal, as opposed to the energy that was captured by the crops that were grown on the land. As we saw in Chapter 4, the population of England grew at a rate that was appreciably faster than 0.5 per cent during the nineteenth century.[7] However, the standard of living also improved at an unprecedentedly fast rate. This was because the exploitation of coal led to an increasingly complex and prosperous economy in which Malthusian constraints in agriculture were no longer a major check on the rate of economic growth (see Wrigley 1988).

The relatively slow (by modern standards) rates of population growth that were experienced during other 'historical' demographic transitions also seem to have had little impact on the rates of economic growth that were experienced. Thus in the countries of western Europe in the nineteenth century rates of population growth and per capita income growth both tended to increase (Easterlin 1996: 91–2). The advent of modern economic growth in Europe – based as it was upon the exploitation of coal – meant that populations were able to expand during the nineteenth century with no obvious negative effect on the general rise in living standards. It is important to emphasize that the rates of per capita income growth that were being experienced at this time were without precedent, and they were appreciably higher than the rates of population growth. In short, a new economic era had arrived. Of course, it was in agriculture that diminishing returns were mostly likely to set in. But the thrust of events was very much away from agriculture, towards industry and the growing towns. Turning to the other notable historical demographic transition, that of Japan, it appears that the growth rate of per capita income attained during the Meiji period (i.e. 1868–1912) would have been reduced only slightly even if the rate of population growth had been very much higher than it actually was (Kelley and Williamson 1974). In short, economic growth in Japan had such force that it was largely unaffected by the rate of population growth.

In countries such as the United States, Canada and Australia, population growth during the nineteenth and early twentieth centuries almost certainly made a significant positive contribution to economic growth and living standards – by helping to open up vast territories, providing a youthful and growing labour force, creating demand, and generating economies of scale. Nevertheless, as we have stressed, the 'frontier' circumstances of these countries were unusual.

Looking at Europe and Japan, there is little evidence that any economies of scale or technological advances that occurred as a result of population growth in the nineteenth century were of sufficient size to have a major net positive effect on per capita income growth. Even in Japan in the decades around 1900 it seems that a higher rate of population growth may have had a small negative effect on per capita income growth. Furthermore, although urban growth in Europe and Japan helped to stimulate a rise in their own levels of agricultural productivity, with growing populations and limited supplies of land, these countries often found that they had to obtain supplies of food from elsewhere – for instance, through imports from Russia and North America. Thus as early as the 1860s England had changed from being a country in which food imports were negligible, to one in which they were equivalent to about 12 per cent of national income (Clark 2007: 248–9).

Turning to the much higher population growth rates that have been experienced in developing countries since the middle of the twentieth century, economists have often implied that these rates of growth have had little impact on per capita income growth – a view that is sometimes described as 'neutralist' or 'revisionist' (see, for example, Kuznets 1967;

Kelley 1988; Kelley and McGreevey 1994). Indeed, it has been suggested that this population growth may have had a positive effect on per capita income growth in the long run – a view that has been quite influential at times (see, for example, Simon 1981, 1989). A key reason why some researchers have tended to take a fairly neutral, or even a positive, position on the issue has been the failure of analyses of international cross-sectional data to detect a negative relationship between rates of population growth and per capita income growth.

The absence of a negative relationship in simple two-variable plots was typical of the data that were available for analysis until the early 1990s. However, as more data have become available so a fairly strong *negative* relationship has emerged – and, in turn, this has contributed to a distinct change in the balance of views prevailing among economists. In short, so-called 'revisionist' thinking has had to be revised (Kelley 2001). It is fair to say that there is now a considerable degree of consensus around the view that rapid population growth has exercised 'a quantitatively important negative impact on the pace of aggregate economic growth in developing countries' (Birdsall and Sinding 2001: 6; see also, for example, Barro and Sala-i-Martin 2004; Sachs 2008; Headey and Hodge 2009).

By way of illustration, Figure 7.1 shows the least-squares linear relationship between the rate of population growth and the rate of per capita income growth over the period 1975–2005 for the fifty-six countries used in this book. Partly because of the difficulties involved in estimating per capita income growth, and partly because of the effects of other variables on this growth, there is a lot of scatter in the diagram. Nevertheless, the linear relationship shown is statistically significant and decidedly negative. It suggests that an increase of 1 per cent in the annual rate of population growth during 1975–2005 was associated with an annual rate of per capita income growth that was lower by about 0.7 per cent per year – i.e. a sizeable amount.[8]

The failure of earlier analyses to find a negative relationship was probably partly because of the unprecedentedly rapid growth of the world economy between the end of the Second World War and the first 'oil crisis' of 1973. At no time in history has the global rate of per capita income growth approached the level that was achieved during this period. For example, according to Maddison's estimates, world per capita income rose at an average annual rate of about 2.9 per cent per year between 1950 and 1973, compared to just 1.7 per cent between 1973 and 2006 (Maddison 2009). The remarkable economic growth experienced in the exceptional decades of the 1950s and 1960s helped to obscure the

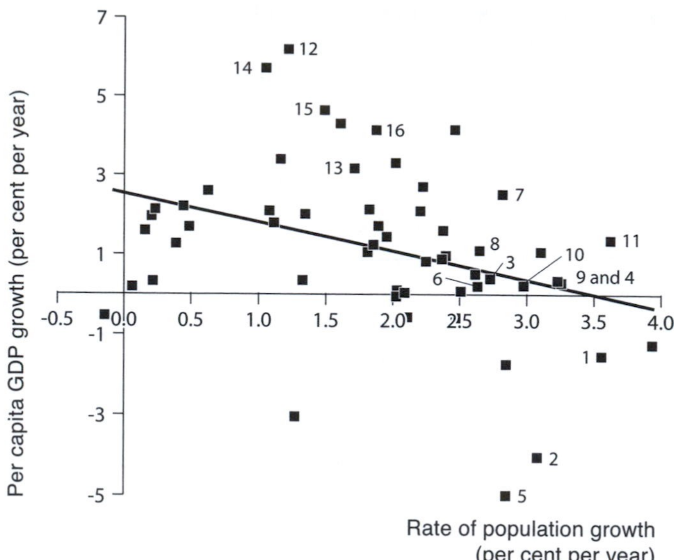


*Notes*: The countries identified with numbers are:
1 = Côte d'Ivoire, 2 = Democratic Republic of Congo, 3 = Ethiopia, 4 = Kenya, 5 = Madagascar, 6 = Nigeria, 7 = Pakistan, 8 = Sudan, 9 = Uganda, 10 = Tanzania, 11 = Yemen, 12 = China, 13 = Indonesia, 14 = South Korea, 15 = Thailand, 16 = Vietnam.

*Principle sources*: United Nations (2009), Maddison (2009)

**Figure 7.1 Population growth and economic growth, fifty-six countries, 1975–2005**

influence of population growth on per capita income growth (Fox and Dyson 2008). However, slower economic growth in more recent times has allowed a negative relationship to show through.

One explanation for the current negative cross-sectional relationship certainly relates to the consequences of sustained and unprecedentedly rapid population growth in very poor countries – the likes of Côte d'Ivoire, Democratic Republic of Congo, Ethiopia, Kenya, Madagascar, Nigeria, Pakistan, Sudan, Uganda, Tanzania and Yemen, all countries represented in Figure 7.1. In such countries agriculture remains a sizeable part of the overall economy, and it remains *very* difficult to raise levels of agricultural productivity at rates that are higher than the prevailing rates of population growth. Moreover, the task is often made even more difficult because rapid population growth contributes to various forms of *environmental* deterioration which themselves almost certainly have negative effects on the economic welfare of poor rural people in the long run – for example, problems like soil erosion, water pollution, falling water tables, fuel-wood losses and deforestation.

In short, in poor settings, rapid population growth arising from the demographic transition exerts a negative effect on people's economic welfare, other things equal. Whatever economic growth is sometimes achieved in such settings tends to be *despite* rapid population growth, rather than because of it. There is very little doubt about that.[9]

*Fertility decline and age-structural change* Of course, fertility decline is the main cause of population ageing within the demographic transition. This fact is reflected, for example, in the population age structures presented in Chapter 3. Fertility decline produces a fall in the proportion of children in the population (e.g. those aged under 15 years) and a rise in the proportion of older people (e.g. those aged 65 years and above).

Therefore, as fertility decline proceeds so there is initially a significant fall in the total age dependency ratio of the population (because of the fall in the *child* dependency ratio) and later there is a rise in the overall dependency ratio (because of the rise in the *old age* dependency ratio). Also, as fertility decline proceeds there is a period – lasting at least several decades – during which the number of people in the main working ages (e.g. those aged 15–64) grows at a faster rate than the total number of people in the other two age groups (i.e. those containing children, and older people).

Figure 7.2 illustrates these trends in age dependency ratios using data for East Asia – a region that has experienced particularly rapid fertility decline, and therefore particularly rapid changes in its age composition and dependency ratios. That said, broadly analogous trends have occurred, and are occurring, in the other developing regions of the world as a result of the demographic transition (see Bongaarts 2001b; United Nations 2009).[10]

The initial short-lived rise in the total dependency ratio shown in Figure 7.2 during the 1950s reflects mortality decline – as the deaths of infants and young children were increasingly brought under control, so bringing about a modest rejuvenating effect on the population age structure. However, the effect of fertility decline on the age dependency ratios is easily the most important one. Thus the major fall in the child dependency ratio, starting from the early 1970s, chiefly reflects the rapid fall of fertility in China at around that time.[11] Notice, however, that an inevitable and delayed outcome of this rapid fertility decline is that from about 2010 onwards East Asia will experience a fast rise in its old-age dependency ratio, and therefore its total age dependency ratio.

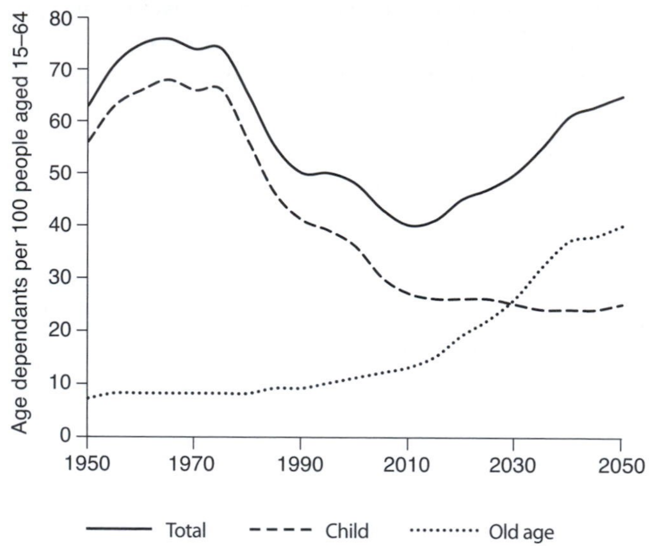


*Note*: The total dependency ratio is the sum of the child and old-age ratios.

*Source*: United Nations (2009)

**Figure 7.2 Past and projected dependency ratios for East Asia, 1950–2050**

With a lag, rapid fertility decline produces rapid population ageing (see Figure 7.2).

These basic facts of the transition help to provide a second explanation for the negative relationship between population growth and per capita income growth shown in Figure 7.1. This explanation was proposed by Coale and Hoover back in 1958. Using a simulation approach, they considered the prospects for future per capita income growth in developing countries (India and Mexico were the examples chosen) under two quite different demographic scenarios. In the first scenario fertility remained high, and therefore a country's population continued to grow at a fairly rapid rate, and the age structure remained young. In the second scenario fertility declined, and therefore both the population growth rate and the overall age dependency ratio declined (because of the fall in the child dependency ratio). Coale and Hoover argued that the second scenario allowed more resources to be saved and invested in the economy – rather than being spent, for example, on a steadily rising number of children. Accordingly, there was significantly faster per capita income growth in the second scenario.

In recent years, and particularly with reference to the experience of developing countries in Asia and Latin America, much research has confirmed the basic validity of the argument proposed by Coale and Hoover (see, for example, Higgins and Williamson 1997; Mason 1997; Bloom and Canning 2001). In short, fertility decline reduces a country's dependency ratio, and thereby raises the potential for faster economic growth – through higher levels of saving and investment – during an extended period during which the labour force expands at a faster rate than the number of people in the other, more dependent age groups. The result can be greater investment in both physical capital (e.g. roads, factories, etc.) and human capital (e.g. through higher levels of education and training provided to each young person).

However, because the total age dependency ratio will eventually increase, the facts of the transition produce only a 'window of opportunity' for economic betterment in this respect. The window will eventually begin to close – with the rise in old-age dependency (see, for example, Figure 7.2). The extent to which the potential for faster economic growth is actually realized, while the window is open, is likely to vary between different societies (e.g. according to institutional and political considerations). It appears that countries in Europe, and Japan, did benefit from this opportunity in the late nineteenth and early twentieth centuries; and it has been estimated that between a quarter and a third of the per capita income growth experienced in East Asia (including China) since about 1970 may be attributable to the successful exploitation of this opportunity (see Williamson 1998; also Bloom and Canning 2001). The economic gain made possible by these age-structural changes is sometimes referred to as a demographic 'bonus' or 'dividend'. It is important to stress, however, that it is far from guaranteed.

Returning to the association between population growth and economic growth in the period since the 1970s, part of the explanation for the emergence of a negative relationship in the international cross-sectional data is that, with fertility decline, some societies have experienced *both* reduced rates of population growth and accelerated rates of per capita income growth – partly because they have made good use of this one-time opportunity. Likely illustrations of this among the countries represented in Figure 7.1 are China, Indonesia, South Korea, Thailand and Vietnam.

It is worth adding that even if governments prove themselves incapable of taking advantage of this period of low age dependency –

for example, by squandering resources on military expenditure – it is reasonable to think that some economic gains may nevertheless arise because of the broadly analogous changes that can take place within households. For instance, there is a considerable amount of research which indicates that fertility decline improves the lives of children within families – e.g. in terms of food consumption, nutritional status and, of course, their education (see, for example, Montgomery and Lloyd 1999; Merrick 2001; Eloundou-Enyegue and Williams 2006). In time, and other things equal, these improvements for children should feed through to benefit a country's economy. Moreover, it is reasonable to think that household enterprises in general may experience higher levels of savings and investment as a result of such age-structural effects.

Furthermore, as we saw in Chapter 6, fertility decline has particular implications for the educational levels of women and their participation in the formal labour force. Fertility decline tends to raise the number of years that women are able to work – unencumbered by bearing and looking after children. These developments are also likely to have positive economic effects.

Finally, the total age dependency ratio eventually increases, because of the rise in old-age dependency. And, towards the end of the demographic transition, when fertility decline is essentially complete, declines in death rates at older ages can make a significant contribution to further population ageing. During the period when the age dependency ratio is increasing, the population at older ages (e.g. 65 years and above) is growing faster than the population in the main working ages (e.g. ages 15–64). During this period what we have referred to as a 'window of opportunity' is closing, and levels of saving and investment may begin to reduce. Other things equal, these developments may exert a dampening effect on economic growth – compared to the preceding period when the age dependency ratio was falling. And, indeed, there is evidence that population ageing may now be exerting such a negative effect in both Europe and Japan (see, for example, Bloom et al. 2009). In this context, notice that in Figure 7.1 the relationship between population growth and per capita income growth seems to be *positive* at low rates of population growth (e.g. below about 1.2 per cent per year).[12] Nevertheless, so far as developing countries are concerned, Figure 7.2 shows that even in the advanced case of East Asia (including China) it will take several decades for the total age dependency ratio to return to its pre-transitional level.

If one compares pre-transitional circumstances in which the total age dependency ratio in a population is high because of a high level of child dependency with post-transitional circumstances in which the total age dependency ratio is high because of a high level of old age dependency, there is little reason to think that the overall change in age structure *in itself* is particularly harmful for the economy (see, for example, Easterlin 1996: 113–27; Mullan 2002). Naturally, in a young population more time and effort will be devoted to the rearing of children; and in an old population more resources will be devoted to caring for elderly people. It is unclear, however, whether the second situation is economically any worse than the first. Indeed, although a society must inevitably adapt to the fact of having an old population – a process that can be accomplished with varying degrees of efficiency – there may be significant flexibilities in the situation. Thus many older people are likely to be quite healthy and capable of working at later ages; and, of course, they have valuable experience. In addition, the age of retirement in a society – if one exists – can be raised in order to help fund pensions and healthcare for older old people.

That said, the process of population ageing may well involve significant difficulties of adaptation. For example, it was relatively easy and straightforward for developed countries to introduce public pension schemes in the past – i.e. when the number of people in the main working ages was growing at a faster rate than the number of people in the older age groups (e.g. 65 years and above). However, reform of such schemes is virtually inevitable in circumstances where the number of people at older ages is increasing faster than the number in the main working ages, as is now generally the case (see Lee 2003).

Of course, severe population ageing and rapid population decline, as a result of sustained and exceptionally low levels of fertility, may well have extremely harmful effects for the economy.[13] However, the degree to which such acute circumstances will actually occur remains to be seen – and considering them would take us beyond the terrain that is of concern here. Extreme circumstances aside, having an old population is the result of having progressed through the demographic transition – and therefore any economic difficulties that may attach to such a situation are relatively good difficulties to have.

*Urban growth/urbanization* Although towns are often places where many people live in conditions of great poverty, the question here is whether urban growth and urbanization have a positive or a negative effect on per capita income growth, other things equal. The answer that is generally given to this question is that the net effect is positive. Thus in nineteenth-century Europe the growing urban population probably contributed to economic growth. And, although urban growth in contemporary developing countries raises and contributes to many problems – e.g. congestion, pollution, slum settlements, etc. – the urban areas are usually seen as the centres for whatever economic growth there is. Indeed, the towns are frequently depicted as 'engines' of growth. Therefore, while urban areas are often concentrators of extreme hardship, in the longer run they may also provide the best way for people to escape from these conditions (see, for example, Jacobs 1972; Crook 1997; UNFPA 2008; Beall and Fox 2009).

As we saw in Chapters 5 and 6, the literature linking the concentration of people in towns with increased specialization, and therefore increased economic productivity per person per hour, stretches back a very long way. Urban areas represent comparatively large and concentrated markets. They enable economies of scale in terms of manufacture, and reduced costs in terms of transportation. Banking and credit facilities tend to be located in urban areas. Towns are also places where firms can share inputs, and where it is easier for them to match their labour needs with the skills that are in supply. The concentration of industries and firms in urban areas means that the returns to capital invested in shared infrastructure – e.g. roads, port facilities, electricity grids – are increased. Moreover, it is easier to provide education and healthcare to urban populations – and these are services that tend to promote economic growth. It is also important to recall the dynamic nature of the economic benefits that can come from urban growth – economic growth and urban growth often interacting in mutually reinforcing ways.

Although the issue is difficult to assess, it seems likely that the economic welfare of people living in urban areas of developing countries today is generally somewhat higher than that of people living in rural areas. Urban inhabitants certainly tend to do better in terms of access to modern healthcare, education, water and sanitation. They tend to live longer. And they tend to have food supplies that are more secure.[14] To the extent that living standards are indeed higher in urban areas, then clearly the higher the level of urbanization in a country the higher will be the overall standard of living. There is no doubt that more urbanized countries tend to be wealthier ones. And analysis of international data for the period since 1975 suggests that the urban share of population growth in countries has been positively associated with per capita income growth (Fox and Dyson 2008). In other words, for any given increment in a country's total population, the greater the proportion of it that occurs in urban areas, the greater will be the country's overall rate of per capita income growth. Again, this is probably because population growth in the urban sector contributes disproportionately to economic growth, and because economic growth in the urban sector tends to heighten the attraction of urban areas for rural outmigrants (i.e. causation works in both directions). In general, however, it seems that a given addition to a country's total population will be more favourable – *or less unfavourable* – to economic growth if it ends up living in the urban rather than the rural sector.

None of this is to deny that rapid urban growth, and large additions to already very crowded and populous towns – e.g. places like Dhaka, Karachi, Lagos and Lima – can generate extremely serious economic (and other) problems (see, for example, Brockerhoff and Brennan 1998; Massey 1996). In many poor countries the rate of growth of per capita income would probably benefit considerably from slower urban growth – more than enough urban dwellers are 'in supply' already. Moreover, it is crucial to recall the principal message of Chapter 5 – namely that, given the demographic transition, both urban growth and urbanization will happen anyway, i.e. largely irrespective of the extent of economic growth. A country's economy will almost certainly benefit more if urbanization is achieved with less rather than with more urban growth. Nevertheless, with these very important reservations, urban growth and urbanization are probably best viewed as having positive economic effects.

## Political effects

Little has been written on the relationship between the demographic transition and what is sometimes referred to as the 'democratic transition' (i.e. the emergence of modern political democracy). This is somewhat surprising – partly because in Europe and North America these two phenomena unfolded over roughly the same stretch of time.[15]

Of course, both 'demography' and 'democracy' draw on the Greek word *demos*, meaning people. And the *idea* of democracy – in the sense of every adult citizen having an equal say in political affairs – has been present in Western thought since at least the time of classical Athens, with similar ideas occurring in other cultures (Keane 2009). Nevertheless, Athens 2,000 years ago was far from being a democracy in the modern sense. Thus only a small minority of men could vote in the assembly and, as one might expect, neither women nor slaves could vote.

The modern process of democratization – i.e. the movement away from autocracy, towards a situation in which every adult citizen has an equal right to vote – has its origins in the societies of north-western Europe and North America in the eighteenth century.[16] The political systems of these populations were fairly autocratic at the start of that century – that is, they were controlled by a small number of people, usually monarchs and other wealthy landowning aristocrats. Nevertheless, influenced by Enlightenment thinking, the American and French Revolutions reflected the beginnings of change. During the nineteenth century the process of democratization gained momentum in Europe and North America, and political thinkers were increasingly confronted with the emergence of a *condition* rather than just the existence of an idea (Laski 1937: 80).

That said, it was not until the twentieth century that full representative democracy was attained in most Western countries. For example, it is worth recalling that in the United States and the United Kingdom, political democracy in the sense of 'one person, one equal vote' was not really achieved until the 1960s and the 1970s respectively. Also, nations like Greece, Portugal and Spain did not attain their present status of established, stable democracies until the 1970s.[17] In short, modern representative democracy is a very young flower.

It is even trickier to estimate a country's level of democracy than it is to gauge its standard of living. To a large degree, it is a matter of judgement; and many countries have experienced abrupt changes in their democratic status – in both directions. Nevertheless, the demographic and the democratic transitions are certainly related. And although an element of speculation is involved, it is interesting to consider some of the connections.

*Mortality decline* As with respect to so many aspects of human progress, it is plausible to think that mortality decline assisted the long-run growth of democracy in Europe and North America.[18] The increased strength of people's hold on life, and the gradual rise in the number of years that they could reasonably expect to live, surely had an influence in helping people to think more about issues of justice and political equity. We have seen too that mortality decline probably promotes the spread of mass education. And there are good reasons to think that better-educated people are more likely to press for a more equitable distribution of political power.[19]

Needless to say, to suggest that mortality decline assists the process of democratization is not to say that the former process leads swiftly and inevitably to the latter. Many countries that have experienced mortality decline remain far from being democratic (e.g. think of Russia and China). On the other hand, a country with fairly high mortality, and a low level of education, can also be fairly democratic. India, for example, has been a parliamentary democracy since soon after 1947. Yet life expectancy at that time was only about 35 years, and only around 16 per cent of the country's people were literate. India in the late 1940s, however, is a very rare instance of a democracy with relatively high mortality – and it is one that can only really be explained with reference to the country's particular history.[20]

It is interesting to note that analysis of international cross-sectional data provides some support for the idea that the attainment of democracy helps to facilitate the improvement of health and mortality (see, for example, Waldmann 1995; Franco et al. 2004). This may partly be because democratic states are more responsive to the needs and wishes of their people. Therefore, it may be that the emergence of democracy in Europe and North America in the nineteenth and twentieth centuries assisted the process of mortality decline to some degree.

*Population growth* There seems little reason to believe that population growth by itself helps much in the process of democratization. Few would argue that the natural increase produced by the historical demographic transitions in Europe assisted the emergence of modern democracy.[21] Moreover, there are reasons for believing that rapid population growth has sometimes made it more difficult for developing countries to establish and maintain democratic political systems.

For example, in many developing countries systems of government and administration have had to be revised in order to try to accommodate the rapid expansion of populations. In some cases such revisions have either not occurred, or they have been delayed – with the result that 'administrative overextension' has become a problem (see McNicoll 1984). Natural increase can also mean that the population of a small minority grows to such a size that it finds its own political 'voice' and therefore begins to argue for its own political jurisdiction (see, for example, Dyson et al. 2004: 344–56). Relatedly, natural increase has often had an adverse impact on democratization in that it has helped to cause conflict between different ethnic and religious groups. Thus if the population of one major group in a society is seen to be growing – or is thought to be growing – at a faster rate than another group, then experience from many countries suggests that this can be a source of social and political tension.[22]

Studies of international cross-sectional data often conclude that rapid population growth has an adverse effect on a country's level of democracy, other things equal (see, for example, Cincotta 2008; Doces 2007; also Sachs 2008). A potentially difficult feature of a rapidly growing population is the expansion of the number of young adults – say, those in the age range 15–24. Particularly if employment is hard to find, people in this age range can be especially challenging in terms of expressing discontent, and therefore the maintenance of socio-political stability. It has been suggested that young adults may be less willing to compromise, and that governments may see them as a particular threat – perhaps leading to the imposition of authoritarian measures (Doces 2009). These ideas lead us to a consideration of how fertility decline may assist in the emergence of democracy.

*Fertility decline and age-structural change* Almost by definition, democracy involves the extension of voting rights to the adult members of a society. Children are specifically excluded from this development. In this context, fertility decline obviously causes both a fall in the proportion of children in a population, and a corresponding rise in the proportion of adults. Also, the process eventually stops growth in the number of *young* adults (e.g. those aged 15–24). As we saw in Chapter 3, the change in age structure caused by fertility decline is considerable. Moreover, the eventual rise in the proportion of people at later ages (e.g. 65 years and above) may have a positive role in relation to democratization, because these people are adults who may well want to express their 'voice'.

A possible connection between population ageing and democratization has not gone unremarked. For example, it has been observed that '[d]emocracy has often accompanied population ageing' (Wilson 2000: 1). Addressing the rise of modern democracy in Western societies, Francis Fukuyama (1992: xiv) notes that people come to 'demand democratic governments that treat them like adults rather than children'. And, of course, what the demographic transition does is raise the proportion of adults in society, and reduce the proportion of children. In a very real sense, therefore, the transition involves a society's 'growing up'. A study of variation in the extent of democracy in the modern world comes to the plausible conclusion that 'a country's chances for meaningful democracy increase as its population ages' (Cincotta 2008: 80).

It is also worth noting that, through the changes that it caused with respect to the lives of women in Western countries, it is plausible to suggest that the process of fertility decline may have assisted the extension of voting rights to women (Garrard et al. 2000: 272). With few exceptions, women in Europe and North America began to achieve the same right to vote as men only from about the 1920s onwards, i.e. from around the time that conditions of low fertility began to be achieved.[23]

*Urban growth/urbanization* The idea of democracy has long been associated with the conditions of urban life – think, for example, of Athens, and the city republics of northern Italy in the late Middle Ages (e.g. Venice and Florence). However, this association is partly due to the fact that towns have always been the centres of power, and therefore the sites of *any* degree of political experimentation (no matter how limited). In reality, over the centuries urban areas have usually been the bases for highly autocratic regimes. This was true in pre-transitional societies – where the control of a single major town was normally vital for the control of power – and it is sometimes the case today.

Nevertheless, political scientists have often considered that more urban societies are more likely to be democratic (see, for example, Laski 1937; Lipset 1963; Smith 1969). In this context, for the fifty-six countries used in this book, Figure 7.3 shows the relationship around the year 2005 between the level of urbanization and an estimated measure of democracy produced by Freedom House (2007). The association is positive and reasonably strong.[24] There are several reasons – working either alone or in combination – why a causal relationship may exist.

One possible explanation for a positive relationship is that urban growth has the effect of widening – and heightening the visibility of – the socio-economic inequalities that exist between a ruling class and the people it controls. Indeed, urban growth may well involve a decline in the ratio of the number of 'rulers' to 'ruled' within the urban sector. And,

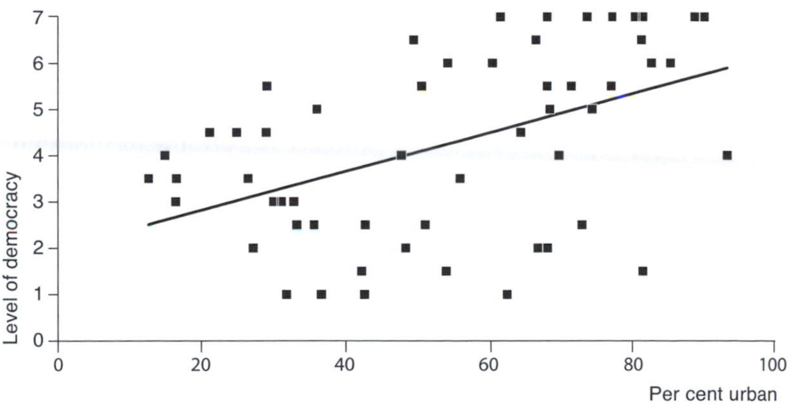


*Note*: The measure of democracy is the combined average freedom rating of Freedom House. For presentational reasons the rating has been reversed, i.e. the highest level of democracy is given a score of 7, and the lowest a score of 1.

*Sources*: Freedom House (2007); United Nations (2008)

**Figure 7.3 The relationship between urbanization and democracy, fifty-six countries, around 2005**

in turn, on this line of reasoning, democracy is eventually brought about through some form of *struggle* – for example, by means of revolution, or through a lengthy and reluctant surrendering of power by the ruling elite. Certainly, the organized urban working class has often played a key role in bringing about this transfer of power (see, for example, Rueschemeyer et al. 1992).

A second possible explanation for the relationship is that the towns are the places where the middle class comes into being (see, for example, Lipset 1963). Middle-class people tend to be relatively educated, articulate and prosperous. On this line of reasoning, towns are locations where socio-economic inequalities are eventually reduced, and this is considered to be inherently conducive to the devolution of political power away from the ruling class. In addition, for reasons already discussed, the urban sector is usually where most economic growth occurs. And an improved standard of living may itself be favourable to the emergence of democracy, although the reasons why this may be so are not always clear (see Barro 1999). Nevertheless, research generally finds that the propensity for democracy tends to rise with the level of per capita income (see, for example, Smith 1969; Feng and Zak 1999).

Finally, countries with autocratic political systems are more likely to have urban structures in which there is a high level of urban primacy – i.e. circumstances in which a single town dominates the urban hierarchy (Beall and Fox 2009: 73–5). In effect, those who control the major town control the whole political system. With the overall rise in the level of urbanization, however, the degree of urban primacy is likely to decline. And it may be harder to maintain autocratic rule in circumstances where there are several major towns.

There may be other reasons for the existence of a positive relationship between urbanization and the level of democracy. And those mentioned above are not mutually exclusive. Indeed, to some degree they may all apply. It is clear, however, that towns are particularly conducive to political action – i.e. places where it is easier for like-minded people to communicate and meet. Moreover, it is probably harder for autocratic rulers to suppress people who live in towns. Alternative bases of power (e.g. merchants and traders), with the potential to challenge autocratic rule, have usually emerged first in urban areas. And in most countries the activities that have underpinned the process of democratization have happened chiefly in the towns. Thus, '[t]o effect large-scale protests, people must be mobilized, money must be raised, information must be shared. These are quintessentially urban services' (Hohenberg and Lees 1985: 284; see also Potter et al. 1997). It is notable that in much of Europe voting rights were extended first to people in urban areas, before they were given to rural people.[25]

For broad periods of time, Figure 7.4 compares trends in urbanization and democracy for four major world regions between 1800 and the 1990s. The estimates of long-run trends in urbanization are those of Grauman (1977), and the historical scores of democracy – which here vary between 0 and 100 per cent – are derived from the Polity 3 database (see Polity 3 2001; also Jaggers and Gurr 1995). A regional approach is



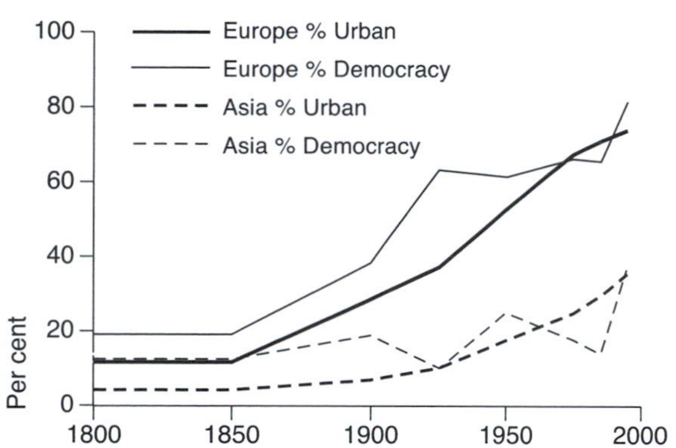


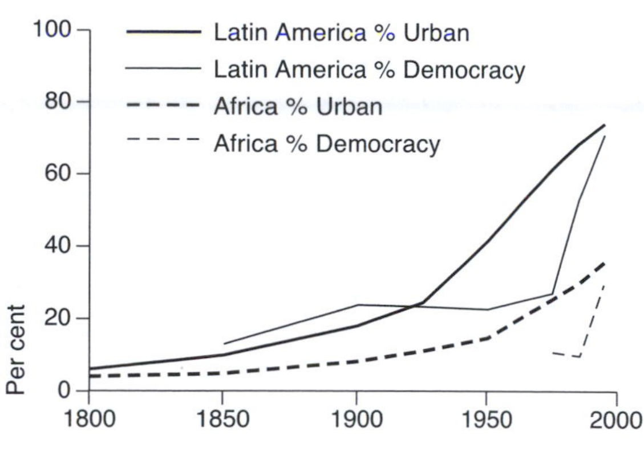


*Source*: Dyson (2001)

**Figure 7.4 Urbanization and the growth of democracy in major world regions since about 1800**

used partly because individual countries can experience sudden changes in the nature of their political systems – a fact which underscores that there are both proximate and underlying causes of political change. Since we are interested in the impact of a slow and remote process (i.e. urbanization), however, the issue of its relationship to democratization is best approached in aggregate terms. Use of the particular regions shown in Figure 7.4 simply reflects the geographical areas for which estimates of long-run trends in urbanization and democracy are available. It should be noted that while the 'per cent urban' figures for any period relate to the total population of each region, the 'per cent democracy' figures relate only to the countries that were politically independent units at the time (democracy scores not being produced for colonies).[26] Naturally, the comparisons shown are only suggestive. Nevertheless, with these reservations, several observations can be made.

The most important point is that there is a broad correspondence between both the level and the trend of urbanization and democracy in each region. By the mid-1990s Europe was the most urban and the most democratic of these regions. It was followed, fairly closely in both respects, by Latin America. Some way behind were Asia, and then Africa – although these regions were both experiencing upward trends. Figure 7.4 also reflects the important fact that, of course, other factors influence the progress of events. For example, in Europe between the 1920s and about 1990 democratization stalled because of the rise of fascist and communist regimes. Similarly, in Latin America the economic depression of the 1930s contributed to the establishment of military dictatorships – many of which lasted until the 1970s. In addition, the very short timescale of the democracy estimates available for Africa obviously reflects the existence of colonial regimes – which were undemocratic by their very nature (Dyson 2001).[27]

*Conclusions* To conclude this discussion of the relationship between the demographic and democratic transitions, in pre-transitional societies populations were young and largely dispersed in rural areas. These conditions are probably conducive to autocratic rule – provided, of course, that some form of central political system exists. In such conditions, power is likely to lie in the hands of those who control the relatively small urban sector. And the members of such a society are *subjects* – that is, they are ultimately ruled by some kind of autocratic elite (often headed by an emperor or king). However, the demographic transition has the effect of expanding the size of the total population, concentrating it in urban areas, and making it appreciably older. These are relatively slow but fundamental changes. And, in a nutshell, the argument here is that they eventually lead to the redistribution of political power in society – away from the command of an autocratic elite.

At the start of this discussion of the political effects of the demographic transition, the concept of democracy was introduced with specific reference to the role of *adult citizens*. These are people with responsibilities as well as rights. The distribution of power in society is not something of direct concern to children. And it is hardly a coincidence that, first and foremost, the definition of 'citizen' is simply someone who lives in a city.

However, to argue that the demographic transition has underlain the democratic transition is not to say that the mechanisms involved are always the same. Thus sometimes violent struggle is entailed, whereas at other times the process of democratization unfolds in a gradual, almost an evolutionary way. Moreover, countries with fairly old and fairly urban populations have nevertheless thrown up terrible totalitarian regimes – as experience in Europe during the twentieth century attests. On the other hand, countries with fairly young and fairly rural populations have managed to reach quite high levels of democracy in recent times. For example, according to the Freedom House measures for around the year 2005 used in Figure 7.3, several countries in Africa (e.g. Ghana, Mozambique, Kenya, Madagascar, Tanzania) have achieved fairly high democracy ratings, despite their demographic characteristics.[28]

Therefore, in the modern world, it is clearly possible for countries to 'jump ahead' of their demographic status in democratic terms. However, that said, there can be a big difference between a new young democracy, and one that has been long established. In a 'mature' democracy the fact of having a relatively old and urban population is likely to constitute a significant underpinning. And it is important to keep in mind that population ageing and urbanization are processes that take many decades to unfold. Even in relation to 'mature' democracies, however, it is as well to recall just how recently this status was usually achieved.

## Discussion

It seems reasonable to assume that, given the chance, people would always have wanted to improve their economic circumstances and have a say in the wider decisions that shape their lives. And it has been stressed repeatedly that non-demographic considerations have a major influence on economic growth and democratization. That said, here we have been concerned with the effects of the demographic transition. And, with respect to both economic growth and democratization, these effects appear to be broadly similar, significant, and in many ways positive.

Almost certainly, mortality decline has been beneficial to economic growth and the gradual movement of societies away from autocracy towards democracy. Indeed, the existence of modern forms of economic growth and democracy is hard to imagine in conditions of pre-transitional mortality.

The population growth that has resulted from mortality decline, however, presents a different picture. In certain exceptional conditions (e.g. those of the United States) population growth has benefited economic growth. And in other circumstances economic growth has been so strong that it has not been affected much by population growth. It is also possible to imagine circumstances in which population growth may have worked to the advantage of democratization – for example, insofar as very low population densities may make the development of democracy harder.[29]

Nevertheless, we have also argued that *rapid* population growth probably does little to help in the process of democratization. And there is now considerable agreement that rapid population growth has negative consequences for economic growth in most settings. We noted some countries that help to illustrate this point in Figure 7.1. And there is no shortage of other examples. Essentially, these are cases where there has been a significant measure of death control, but with relatively little progress being made with respect to birth control (by the standards that have generally prevailed in developing countries in recent decades). It seems likely that rapid and sustained population growth in some countries will do much to negate any positive economic effects arising from other aspects of the demographic transition.

That said, there are good reasons for believing that fertility decline, and the changes in age structure it brings about, have positive consequences for both economic growth and the chances of democracy. So far as economic growth is concerned, this is the potential for a demographic 'bonus' – an effect predicted by Coale and Hoover decades ago. This bonus is now largely accepted as a possibility, although it is an effect that is far from guaranteed. It is true that population ageing may have some economic drawbacks, eventually. But these are mainly drawbacks compared to the period during which the age dependency ratio is reduced. It is not clear that they are drawbacks compared to the situation earlier in the demographic transition when the level of child dependency was high. Moreover, as we have noted, there is scope for societies to adapt to population ageing. So far as the redistribution of political power in society is concerned, the relative growth of the adult population is likely to work to advantageous effect. And the fact that fertility decline releases women from concerns of the domestic domain probably has beneficial effects for both the economy and the growth of democracy.

Finally, there is urban growth and urbanization. Some urban growth appears to be positive – both for economic growth and democratization. For any volume of population growth in a country, it is probably better if that growth end up living in the urban areas – where positive economic processes, such as specialization and the sharing of infrastructure by firms, can have some effect. Having said that, however, rapid urban growth is something to be avoided. So far as the distribution of political power in society is concerned, there are reasons for believing that urban growth and urbanization have often been important underlying considerations in the process of democratization in the past. However, towns with rapidly growing numbers of poor and illiterate people can also be very receptive to autocratic rule. So, again, rapid urban growth may present distinct difficulties. There has been quite a lot of research linking the rise of democracy to economic growth; there has been relatively little work on democracy's various demographic underpinnings.[30]

# PART FOUR

# Conclusion

# 8 · Conclusions, discussion, the future

This chapter provides a short outline of the book's conclusions and discusses several points that may be raised about them. It finishes with some brief remarks on the demographic transition and the future of the world.

## Conclusions

The demographic transition provides a unique framework with which to understand the modern world. Its major processes are causally related, and they unfold over very long periods. The processes are extremely important in themselves, and they also have huge consequences for the nature of human society. However, because they are slow, and because they affect other aspects of society in remote ways, their influence is often unseen. Yet looking at the period from the eighteenth century onwards, not even the Industrial Revolution and the modern economic growth to which it gave rise have been more important for the course of world development.

The origins of almost everything discussed in this book lie in the Enlightenment. In particular, the more secular and scientific way of thinking about life, which began to gather pace during the eighteenth century, underpinned the process of mortality decline. A crucial element was progress in the understanding of infectious diseases, and how they could be prevented, controlled and treated. This has been central to all cases of mortality decline.

If mortality falls, and the birth rate stays high, then natural increase occurs – i.e. there is population growth. And, in turn, the pressures that arise from this growth eventually lead adults of reproductive age to reduce their fertility. In its early stages, fertility decline often occurs because of a rise in the age of marriage. However, in the long run people always resort to the use of some form of birth control. The stresses and strains that lead people to adopt birth control vary. Pressures come both from within households (e.g. rises in the number of surviving children, and shortages of living space) and from outside of households (e.g. land fragmentation, and greater competition for employment).

In every case where there are reasonably good data, there is some mortality decline before the onset of fertility decline. To state that mortality decline is the remote cause of fertility decline is not to say that exactly the same mechanisms always link the two processes. Nor is it necessary for couples to appreciate that mortality decline has occurred for them to reduce their fertility. Instead, people delay marriage and turn to birth control because of more immediate pressures which arise in their day-to-day lives.

Moving on, the process of fertility decline causes the age structure of society to become very much older. Populations move from having young age distributions to having old age distributions because of fertility decline.

Before the demographic transition people died mainly from infectious diseases. These diseases thrived in the towns, where the population density was high. Therefore, with exceptionally high death rates, and sometimes comparatively low birth rates, urban areas tended to be places of negative natural increase, i.e. they were demographic sinks. Migration from rural areas kept the urban sector in existence, and there was a limit on how urban any major population could become.

However, when mortality decline occurs within the demographic transition, there comes a point where the urban death rate falls below the urban birth rate. The towns cease to be sinks, and their populations expand both from their own natural increase and from a continuing flow of migrants from rural areas. The urban population grows faster than the rural population – i.e. there is urbanization.

Most of the changes in society that are held to constitute 'development' either occur in, or have their origins in, the urban sector. Therefore, to a very considerable degree, what comprises development can be seen as being dependent upon the level of mortality becoming free from the influence of population density. There was a severe limit to human progress while the towns were such very unhealthy places.

Provided there is sustained mortality decline from high to low levels, it is inevitable that all of the transition's other processes will occur in the long run. There can be no doubt as to the critical importance of mortality decline. However, we have seen that different sections of humanity have joined the transition's central causal pathway at different times, and from different initial conditions. And, of course, there is tremendous variation – institutional, cultural, economic, geographical, etc. – between different societies.

Therefore, there is great variation in the experience of the demographic transition. This was true with respect to the historical transitions, and it is even more true with respect to those we have termed the contemporary ones. More recent cases of mortality decline and fertility decline have tended to be faster – essentially because they benefit from the experience that has gone before. In many developing countries there are signs of an element of compression in the overall length of the transition. In other words, the reduction in vital rates from high to low levels appears to be occurring over somewhat shorter lengths of time. However, contemporary transitions involve faster rates of population growth compared to the historical ones. And there are reasons for thinking that some societies – especially in sub-Saharan Africa – are going to experience natural increase of exceptional scale, even by modern standards. This will happen because of an unprecedentedly large and lengthy gap between their vital rates as they proceed through the transition.[1]

At the world level, it seems reasonable to suggest that the demographic transition will lead to roughly a tenfold increase in the size of the human population (perhaps slightly more). The 'growth multiples' of countries in Europe were sometimes less than four. In some cases, however, such as England and the Netherlands, the multiples were appreciably higher – perhaps in the vicinity of seven or eight (particularly if an allowance is made for emigration). Although China and India have both experienced fairly rapid rates of population growth at times, it seems that China's population may increase by a factor of only about four as a result of the transition, and India's population may increase by a factor of roughly five or six. These multiples are lower than some of those experienced in Europe – the higher contemporary growth rates of population being counteracted by what we have termed a greater degree of compression. Quite a few other developing countries, for example in East and South-East Asia, and Latin America, seem likely to experience population growth multiples of around or less than ten.

However, there are also quite a few countries where the growth multiples are going to be *much* greater than ten. Thus estimates and projections produced by the United Nations suggest that, just for the century 1950–2050, the populations of eight of the fifty-six countries used in this book will increase by factors varying between ten and seventeen.[2] In 1950 these eight populations had certainly grown already because of the demographic transition, and in 2050 they will still be growing because of it. In some of these cases eventual growth multiples of twenty, thirty, perhaps even more, are possible.[3] At the other end of the scale, France's population did not even double in size as it went through the transition.

With the faster population growth of the contemporary demographic transitions, there has also been appreciably faster urban growth than applied historically. This point is known. However, we have also seen that the pace of urbanization in the modern world appears to be somewhat quicker than it was in developed countries in the past. Moreover, there are theoretical reasons for thinking that faster population growth should produce faster urbanization.

Turning to the transition's wider effects, they have mostly been discussed in general terms here. Hugely important in itself, the process of mortality decline has underlain progress in almost every aspect of human affairs. The fall in death rates from high to low levels, and the virtual banishment of death from the first fifty years of life, has led to the creation of a much more stable and predictable world. The socio-psychological consequences of this should not be underestimated. People have become increasingly confident and secure in themselves. They are more likely to plan, save, and invest as regards their material future. These socio-psychological changes go unnoticed. Indeed, even the mortality decline that underpins them is unlikely to be recognized by people themselves. In addition, mortality decline increases the strength of the relationship between parents and children. More generally, the process has probably heightened the value that is attached to human life at all but the highest ages.

The demographic transition means that horizontal relationships between family and kin members tend to become less important in people's lives. On the other hand, vertical relationships across the generations become more prominent. Mortality decline produces upward pressure on household size, and tends to spur migration. With fertility decline, however, this pressure is reduced. There are reasons to think that the transition is contributing to a degree of convergence in household forms in many different societies – including a move towards smaller units.

Fertility decline and mortality decline have led to a weakening of the institution of marriage. Divorce, separation, remarriage, consensual unions and one-parent households become more common. And where new unions follow earlier ones, in certain respects households can become more complex.

Women gain greater autonomy and independence from men. And, consequently, gender differentiation tends to be reduced. The lives of women become more like those of men. Societies that have progressed through the demographic transition are unquestionably more adult in their composition. This is a significant fact, the broader implications of which are rarely observed, let alone discussed.[4]

On a wider canvas, the increase in population scale which results from the transition underlies a general increase in societal complexity. This is especially evident in urban areas – where, of course, the overall increase in population is concentrated. Urban growth tends to produce greater differentiation with respect to most dimensions of life – e.g. the artistic, administrative, economic, educational and political. Urban growth also leads to the creation of new forms of activity – e.g. in relation to the provisioning of towns and waste disposal. Such developments contribute to the general expansion of the division of labour in society, and probably higher levels of competition as well. Rates of social interaction are generally higher in the towns. And more of the interactions that people engage in are relatively specific and short-term. Yet another outcome of greater urban residence is that people's horizons are expanded to take in more of the wider world. In a post-transitional society there is little difference between people who live in urban and rural areas because, effectively, everyone has fairly urban characteristics irrespective of where they reside.

It has also been argued that the processes of the demographic transition have contributed to the decline of status ascription in society, and greater emphasis on achievement. Formal education and training become more important in circumstances where life is secure and long, and where specialization and competition are increased. There are many reasons for believing that economic growth has benefited greatly from the processes of the transition. Indeed, it is unlikely that a predominantly rural population with high mortality could experience sustained economic growth in any meaningful sense. Urban growth and urbanization arise out of the transition. And economic growth is probably more dependent on urban growth and urbanization than the reverse. Moreover, the general progression from autocratic to more democratic systems of government owes much to the demographic transition.

Most of the outcomes of the demographic transition have been favourable. Nevertheless, it is important to acknowledge that the phenomenon has often had the effect of advancing good things which, to a certain extent, were present in society already. For instance, it is important to recall that most pre-transitional societies had a small urban sector, with some degree of social and economic differentiation. Also, in some pre-transitional societies women enjoyed a measure of independence and autonomy. Moreover, at least ideas relating to, say, sexual equality, or democracy, were sometimes there already. That said, 'development' in a modern, rounded sense is almost inconceivable in the absence of the demographic transition.

We have also remarked on some of the transition's downsides –

such as difficulties arising from urban growth and population ageing. Nevertheless, as has been noted, some of these problems – like those of population ageing – can be overstated. Moreover, given the huge benefits of the demographic transition, they are probably comparatively good problems to have to confront.

The most important difficulty posed by the transition pertains to the amount of population growth that it sometimes entails. In a few situations this growth has been beneficial to economic development. Moreover, many societies, both developed and developing, which are comparatively well established, and with relatively sophisticated administrative infrastructures, have limited this growth partly by facilitating the process of fertility decline in a variety of ways. However, some other societies have been much less successful in this respect – and, other things equal, the implications for their economic development are likely to be negative. In some countries the scale of future population growth may be so great as to far outweigh any potential economic 'bonus' or 'dividend' arising from the transition.

## Discussion

It is often said that processes of population and development interact. In other words, population processes affect development processes, and development processes affect population ones. That is true. But it is important to emphasize that the present argument is that *if* mortality decline occurs in a pre-transitional society, then the population will grow, fertility will decline sooner or later, and the society will eventually both urbanize and age. Thus while development processes (e.g. economic growth, the spread of modern education) and the overall context (e.g. the culture and institutions) will be significant in conditioning the details of the transition – including the extent of population growth – in the final resort such considerations are secondary. In short, the demographic transition has its own causal pathway. Relatedly, policies and programmes can help a society to move down this pathway more efficiently – especially by influencing how closely mortality decline is followed by the adaptive process that is fertility decline.[5] However, such policies and programmes are also essentially conditioning factors, rather than being central to the main chain of events.

In this context, it is worth underlining just how modest a role economic growth plays in the overall story.[6] Rises in the standard of living have certainly assisted the process of mortality decline to some degree. But most mortality decline in the world, past and present, has occurred for reasons that have little direct connection with improvements in the standard of living. Some very poor countries have experienced very substantial mortality decline.[7] Similarly, the once widely held view that significant rises in the standard of living would be required for people in developing countries to adopt birth control has been largely dispelled. Some very poor populations have experienced fertility decline, and they have done so at speeds that bear little or no correspondence to their experience of economic growth. The process of population ageing is almost completely independent of economic growth. And we have also seen that urbanization is happening in every world region – largely irrespective of the amount of economic growth. Some researchers have reacted to this with a degree of surprise. But it is only surprising if the basic causal processes that underpin the process are unknown.

On the other hand, the demographic processes of the transition have very considerable consequences for the economy. Thus we have argued that mortality decline is necessary for economic development in any meaningful sense. Urbanization certainly benefits the economy. And the decline in age dependency ratios that occurs during the transition also seems to have had a positive economic effect – i.e. a bonus, or dividend – in some countries. On the downside, however, prolonged population growth at rapid rates almost always has a decidedly negative effect on people's material welfare.

Despite the modest influence of economic growth on the processes of the demographic transition, it is important to emphasize that there are two decisions, which often have an economic dimension, that are crucial to the present argument. One is the choice of some people (especially young adults) to migrate from rural to urban areas. This is required for urbanization. However, as we have seen, this is not a new decision – in the sense that there has always been a net flow of people from rural to urban areas (i.e. both before and during the transition). Rural-to-urban migration occurs in both good times and bad; and it can be 'explained' in a rather descriptive and superficial way in either event. However, the fact that there is usually a net flow of people to the towns suggests that they may be moving for some other fundamental end. And many of the reasons why young people migrate are not closely related to their economic circumstances.[8]

The second decision with an economic dimension is that of couples to restrict their fertility. There is no doubt that economic considerations feature prominently in the reasons people give for why they adopt birth control. However, these considerations are themselves ultimately induced by the fact of mortality decline. And, again, what are essentially plausible rationalizations for the adoption of birth control can be made irrespective of whether economic conditions are improving or deteriorating. In a sense, then, economics provides the idiom of account for the change in behaviour, rather than revealing its underlying cause.

The explanations provided by researchers for fundamental demographic processes are frequently rather shallow. They often lack time depth. And they often fail to recognize that, within the transition, one process leads to another in a sequence that is essentially self-contained. For example, there has been a widespread tendency to try to explain the occurrence of fertility decline in terms of various socio-economic factors. But this misses the point that, despite variation in experience, the same remote causal force is operating at a high level to bring about the same general effect. Relatedly, research tends to focus on studying differentials in behaviour – e.g. between couples, households or countries. It misses the point that fertility decline is something which is ultimately homogeneous. That is, in the end, the process is both uniform and shared.

To state that the origins of the demographic transition lie in the European Enlightenment, although a simplification, is largely a matter of fact. A similar statement could be made with respect to the origins of the Industrial Revolution, and modern economic growth. Naturally, one could go still further back in time – and consider the antecedents of the Enlightenment. But while these antecedents should be recognized, for present purposes addressing them here would a step too far. The processes of mortality decline and fertility decline began in Europe and its offshoot populations. And, until recent decades, developments originating from Europe and North America have exerted the main influence on the course of what has become a global demographic transition. However, as time has gone by, and starting with Japan, more and more countries have become involved in, and have contributed to, this global phenomenon.

Nevertheless, because the present argument has revolved around a central pathway of cause and effect, it is important to state that if the process of sustained mortality decline had occurred first in some other part of the world – say in Japan, or China – then the implication of the argument is that, sooner or later, it would have resulted in the same basic sequence of events, i.e. natural increase, fertility decline, urbanization and population ageing. Moreover, eventually the transition would probably have gone on to affect the rest of the world. Of course, to make this assertion is to raise a massive historical counterfactual.[9] But the assertion is warranted because of the strength of the central chain of cause and effect.

Although the point has been made repeatedly, it is worth restating that other phenomena, notably modern economic growth and technological change, have made huge contributions to world development. The transition's impact on societal developments can never be neatly isolated from those of these other forces. Furthermore, we have been at pains to stress that, in the modern world, countries are sometimes able to jump ahead of their stage in the demographic transition in relation to developmental changes that were once tied much more closely to progress within the transition. For instance, changes in attitudes towards women, or the idea that every adult should have the vote – changes that were once assisted greatly by the processes of the transition – now have an independent dynamic of their own.

We have certainly been concerned with the *very* 'big picture' in this book – as, indeed, was promised at the start. The argument has mostly been framed at a high level of aggregation, and with respect to the very long run. As a result, there has been little discussion of the many detailed, important, yet mundane implications that arise from the phenomenon.[10] Another consequence of dealing with the very big picture is that there has been little consideration of variation in experience within both the historical and the contemporary transitions. Indeed, while we have noted that there are significant differences between the historical and the contemporary transitions, in many respects the phenomenon has been treated here as a whole. There may be those who consider that the historical experience is so distinct as to be deserving of separate treatment. However, that is not the view taken here. The historical and the contemporary transitions are ultimately the same. Moreover, to repeat a point just made: there has been plenty of attention to variation; there has been too little attention to uniformity.

A key proviso which – more or less explicitly – has been interspersed throughout the present argument is 'other things equal'. Naturally, this pertains to every statement involving cause and effect – even those of the transition's main causal pathway. In reality, of course, other things are never exactly equal. And this explains why experiences of the demographic transition are never exactly the same. At several points we have also remarked on 'third factors' which have intervened to affect the workings of the transition. These factors are often – although not always – political in kind.[11] For example, in China, at various times, government policies have hastened fertility decline, and tried to control the process of urbanization. However, even in China there are strong grounds for thinking that, because mortality decline had occurred, fertility would have declined anyway (although at a slower pace). Moreover, the Chinese government discovered that there were limits to the degree to which urbanization could be controlled. In general, although they occur at different speeds in different contexts, the main processes of the transition are usually pretty inexorable once they have begun.

Turning to the transition's social, economic and political effects, however, the complicating influence of 'third factors' – and differences of context – can undoubtedly be *much* more important. Sometimes an effect can probably be regarded as almost inevitable, to some degree. For example, an increase in occupational differentiation is probably an unavoidable consequence of urban growth. However, often an assumption of inevitability will be much less warranted. For example, many would point out that population ageing has not always been followed by democratization.

We have been unable to do justice to the influence of third factors and contextual variation here. However, consider, for example, the proposition that rapid population growth has a negative influence on per capita income growth. Clearly, the statement is made other things equal. It does not preclude the possibility that some, or indeed all, countries with rapidly growing populations can experience per capita income growth – either because of the operation of other specific factors, or because of contextual considerations. Equally, however, the proposition is not falsified by the fact that there happen to be rapidly growing populations in which incomes are rising.[12]

To make a related point, consider the proposition that sustained conditions of low mortality and low fertility eventually produce a reduction in gender differentiation. Even in favourable social circumstances, this may take a long time. And in some societies it may take an extremely long time. Indeed, the extent to which gender differentiation can be reduced may itself be restricted by the social context. These sorts of consideration account for the use of the word 'eventually' above, and throughout these pages. On the other hand, *given enough time* the proposition may turn out to be true – even in the most testing of circumstances. And the same may apply with respect to population ageing and democratization. It is important to appreciate that many of the arguments made here regarding the transition's effects need be evaluated against a suitable timescale. Rarely can they be dismissed on the basis of evidence for just a few decades.

## The future

We can be fairly confident about broad population trends over the next few decades. However, for the reasons mentioned, what we have termed the societal effects of the demographic transition are usually less assured, at least in relation to comparatively short periods. In general, with respect to both demographic and non-demographic developments, we can probably be more confident about the prospects for large populations – such as the world and its main regions. Of course, the further one looks into the future, the more uncertain things become. And events will definitely occur which take everyone by surprise. Nevertheless, a few words on the future are appropriate in concluding.

As we saw in Chapter 3, the projections of the United Nations suggest that the world's population will rise from 6.9 billion in 2010 to reach about 9.2 billion in 2050. However, due to the continuation of fertility decline, by the middle of this century the human population will be growing at a much lower rate than it is today. Indeed, the population may begin to decline in size before the end of this century – signifying that the world's birth rate will have fallen below its death rate (United Nations 2004). Fertility decline will mean that most population growth in the next few decades will occur at adult ages – for example, the number of people aged 0–14 in the world is not expected to change by much. Relatedly, humanity will become appreciably older. The median age is projected to rise from 29 years in 2010 to about 38 in 2050. More speculatively, the UN projections suggest that over the same period the global level of urbanization will rise from about 50 to around 70 per cent.

Much of the coming growth in the world's population is inevitable – the result of population momentum. But the speed at which fertility falls in the next few decades can still exert a significant influence on the extent of future growth. Thus the UN's low and high projections for 2050 are 8.0 and 10.5 billion people respectively, although a figure towards the centre of this range is most likely.

At the regional level, sub-Saharan Africa lies well behind with respect to its demographic measures – including life expectancy. The region has by far the highest level of fertility. It will experience by far the highest rate of population growth in the period to 2050. In fact, sub-Saharan Africa could experience the largest absolute addition to its population of any of the regions considered here.

The other developing regions will mostly experience relatively modest population growth during the next few decades. Their average levels of fertility are already fairly low, and they are generally still falling. Because these regions have experienced relatively rapid fertility declines, they will also experience relatively rapid population ageing in the future. This is especially true for East Asia, which is about to experience population ageing of unparalleled speed. Indeed, with very low fertility, the population of East Asia in 2050 may be no larger than it was in 2010. Europe's population may decrease significantly over the same period. Because of different growth rates, the proportional composition of the human population will change appreciably in the coming decades.

It is virtually certain that the UN projections reflect the broad thrust of where the world's population is heading. In brief, mortality is generally improving, fertility is generally declining, birth rates are coming down faster than death rates, rates of natural increase are therefore falling, and populations are urbanizing and getting older. Such population projections provide a valuable starting point from which to assess the future – one that is generally unequalled in terms of its relative surety. Essentially, these projections are made within the framework of the demographic transition. Thus, looking at past experience, assumptions are made about future trends in mortality and fertility – and these assumptions then determine both the scale of the projected population growth and the extent of future population ageing. The framework of the demographic transition suggests that there will eventually be a time when mortality and fertility are fairly low everywhere – largely irrespective of the characteristics of the populations concerned.[13] Indeed, by 2010 the world had already reached a situation where fertility in some major developing countries was lower than in some major developed countries – something that was not generally anticipated.[14]

Nevertheless, although we are heading in the direction of comparatively little variation in mortality and fertility between regions (and countries), and comparatively low rates of natural increase everywhere (including negative rates), it will take many decades before every region experiences a low rate of population growth. And differences in growth rates – i.e. essentially rates of natural increase – can have important implications. Thus when a region (or country) reaches the point where its vital rates are low and equal, then changes in population size are determined solely by migration. The role of international migration is likely to become even more prominent in the future – when the populations of different regions are growing (or declining) at quite different rates.[15] In this context, we saw that European countries tended to export people as they went through their transitions. Analogous pressures to export people exist in many developing countries today. Thus, along with differences in the standard of living, differences in the timing and characteristics of the demographic transition will be a major consideration influencing future flows of international migration.

Assuming that the transition continues to unfold more or less as projected, then in most countries most of its main societal effects are likely to occur, other things equal. Moreover, most of these effects will be beneficial (see, for example, Figure 2.1). However, it is important to underscore the fact that very significant time lags are likely to be involved. Indeed, the full consequences of the transition are still not completely played out even in more developed regions. So far as the world's less developed regions are concerned, the continuing demographic transition can be expected to underpin 'development' in many ways. For example: people are likely to gradually become more confident and assured as a result of mortality decline; more and more women will be released from lives dominated by childbearing; the institution of marriage will become weaker; to varying degrees, countries will benefit economically from the window of opportunity that is provided by age-structural change within the transition; and the lengthy and often contorted process that is democratization will gradually be put on a firmer basis. In short, and of course other things equal, the societal effects of the demographic transition are likely to be transformational in the very long run.

That said, the modern world is such an increasingly complex and interconnected place that it will often be impossible to isolate the specific influence of the transition on development from the influence of other forces. Moreover, it is important to stress that in the future, as in the past, the course of many aspects of development will be bumpy – even if the general direction of change is as expected. This is not the place to speculate in detail about the future effects of the transition for major regions and countries. But there is no doubt that all societies will undergo adaptive changes in response to the processes of the demographic transition. And poor countries with high fertility and rapidly growing populations will find development of all kinds much harder to achieve.

If there is a phenomenon with the potential to disrupt everything, then it is surely global warming and climate change. The occurrence of a substantial rise in the temperature of the Earth, or a sudden major shift in the world's climate system, might well mean that most of the generally positive chains of cause and effect discussed in these pages would cease to be relevant. Of course, no one knows what will happen during the rest of this century, let alone beyond. Perhaps only a gradual and modest warming of the Earth will occur – a trajectory that is devoutly to be wished.

However, it is also clear that a major change in climate could well occur. And, should this happen, then the world's population will face difficulties that are completely unprecedented in terms of their severity and their scale (Dyson 2005; IPCC 2007). In particular, hundreds of millions of people alive today already have only meagre access to supplies of food and water. And even should the world's climate remain relatively unchanged, there are reasons to think that this situation may not improve greatly in the coming decades – not least because of the environmental and economic effects of rapid population growth in poor countries. Pictures of forlorn adults, surrounded by hungry children, are most unlikely to go away. However, the occurrence of major climate change would almost certainly make things very much worse. Indeed, supplies of food and water could become badly disrupted almost everywhere, i.e. in both developing and developed countries. In such conditions, assumptions about future mortality trends would have to be seriously revised. Moreover, should such a calamity occur, it would not be entirely due to a 'third factor' that is independent of the transition.

The Enlightenment saw the birth of both the demographic transition and the Industrial Revolution – the latter with its attendant modern economic growth, a phenomenon that is highly dependent upon the burning of fossil fuels. Much of what has been said in these pages has stressed the relative independence of these two phenomena. In relation to global warming and climate change, however, they both combine to produce an effect – an effect which, importantly and again, seems likely to involve a fairly long time lag (making it easier for people to indulge a natural inclination for avoidance and denial). There is no doubt that economic growth – mainly in developed countries, but increasingly in developing countries as well – has been the first engine of the increase in the emission of greenhouse gases, such as $CO_2$, which underlies global warming and the threat of climate change. However, the second-most important engine has been the growth in the world's population that has resulted from the demographic transition – again, in developed countries initially, but then in developing countries too.[16]

The demographic transition has been a terrifically important and largely advantageous affair. But the world would probably be a more secure place if there were somewhat fewer of us around. And, provided that the world's climate remains relatively unchanged, then the lives of many people will benefit in all sorts of ways if large and long gaps between death rates and birth rates can be reduced, as their countries pass through the demographic transition.

# Appendix: remarks on data and approach

This work deals with a phenomenon that is still affecting every country either directly or indirectly. Therefore it is inevitable that generalizations are made without providing reams of qualification. And, for similar reasons, a degree of licence – hopefully not too great – has occasionally been taken in relation to the use of some demographic terms.

Several scatter-plots are employed to illustrate key points. It is important to note that they are meant to be only broadly illustrative. They are not intended as exercises in the estimation of quantitative effects. To underscore this point, the regression equations, which are given mainly for reasons of completeness, have been placed in the chapter notes. Some of the measures used in the scatter-plots are far from concrete and, of course, one should always be cautious in drawing dynamic inferences from what are essentially cross-sectional data.

The scatter-plots are based on the fifty-six countries in the world that according to the United Nations (2009) had populations of 20 million or more in the year 2010. These countries contain about 90 per cent of the world's population. They are: Afghanistan, Algeria, Argentina, Australia, Bangladesh, Brazil, Canada, China, Colombia, Côte d'Ivoire, Democratic Republic of Congo, Egypt, Ethiopia, France, Germany, Ghana, India, Indonesia, Iran, Iraq, Italy, Japan, Kenya, Madagascar, Malaysia, Mexico, Morocco, Mozambique, Myanmar, Nepal, Nigeria, North Korea, Pakistan, Peru, the Philippines, Poland, South Korea, Romania, the Russian Federation, Saudi Arabia, South Africa, Spain, Sri Lanka, Sudan, Syria, Tanzania, Thailand, Turkey, Uganda, Ukraine, the United Kingdom, the United States, Uzbekistan, Venezuela, Vietnam and Yemen. In some of the scatter-plots a few countries are omitted owing to lack of data.

Several figures depict processes that unfold over very long periods. Therefore it was sometimes necessary to go beyond the above list of countries in order to find suitable illustrations. Accordingly, data for Chile, Costa Rica, Sweden, Taiwan, New Zealand and a region of central India have also been used. Data for England and Wales (i.e. most of the population of the United Kingdom) are employed in this context as well.

The discussion in Chapter 3, in particular, is conducted partly with reference to demographic estimates for around the year 2010. These estimates involve a small element of projection – because they are drawn mostly from the United Nations (2009). However, 2010 constitutes an appropriate base year for this work, and any inaccuracies resulting from the use of these figures are likely to be small, and can safely be ignored for present purposes.

# Notes

## 1 Introduction

1 See the Glossary for information on terms used in this paragraph (e.g. the distinction between population growth and natural increase). As will be elaborated in Chapter 3, death rates and birth rates are influenced by changes in population age structure as well as by changes in mortality and fertility. Urbanization, and urban growth, are often not seen in the context of the demographic transition. For reasons discussed in Chapter 5, however, they are seen as components of the transition here.

## 2 The demographic transition – origins, processes, effects

1 For an initial foray into this territory, see Dyson (2001).

2 For more information on demographic terms and concepts, see the Glossary, and also Chapter 3.

3 For the term 'offshoot', see Maddison (2007). The countries of western Europe are followed in this respect by others in Europe, and by Japan.

4 The actual growth multiple was probably significantly greater, owing to natural increase *before* 1800, and because there is no allowance for emigration in this calculation.

5 This sketch draws on Livi Bacci (2000), Reader (2005), Thomas (1941) and United Nations (2008, 2009). It should be stressed that mortality decline – and therefore the transition – probably began before 1800 in Sweden.

6 This sketch draws on Sarkar (1957) and United Nations (2008, 2009). Again, there was probably some dampening of death rate fluctuations before 1920. The transition may have begun in the last decades of the nineteenth century and, relatedly, the pre-transitional level of life expectancy was probably lower than 36 years.

7 Sri Lanka's growth multiple of 5.7 (as of 2005) is fairly low for a contemporary transition.

8 Sweden here representing the experience of western Europe, of which it is part.

9 This subject is discussed in Chapter 4.

10 Here and subsequently, the word 'marriage' refers to socially recognized forms of stable sexual union, whether or not they are legally sanctioned. There is little evidence of the widespread use of contraception in pre-transitional populations.

11 Many people incorrectly ascribe population ageing within the transition to mortality decline.

12 This discussion ignores the effects on age structure of migration and very low fertility. In the present context, however, these effects are secondary.

13 A similar limited 'rejuvenating' effect can come from a temporary rise in fertility during early stages of the transition. Again, however, for present purposes such an effect is secondary.

14 The equation for the line

shown in Figure 2.4 is y = 1.301x + 0.384 ($R^2$ = 0.70).

15 There were pre-transitional societies where women and men were of roughly equal status, although they were the exception. No pre-transitional society was democratic in the modern sense of the term (see Chapter 7).

16 Average *household* size, however, may well be smaller after the transition, for reasons touched on below. See also Chapter 6.

17 For simplicity, the discussion here assumes monogamy. Circumstances of widespread polygyny are discussed briefly in Chapter 6. See also note 10.

18 Inevitably, there is a degree of speculation in addressing the socio-psychological characteristics of pre-transitional societies (see Chapter 6).

19 This is not to deny the influence of other factors – such as modern economic growth – in contributing to the increase in value that is attached to education (see, for example, Easterlin 1996).

20 The words 'by itself' are italicized because mortality decline causes population growth.

21 It is possible to construct a hypothetical scenario in which the costs of caring for elderly people produce financial ruin. In practice, however, all societies adapt and restrict the resources allocated for this end.

22 The discussion here excludes considerations of migration, extreme population ageing and rapid population decline – the last two, in particular, being regarded as *beyond* the demographic transition.

23 The expression 'almost always' is used here partly because in the case of China couples were coerced into limiting their fertility.

24 Of course, people can migrate to urban areas for many reasons. These issues are discussed in Chapter 5.

25 The Millennium Development Goals are an example of this.

### 3 World population and the transition

1 All figures for 1950 and later used here are estimates and projections made by the United Nations (see especially United Nations 2009). The approximate nature of the figures must be stressed. The UN revises its figures biennially, and they are available online at esa.un.org/esa/population/.

2 We use the simple terms 'death rate' and 'birth rate' here for reasons of exposition. These rates, however, are formally referred to as the *crude* death and birth rates (see the Glossary).

3 Replacement-level fertility is formally defined in terms of women and daughters (see the Glossary).

4 Part of the increase in the growth rate in the eighteenth century – which is reflected, for example, in population estimates for China – may have mirrored a warming of the world's climate (see Galloway 1986).

5 Fertility decline also produces a modest initial rise in the proportion of the population in the childbearing ages.

6 This fact is somewhat obscured in Figure 3.2 because the growth rates relate to periods of fifty years.

7 Note too in Figure 3.3 that since about 1990 the death rate has been higher in the more developed regions than in the less developed regions – reflecting the much older populations of the former.

8 Perhaps the most important exception to this generalization

is Japan, which is located in East Asia. For a listing of countries by region, and demographic estimates for individual countries, see United Nations (2009).

9 Some settlements with tens of thousands of people are classed as rural (see Dyson and Visaria 2004: 115–16).

10 The figure can, however, be substantially higher than 2.1 births in a few places where mortality is still relatively high (see Espenshade et al. 2003). See also note 3 above.

11 In much of this book the demographic transition is taken as complete when the vital rates in a population are low and roughly equal. But there is also a presumption that the population will be fairly old, and the level of urbanization high, and these processes may take some time. It should also be clear that mortality especially, but also fertility, can continue to decline after a population has gone through the transition.

12 As was observed with reference to South-Central Asia (see note 9).

13 In both cases the exceptionally low death rate of 6 per thousand reflects the still quite young age structure.

14 Mortality decline does contribute significantly to ageing in a population with already low fertility.

15 In 2010 there were about 1.86 billion people aged 0–14. According to the medium projection the figure will still be 1.80 billion in 2050.

16 An increase in population of about 3.4 per cent is suggested for 2050–75 (see United Nations 2004: 179).

17 The projections discussed in this chapter are for large populations. Projections for smaller populations tend to be less reliable because they are more open to the effects of migration.

18 The detailed projections for individual countries should be viewed with special caution. Here we are chiefly concerned with the broad picture.

19 A 'growth multiple' of roughly ten results if one uses a world population estimate of 954 million in 1800 as the base (see Table 3.1). Using an estimate of 770 million for 1750 as the base, however, would raise the multiple to twelve (but see also, for example, note 4 above). The very approximate nature of the calculation should require no emphasis.

20 These statements regarding growth multiples are deliberately imprecise. They are made mainly on the basis of population estimates contained in Livi Bacci (2000), Maddison (2007) and United Nations (2004, 2009). Data on population size at the start of the transition, if they exist at all, are usually very rough. And migration can complicate the calculation. The time when the transition is assumed to start can also have a big effect on the resulting multiple. For a formal treatment of the issue, see Chesnais (1992: 302–20). See also note 19.

## 4 The demographic transition – facts and theory

1 His book, written in French, appeared in 1986. It is *La Transition Démographique – Étapes, Formes, Implications Économiques*, Presses Universitaires de France, Paris. The 1992 English translation is by Elizabeth and Philip Kreager.

2 The UN estimates refer to a period of just sixty years, and they are often derived from various, rather patchy, data sources,

including different types of survey (hence the term 'manufactured').

3 For example, people may see no point in registering a vital event, or the place of registration may be difficult to reach.

4 Because this chapter deals with mortality and fertility, this is the main sense in which completion of the transition will be referred to here. As we noted in Chapter 3, however, population ageing and urbanization can still be occurring.

5 The level of the vital rates in Figure 4.1 is sometimes deficient. Their use here is mainly to illustrate the general *form* of the phenomenon. Notice that there are gaps in the series for Spain and Taiwan, and the series for central India ends in 1980. There are some comparatively good examples of the transition for small, often island, populations. But the temptation to use them here has been resisted. For data on sixty-seven cases, most of them far from complete (in several senses), see Chesnais (1992: 225–77).

6 The area consists of four districts in the modern Indian state of Maharashtra. In 1981 it contained about seven million people. For further details, see Dyson (1989).

7 The death rate in both countries remained high during 1940–45 and then fell abruptly in the late 1940s and early 1950s. The effect of both world wars on death rates can be detected in many countries (see Dyson and Murphy 1991).

8 Before 1838 the time series for England in Figure 4.1 is based on ecclesiastical data. Ecclesiastical records also form part of the basis for the Swedish and French series in Figures 2.2 and 4.5 respectively.

9 In 1900 and 1918 the registered death rates were 82 and 111 per thousand respectively, going well beyond the vertical scale used in Figure 4.1. Some of the fall in vital rates in the 1960s and 1970s shown for this area of India probably reflects a deterioration in registration coverage (see Dyson 1989).

10 Most north-western European countries had reached replacement-level fertility by the 1930s. After the Second World War, England and other Western countries, in Europe and elsewhere, experienced an extended baby boom which lasted into the 1960s. This boom complicates the interpretation of birth-rate trends in relation to the ending of the transition. In this context, see also Figures 4.4 and 4.5.

11 See note 9 above.

12 Rates of natural increase can be calculated for Japan from the 1870s onwards. The registered birth and death rates were probably under-registered in the 1870s and 1880s, but the rate of natural increase (i.e. the difference between them) is less affected. Egypt and central India are excluded from Figure 4.2 because their transitions are insufficiently complete for present purposes.

13 In fact it is often skewed somewhat towards the right, owing to the influence of population age structure in slowing the decline in the birth rate.

14 This may have reflected an increasing degree of social integration within north-western Europe.

15 The rates were read from Figure 8.7(c) in Chesnais (1992: 265); for their sources see Chesnais (1992: 620).

16 Indeed, probably at younger ages than their ancestors in Europe. That is, migration to North America may well have involved a rise in total fertility per woman.

17 The point cannot be pushed too far back in time owing to the much later peopling, by Europeans, of Australia and New Zealand. Natural increase rates for Canada show a similar trend.

18 Thus average life expectancy in England and Wales in the first half of the eighteenth century is put at about 39 years, and by 1871–80 it had increased to about 43 years (Woods 2000: 365).

19 There may be elements of this in relation to France, for example. Thus the argument might be that increases in the degree to which people feel that they can exert control in their own lives to some extent operate simultaneously with regard to behaviour relating to both childcare and the use of birth control.

20 Breastfeeding has an inhibiting effect on ovulation. Many traditional societies had prohibitions relating to sexual intercourse. Thus, for a woman, it might be deemed inappropriate in a period following having given birth, or on becoming a grandmother.

21 In all societies men tend to marry (formally or otherwise) women who are younger than themselves. The process of mortality decline creates younger cohorts that are larger than older cohorts – so producing a 'marriage squeeze' effect, i.e. making it more difficult for women to find a partner. One outcome can be a delay in the age of women at marriage.

22 Sub-Saharan Africa may be a partial – and one suspects temporary – exception to this generalization; see Timaeus and Moultrie (2008).

23 The estimates are taken from United Nations (2007). They relate to all contraceptive methods, including traditional ones; nowadays, however, most usage involves modern methods. The estimate for England and Wales is that for the United Kingdom.

24 Often, but not always. The English case, and for example that of the Netherlands, involved quite a long lag.

25 Pre-transitional fertility also seems to have been moderate in Japan.

26 For example, on the fitful spread of vaccination in India during the nineteenth century, see Banthia and Dyson (1999). The last naturally occurring case of smallpox was in Somalia in 1977.

27 As is noted in Chapter 5, however, the *initial* effects of the Industrial Revolution on urban living conditions and death rates were often deleterious.

28 Population ageing also contributes to the increasing prominence of degenerative diseases.

29 See the Appendix for the fifty-six countries represented. The equation for the line shown for 1950–55 is $y = 10.87\text{Ln}(x) - 32.08$ ($R^2 = 0.67$); that for 2000–05 is $y = 7.48\text{Ln}(x) + 5.71$ ($R^2 = 0.73$).

30 The countries in Figure 4.6 which in 2000–05 had an average life expectancy of below 50 years were Afghanistan, Democratic Republic of Congo, Ethiopia, Kenya, Mozambique, Nigeria, South Africa, Uganda and Tanzania. In many pre-transitional populations life expectancy was well below 30 years.

31 Increased infanticide was a possible response. It is generally agreed that farmer-generated rises in agricultural productivity cannot match modern rates of population growth without a lot of external help (see, for example, Boserup 1965: 118; Pingali and Binswanger 1991: 52).

32 It is possible to interpret both

the rise in England's birth rate up to about 1815 (to the extent that it occurred) and the long delay before the sharp fall in the birth rate from the 1870s onwards as reflecting the country's comparatively favourable economic performance.

33 See the Appendix for the countries represented. The equation for the line shown for 1950–55 is $y = 38.48x^{-0.267}$ ($R^2 = 0.35$); that for 2000–05 is $y = 48.37x^{-0.551}$ ($R^2 = 0.61$).

34 It has been necessary for economic accounts of fertility decline to emphasize structural changes in society (e.g. increases in education, health and urbanization) which are claimed to accompany economic growth, rather than rises in incomes per se (see, for example, Simon 1976). To a considerable extent, however, gains in education and health can occur independently of economic growth, and as is argued in Chapter 5, urbanization can be relatively independent of economic growth as well. There is also the point that rising incomes might be expected to have a positive effect on the demand for children.

35 Of course, the discussion here relates to modern rather than religious education.

36 The evidence consists of urban/rural estimates of fertility contained in United Nations (various years).

37 The absolute numbers of people involved in migration from developing to developed countries today are considerable. Expressed as a proportion of the natural increase in the sending countries, however, the numbers are much smaller than applied in Europe in the past.

38 The point is often downplayed in the interpretation of results from regression analyses (which are rarely complete in terms of the factors and variables considered).

39 The words 'almost always' are used partly because it might be argued that China's government reduced fertility through coercive measures which imposed political and social costs to having children. The government was still responding, however, to the unprecedented population growth of the 1950s and 1960s (see Figure 4.3).

40 See also note 34 above.

41 For world economic growth rates, see Maddison (2007). Reher (2004) argues that in Europe there was a long history of limiting fertility for economic reasons, and that this helps to explain the close temporal association sometimes seen between death and birth rate declines (see, for example, Figure 4.5).

42 We noted the possibility of changes in ideas to some extent having a simultaneous effect on child mortality and fertility. Fertility decline is almost always concurrent with mortality decline to some degree. See also note 41.

43 See note 24. For the reasons emphasized in the notes to Chapter 3, all these statements on growth multiples must be regarded as approximate.

44 On this see, for example, Maddison (2007: 77–87).

## 5 Urbanization and the transition

1 These are not dealt with in detail here, but see, for example, UNCHS (2008) and UNFPA (2008).

2 Rural-to-urban migration often involves the movement of young people in their late teens, twenties and early thirties. These are the prime reproductive age groups, and they also tend to experience low

death rates. Therefore, other things equal, such migration may raise the urban birth rate and lower the urban death rate – so tending to raise the urban rate of natural increase, compared to the rural rate. As is noted in the text, however, urban natural increase rates are often somewhat lower than rural rates.

3 See Figure 5.3 below. Net rural-to-urban migration is the excess of rural-to-urban migration over urban-to-rural migration. Note that the distinction between the rate of population growth (which reflects change due to migration) and the rate of natural increase (which does not reflect migration) is important here (see the Glossary).

4 This statement is true in relation to relatively short time periods, say of a decade. As is noted below, however, the situation is more complicated if the subsequent natural increase of rural-to-urban migrants is taken into account.

5 Here and elsewhere, it seems likely that the process may have originated somewhat earlier than is stated in the text. The origins are difficult to identify, however, and so a cautious view is taken.

6 Grauman's estimates assume that an urban settlement contains at least five thousand people.

7 The location of the Industrial Revolution in England, for example, was determined partly by such considerations, and thus it often occurred initially around small rural settlements (Bairoch 1988: 503).

8 The explanation for such migration has been addressed notably by Todaro (1981). The relatively low price of wheat on the international market has been a significant factor conditioning urban growth in much of sub-Saharan Africa since the 1970s.

9 This statement also applies to examples of urbanization that have been based to some degree upon imported supplies of food. See also, for example, note 8.

10 The account relates to populations that had a significant, though small, urban sector in existence prior to mortality decline. In broad terms this covers Europe, Asia and North Africa. But it may not apply in a straightforward way to parts of sub-Saharan Africa. And, as we saw in Chapter 4, offshoot populations are somewhat distinctive in that they began to experience the transition from a somewhat different position – in the present context, in relation to the degree to which their tiny urban sectors were ever demographic sinks.

11 For research on the demographic basis of urbanization, see also Rogers (1977) and White et al. (2004). For other work relating urbanization to the transition in different ways, see Abu-Lughod (1964), Cochran and O'Kane (1977) and Sharma (1979).

12 The level of the ceiling depends on the degree to which the urban areas were sinks, and rates of net rural-to-urban migration. The level of mortality in pre-transitional north-western Europe was comparatively favourable. It may be that ceilings on urbanization were even lower in other parts of the world.

13 But, and of course, the considerations of note 4 are relevant here.

14 This rate is expressed per thousand *rural* inhabitants and, as we have noted, there comes a point where the size of the rural population declines. On this, see Preston (1979).

15 Ten-year averages are used for Sweden, and five-year averages for Sri Lanka.

16 In the case of Sri Lanka

(formerly Ceylon) migration from India also played a role in maintaining the urban sector. See Dyson (2009) and Dyson (forthcoming) for further details, and note 18 below.

17 For example, some urban residents certainly returned to their natal villages to die.

18 For example, there were significantly more men than women in urban Sri Lanka – owing partly to the presence of immigrant labourers from southern India. This helps to explain the appreciably lower urban birth rate compared to the rural birth rate in Sri Lanka.

19 If the deaths of rural residents in urban hospitals are not excluded from the urban death rates in Figure 5.1 then these rates are raised by approximately 25 per cent, and they are much higher than the rural rates. See Dyson (2009 and forthcoming) for further details.

20 This is partly because of the tendency for reclassification to occur on a lagged basis. According to the United Nations (2008) Sweden's population was 66 per cent urban in 1950; so the figure of 47 per cent is low using current criteria. The UN puts the level of urbanization in Sri Lanka in 1970 at 19.5 per cent, falling to 15 per cent in 2010 – almost certainly reflecting a major change in criteria.

21 Grauman's estimates for periods before 1950 were made within the Population Division of the United Nations. Minor interpolations have been made in relation to Grauman's figures here for reasons of comparability. See also note 6.

22 This probably reflects the rather arbitrary way in which areas are designated as 'urban' in India; see Dyson and Visaria (2004) and relevant discussion in Chapter 3.

23 Even in the case of sub-Saharan Africa, the fact of high rates of natural increase might be expected to quicken the pace of urbanization – for example, by speeding up the rate at which rural settlements exceed the threshold size for a population to be classed as urban. See the relevant discussion under 'Conceptual issues' in the text above.

24 Infectious (and parasitic) diseases tend to depress fertility for several reasons – for example, because they reduce the frequency of sexual intercourse.

25 The basic explanation probably applies in any population that had an urban sector in existence at the start of the demographic transition. See also note 10, and the preceding discussion under 'Conceptual issues'.

26 This is true in practice, although as we have noted in the text above, it is possible to construct a hypothetical scenario in which urbanization occurs simply through population growth and reclassification, i.e. without migration (see the discussion of 'Conceptual issues').

27 This matter was broached in Chapter 4 – although it was also noted that the transition in some parts of the world, particularly sub-Saharan Africa, may not support the idea that there is a general tendency towards compression.

28 For evidence of a systematic increase in the proportion of moves involving the urban sector over time, see, for example, Oucho and Gould (1993) on sub-Saharan Africa, and Dyson and Visaria (2004) on India.

29 See Chapter 4 for discussion of migration as a response to population pressure within the demographic transition.

30 This slowdown of urbanization as a result of HIV/AIDS may, however, be relatively short lived because mortality due to the disease is being increasingly controlled.

31 Of course, in the modern world food availability is often tied closely to energy availability.

## 6 Social effects of the transition

1 As was noted in Chapter 2, it is unlikely that HIV/AIDS has taken mortality back to truly pre-transitional levels.

2 Notice, however, that for elderly people themselves, it becomes increasingly common to hear of the deaths of individuals of their own generation. That is, in developed countries, death is both concentrated and common among old people.

3 The stoic manner in which some societies in Africa appear to have faced the rise in mortality due to HIV/AIDS may partly reflect their closeness in time to pre-transitional mortality conditions – although this suggestion has been questioned (see, for example, Caldwell et al. 1992; Caldwell 1997).

4 The quantity/quality trade-off in relation to having children was mentioned in Chapter 2 in connection with the transition's beneficial effects on the spread of education and economic performance.

5 See the discussion in Chapter 3. It should be noted that the range 40–45 per cent would be rather high for some pre-transitional populations – e.g. those in north-western Europe.

6 Population ageing may have socio-psychological effects additional to those brought about simply by the change in composition, i.e. effects analogous in this respect to those (such as alienation and social isolation) that are alluded to below in relation to conditions in large towns.

7 The general nature of the discussion here probably does not require a formal distinction to be made between households and families. It will suffice to say that in pre-transitional circumstances the family usually was a household, or at least it formed the major part of one.

8 The discussion here relates to societies in which monogamous unions prevail – i.e. all regions, except for sub-Saharan Africa, where polygynous households were, and often still are, common. In societies with widespread polygyny average household size could be relatively large even in pre-transitional conditions. Nevertheless, *horizontal* kin relationships, involving co-wives and their children, still predominated. Conditions in sub-Saharan Africa are touched on at the chapter's end. See also note 14.

9 The point that the demographic transition has had particular implications for women, as more children were borne and survived, has gone largely unnoticed in research.

10 The term 'marriage' is used here to refer to a stable sexual union between a woman and a man for the purpose of having children.

11 The words 'decline' and 'weakening' are not used normatively here.

12 In western Europe in the past the age of women at marriage was often somewhat later, i.e. in the twenties.

13 Survey data for some contemporary developing countries suggest that most births occur at intervals of less than three years

(see, for example, Setty-Venugopal and Upadhyay 2002). However, this may partly reflect the disruption of traditional patterns of breastfeeding and sexual intercourse.

14 In all societies there is a tendency for men to marry women who are younger than themselves. Davis and van den Oever (1982) observe that this is informed by the fact that men of all ages tend to compete for women of reproductive age. Also, following divorce or widowhood, men are more likely to remarry than are women. In sub-Saharan Africa, however, high levels of polygyny are based on a large age gap between married men and married women – and in these conditions it is much more likely both that women will be widowed, and that they will be remarried in some way (e.g. through levirate remarriage). See also the discussion of sub-Saharan Africa at the chapter's end.

15 Of course, the following discussion also applies to Australia and New Zealand. The term 'western Europe' is used loosely here to encompass much of the continent's south, north and west.

16 This resurgence in fertility was noted briefly in Chapter 4.

17 You, the reader, can probably attest to this from your own experience, but see also the age structures for Sweden, Russia and Japan in Figures 2.3 and 3.4. Notice that the lack of men at older ages is one reason why women are less likely to remarry than are men.

18 For example, young people, perhaps especially women, are likely to see this as a potential burden of getting married and having children in the first place. It is important to note that, although smaller and simpler household structures may come to prevail overall, to the extent that *new* partnerships are formed following divorce and separation, then household structures can actually become increasingly complex.

19 In England and Wales in 2006, the mean age of women at first birth was 27.3 years, the mean age at marriage for single women was 29.7 years, and 43.5 per cent of all births occurred outside of marriage (see ONS 2007a, 2007b).

20 New attitudes towards marriage, which arose first in demographically advanced societies, are transferred elsewhere via the media. Policies designed to raise the level of female education contribute to the rising age of female marriage in many countries. It should be clear, however, that the attitude that girls have as much right to education as boys itself results at least partly from the transition.

21 Of the fifty-six countries used in this book, GEM values were unavailable for fifteen – i.e. Afghanistan, Bangladesh, Côte d'Ivoire, North Korea, Democratic Republic of Congo, Ghana, India, Iraq, Kenya, Mozambique, Myanmar, Nigeria, South Africa, Sudan and Uzbekistan. The illustrative line shown in Figure 6.1 is $y = 0.691x^{-0.360}$ ($R^2 = 0.23$).

22 See note 21 for the countries not represented in Figure 6.1 – a majority of which have high fertility (and probably low gender equity).

23 Using life expectancy as a measure of a country's progress through the demographic transition, the increase in gender empowerment is most pronounced at high levels of life expectation (see Dyson 2001: 73; see also McNay 2005: 121).

24 For example, for evidence relating to the United Kingdom, see Walby (1997).

25 For example, this was true with respect to the occurrence of fertility decline in developing countries (see Eberstadt 1981).

26 This is so, notwithstanding the fact that there may be demand for education and new technologies in rural areas. In relation to the role of urban populations in the development of modern agriculture, see the discussion in Chapter 5, and Jacobs (1972).

27 That is, they might be expected to occur independently of these other economic and political effects – at least to some degree.

28 Even towns like Rome, Constantinople and Vijayanagar probably never contained 1 million people. In 1800 perhaps only London and Edo had 1 million inhabitants (Ponting 2007: 294–313).

29 For example, see Hauser (1965), Hawley (1979), UNFPA (2008) and Beall and Fox (2009).

30 Polygyny in this region was, and remains, on a much greater scale than elsewhere in the world. The institution has its own particular demographic basis (see note 14), and while it has undergone change, it remains especially strong in west and central Africa.

31 In this context, see the Indonesian woman's remark in the 'Marriage and gender relations' section of Chapter 2.

32 Notice that while mortality decline may produce a rise in the overall level of confidence prevailing in a society, fertility decline may produce a decline in confidence, at least in this respect.

## 7 Economic and political effects

1 Full information would involve knowledge of pre-transitional mortality conditions. Faced with the choice of either living in the London of today with the mortality conditions of the eighteenth century, or of living in the London of the eighteenth century with the mortality conditions of today, I would certainly prefer the latter.

2 As we noted in Chapter 4, however, there may well have been mortality decline in England in the eighteenth century. For the argument that there was, and that it assisted economic growth, see Razzell (2007). In any case, pre-transitional mortality levels in north-western Europe were relatively favourable.

3 In high mortality conditions, the so-called 'synergy of malnutrition and infectious disease' is likely to account for most deaths at young ages. Because repeated bouts of infection are a major cause of undernutrition, an improvement in a population's nutritional status may to a large degree reflect a decline in the experience of infectious diseases (as opposed to a rise in food consumption).

4 Of course, these considerations are relevant to the interpretation of Figure 4.6.

5 It is important to stress that the words 'relatively fast population growth' here mean relatively fast for pre-transitional conditions.

6 Ester Boserup (1965) argued that population growth leads to advances in agricultural technology and land use. But she did not see improvements in the standard of living as guaranteed, and her arguments referred mostly to slow population growth over the long sweep of history.

7 See, for example, Figures 4.1 and 4.2.

8 It is common to use a linear fit. The linear equation shown is $y = -0.703x + 2.500$ ($R^2 = 0.12$) and

the relationship is significant at the 1 per cent level. A polynomial fit, however, provides the equation $y = -0.593x^2 + 1.387x + 1.260$ ($R^2 = 0.22$). The polynomial fit suggests that at low rates of population growth the relationship between population growth and per capita income growth may be positive, while at high rates of population growth the relationship may be appreciably more negative than is suggested in the text.

9 It should be noted that, in relation to rapid population growth, this has probably always been the view of many economists – including some revisionists. Boserup's work is often cited to support the idea that population growth can stimulate productivity increases (see note 6). But she was well aware that her arguments were unlikely to hold in rural areas with high rates of population growth. See Boserup (1965: 118); also Hayami and Ruttan (1987) and Pingali and Binswanger (1991).

10 As we noted in Chapter 3, however, sub-Saharan Africa has only recently begun to experience fertility decline, and therefore it is well behind in terms of change in population age composition.

11 See the discussion of fertility decline in China in Chapters 3 and 4.

12 There are only fourteen countries with population growth rates less than 1.2 per cent in Figure 7.1. And it should also be noted, in relation to the *direction* of causation, that low economic growth may reduce the rate of population growth by stimulating out-migration. See also the discussion of the polynomial fit in note 8.

13 The possible cases of Japan and, still more, Russia come to mind – see, for example, Figures 3.4 and 3.6.

14 This is not to deny that urban populations can suffer food scarcities and famines. Moreover, the poorest inhabitants of urban areas may be worse off than the poorest people in rural areas.

15 With the proviso that, because of different starting conditions, the experience of the demographic transition was somewhat different in North America (see Chapter 4).

16 Huntington (1991: 6) states that the core of democracy is 'the election of leaders through competitive elections by the people they govern'.

17 In some parts of the United States literacy tests were used to restrict the voting rights of Afro-Americans as late as the early 1960s. In Northern Ireland, in the United Kingdom, the value of the vote of people in the Catholic community was reduced by the practice of gerrymandering in the 1960s. Greece, Portugal and Spain achieved their present democratic status in 1975, 1976 and 1978 respectively.

18 Perhaps especially in Europe, where in the eighteenth century life expectancy was lower than it generally was in the offshoot populations of North America (see Chapter 4).

19 For the impact of education on the propensity for democracy see, for example, Barro (1999).

20 For example, in 1947 India's political elite had been heavily influenced by international ideas. Using Freedom House (2007) figures, and a democracy scale ranging from low (1) to high (7) outlined in note 24 below, in 2006 Russia scored 2.5, China 1.5 and India 5.5.

21 It might, however, be argued that population growth in North America assisted democratization inasmuch as it benefited eco-

nomic growth. There may also be a minimum level of population density necessary for the establishment of democracy. Moreover, as we note in the text below, urban growth may play a role in democratization.

22 Of course, population growth does not need to be rapid for such difficulties to occur, and they also arise in developed countries.

23 The right for women to vote was often introduced initially at a higher age than applied to men (Dyson 2001: 87).

24 The regression line shown is $y = 0.042x + 1.966$ ($R^2 = 0.23$). The relationship is significant at the 1 per cent level. The measure of democracy is the combined average rating of political rights and civil liberties. For presentational reasons, the Freedom House scale has been reversed. Therefore the highest level of democracy scores 7, and the lowest 1.

25 In the United Kingdom, for example, the Reform Acts of 1867 and 1884 provide a clear illustration of this.

26 This difference between the two percentages somewhat reduces the directness of the comparisons that can be made. For further detail on both the data and the comparisons, see Dyson (2001).

27 In Europe during 1900–25, and in Latin America after 1980, there are signs of a democratic 'surge' (see Figure 7.4). Interestingly, in both regions these were periods of unprecedented population ageing.

28 The ratings for 2006 for these countries were Ghana (6), Mozambique (5), Kenya (4.5), Madagascar (4.5) and Tanzania (4.5) (see also note 24). Thus Ghana was categorized by Freedom House (2007) as 'free' and the other countries as 'partly free'. Clearly, however, these scores do not preclude backsliding – which is common, and may already have occurred in some cases.

29 For example, see note 21. To a small degree, it is also conceivable that the increase in population size produced by the demographic transition has contributed to the need for political parties, and representative rather than direct forms of democracy.

30 The median age of a population appears to be much more closely associated with the level of democracy than the level of urbanization (see Dyson 2010).

## 8 Conclusions, discussion, the future

1 There may be no element of compression in relation to some of these transitions, although only time will tell.

2 The countries and their growth multiples for the period 1950–2050 are Côte d'Ivoire (17), Democratic Republic of Congo (12), Kenya (14), Madagascar (10), Saudi Arabia (13), Tanzania (14), Uganda (17), Yemen (12). See United Nations (2009).

3 For data reasons, however, the exact growth multiples will never be known.

4 The increasingly adult composition of society is relevant both when considering how developed countries have changed over time, and when comparing developed and developing countries.

5 Policies and programmes here include measures in areas like education and health, as well as family planning.

6 None of the points made in this paragraph detracts from the general importance of economic growth in development.

7 To put the matter differently, the likes of Jenner and Pasteur have been much more influential in this regard than has Adam Smith. For a clear statement on this point, see Easterlin (1996: 80–82).

8 Non-economic reasons for such migration were mentioned in Chapter 5, as was Preston's suggestion that people may have an innate desire to live in larger groups.

9 That is, what would have happened if the demographic transition had not started in north-western Europe, but rather somewhere else.

10 For example, in relation to population ageing, there has been little discussion of its implications for more practical matters such as the age of retirement, pensions, healthcare provision or international migration.

11 Diseases and climate change are also among these factors.

12 Of course, this point should be obvious. However, one often hears people challenge a generalization simply on the basis that it does not appear to hold in a particular case – with no mention of other considerations that may explain why it is an exception.

13 Of course, to say that mortality and fertility will be fairly low everywhere is not to say that there will an absence of variation.

14 For example, for the period 2005–10 the UN puts total fertility in China and the United States at 1.8 and 2.1 births respectively. The difference in mortality level between these two countries is also quite small – the respective life expectancies being 73 and 78 years.

15 For example, the United Nations medium variant projections imply that in 2040–50 the average annual rates of population growth for Europe, the Middle East and sub-Saharan Africa will be approximately −0.25 per cent, 0.7 per cent and 1.3 per cent respectively.

16 For elaboration of these statements, see Bongaarts (1992) and Dyson (2005). Of course, poor people make little contribution to greenhouse gas emissions on a per capita basis.

# Bibliography


Abu-Lughod, J. (1964) 'Urban–rural differences as a function of the demographic transition: Egyptian data and an analytical model', *American Journal of Sociology*, 69(4): 476–90.

Adnan, S. (1993) '"Birds in a cage": institutional change and women's position in Bangladesh', in N. Frederici, K. O. Mason and S. Sogner (eds), *Women's Position and Demographic Change*, Oxford: Oxford University Press.

Ariès, P. (1960) *L'Enfant et la Vie Familiale sous L'Ancien Régime*, Paris: Librairie Plon.

Australian Bureau of Statistics (2008) *Year Book Australia 2008*, Canberra: Australian Bureau of Statistics, Canberra, www.abs.gov.au/AUSSTATS, accessed May 2009.

Bairoch, P. (1988) *Cities and Economic Development*, Chicago, IL: University of Chicago Press.

Banthia, J. and T. Dyson (1999) 'Smallpox in nineteenth-century India', *Population and Development Review*, 25(4): 649–80.

Barclay, G. W., A. J. Coale, M. A. Stoto and T. J. Trussell (1976) 'A reassessment of the demography of traditional rural China', *Population Index*, 42(4): 606–35.

Barro, R. J. (1999) 'Determinants of democracy', *Journal of Political Economy*, 107(6): S158–83.

Barro, R. J. and X. Sala-i-Martin (2004) *Economic Growth*, Cambridge, MA: MIT Press.

Basu, A. (1986) 'Birth control by assetless workers in Kerala: the possibility of a poverty-induced fertility transition', *Development and Change*, 17(2): 265–82.

Bauer, J. (2001) 'Demographic change, development, and the economic status of women in East Asia', in A. Mason (ed.), *Population Change and Economic Development in East Asia*, Stanford, CA: Stanford University Press.

Beall, J. and S. Fox (2009) *Cities and Development*, London: Routledge.

Beaver, S. (1975) *Demographic Transition Theory Reinterpreted*, Lexington, MA: Lexington Books.

Berger, B. (1971) *Societies in Change*, New York: Basic Books.

Bhat, M. (2002) 'Returning a favour: reciprocity between female education and fertility in India', *World Development*, 30(10): 1791–803.

Bhat, T. N. (2005) 'Demographic change and women's empowerment', in S. Subramanya, M. Chakravorthy and N. S. Viswanath (eds), *Women in Nation Building: Perspectives, Issues, Implications*, Bangalore: Southern Economist.

Biraben, J. (1979) 'Essai sur l'évolution du nombre des hommes', *Population*, 34(1): 13–25.

Birdsall, N. and S. Sinding (2001) 'How and why population matters: new findings, new issues', in N. Birdsall, A. C. Kelley and S. Sinding (eds), *Population Matters: Demographic Change,*

*Economic Growth, and Poverty in the Developing World*, Oxford: Oxford University Press.

Birdsall, N., A. C. Kelley and S. Sinding (eds) (2001) *Population Matters: Demographic Change, Economic Growth, and Poverty in the Developing World*, Oxford: Oxford University Press.

Bloom, D. and D. Canning (2001) 'Cumulative causality, economic growth, and the demographic transition', in N. Birdsall, A. C. Kelley and S. Sinding (eds), *Population Matters: Demographic Change, Economic Growth, and Poverty in the Developing World*, Oxford: Oxford University Press.

Bloom, D., D. Canning, G. Fink and J. E. Finlay (2009) 'The cost of low fertility in Europe', NBER Working Paper no. 14828, Cambridge, MA: National Bureau of Economic Research.

Bongaarts, J. (1987) 'The projection of family composition over the life course within family status life tables', in J. Bongaarts, T. K. Burch and K. Wachter (eds), *Family Demography: Methods and Their Application*, Oxford: Clarendon Press.

— (1992) 'Population growth and global warming', *Population and Development Review*, 18(2): 299–319.

— (1997) 'The role of family planning programmes in contemporary fertility transition', in G. Jones, R. Douglas, J. C. Caldwell and R. D'Souza (eds), *The Continuing Demographic Transition*, Oxford: Clarendon Press.

— (2001a) 'Household size and composition in the developing world in the 1990s', *Population Studies*, 55(3): 263–79.

— (2001b) 'Dependency burdens in the developing world', in N. Birdsall, A. C. Kelley and S. Sinding (eds), *Population Matters: Demographic Change, Economic Growth, and Poverty in the Developing World*, Oxford: Oxford University Press.

— (2008) 'Fertility transition in developing countries: progress or stagnation?', Population Council Working Paper no. 7, New York: Population Council.

Boserup, E. (1965) *The Conditions of Agricultural Growth*, London: George Allen and Unwin.

Brass, W. (1970) 'The growth of world population', in A. Allison (ed.), *Population Control*, Harmondsworth: Penguin Books.

Brockerhoff, M. (1999) 'Urban growth in developing countries: a review of projections and predictions', *Population and Development Review*, 25(4): 757–78.

Brockerhoff, M. and E. Brennan (1998) 'The poverty of cities in developing regions', *Population and Development Review*, 24(1): 75–114.

Burch, T. K. (1967) 'The size and structure of families: a comparative analysis of census data', *American Sociological Review*, 32(3): 347–63.

— (1970) 'Some demographic determinants of average household size: an analytic approach', *Demography*, 7(1): 61–9.

Caldwell, J. C. (1976) 'Toward a restatement of demographic transition theory', *Population and Development Review*, 2(3/4): 321–66.

— (1980) 'Mass education as a determinant of the timing of fertility decline', *Population and Development Review*, 6(2): 225–55.

— (1986) 'Routes to low mortality

in poor countries', *Population and Development Review*, 12(2): 171–220.

— (1997) 'The impact of the African AIDS epidemic', *Health Transition Review*, vol. 7, supplement 2, pp. 169–88.

Caldwell, J. C., I. Orubuloye and P. Caldwell (1992) 'Under-reaction to AIDS in sub-Saharan Africa', *Social Science and Medicine*, 34(1): 1169–82.

Caldwell, J. C., P. H. Reddy and P. Caldwell (1988) *The Causes of Demographic Change*, Madison, WI: University of Wisconsin Press.

Carr-Saunders A. M. (1936) *World Population: Past Growth and Present Trends*, Oxford: Clarendon Press.

Cassen, R. H. (1976) 'Population and development: a survey', *World Development*, 4(10/11): 785–830.

Casterline, J. B. (2003) 'Demographic transition', in P. Demeny and G. McNicoll (eds), *Encyclopedia of Population*, New York: Macmillan Reference.

Ceylon (1923) *Report on the Census of Ceylon, General Tables, Volume IV*, Department of Census and Statistics, Colombo: Government Printer.

— (1967) *Census of Population, Ceylon 1963*, Colombo: Government Press.

— (various years) *Ceylon Administration Report*, Colombo: Government Printer.

CGER (1996) *Use of Reclaimed Water and Sludge in Food Crop Production*, Commission on Geosciences, Environment and Resources, Washington, DC: National Academies Press.

Chen, N., P. Valente and H. Zlotnick (1998) 'What do we know about recent trends in urbanization?', in R. E. Bilsborrow (ed.), *Migration, Urbanization, and Development: New Directions and Issues*, New York: United Nations Population Fund (UNFPA).

Chesnais, J.-C. (1992) *The Demographic Transition – Stages, Patterns and Economic Implications*, Oxford: Clarendon Press.

Cincotta, R. P. (2008) 'How democracies grow up', *Foreign Policy*, 165: 80–82.

Clare, A. (2001) *On Men: Masculinity in Crisis*, London: Arrow Books.

Clark, G. (2007) *A Farewell to Alms – A Brief Economic History of the World*, Princeton, NJ: Princeton University Press.

Cleland, J. (2001) 'The effects of improved survival on fertility: a reassessment', in *Global Fertility Transition*, vol. 27, supplement, *Population and Development Review*, New York: Population Council.

Cleland, J. and C. Wilson (1987) 'Demand theories of the fertility transition. An iconoclastic view', *Population Studies*, 41(1): 5–30.

Coale, A. J. (1964) 'How a population ages or grows younger', in R. Freedman (ed.), *Population: The Vital Revolution*, New York: Doubleday.

— (1973) 'The demographic transition reconsidered', in *International Population Conference*, vol. 1, Liège: International Union for the Scientific Study of Population.

Coale, A. J. and E. Hoover (1958) *Population Growth and Economic Development in Low-Income Countries*, Princeton, NJ: Princeton University Press.

Coale, A. J. and S. C. Watkins (1986) *The Decline of Fertility in Europe*, Princeton, NJ: Princeton University Press.

Cochran, L. T. and J. M. O'Kane (1977) 'Urbanization-industrialization and the theory of demographic transition', *Pacific Sociological Review*, 20(1): 113–34.

Cochrane, S. H. (1979) 'Fertility and education: what do we really know?', World Bank Staff Occasional Papers 26, Washington, DC: Johns Hopkins University Press.

Cohen, B. (2004) 'Urban growth in developing countries: a review of current trends and a caution regarding existing forecasts', *World Development*, 32(1): 1431–61.

Collver, A. (1963) 'The family life cycle in India and the United States', *American Sociological Review*, 28(1): 86–96.

Crook, N. (1997) *Principles of Population and Development*, Oxford: Oxford University Press.

Crutzen, P. and E. Stoermer (2000) 'The "Anthropocene"', *International Geosphere-Biosphere Programme Newsletter*, 41: 17–18, available at www.igbp.net/, accessed October 2009.

Davis, K. (1945) 'The world demographic transition', *Annals of the American Academy of Political and Social Science*, 237: 1–11.

— (1963) 'The theory of change and response in modern demographic history', *Population Index*, 29(4): 345–66.

Davis, K. and A. Casis (1946) 'Urbanization in Latin America, Part 1', *The Milbank Memorial Fund Quarterly*, 24(2): 186–207.

Davis, K. and P. van den Oever (1982) 'Demographic foundations of new sex roles', *Population and Development Review*, 8(3): 495–511.

Davis, M. (2006) *Planet of Slums*, London: Verso.

Demeny, P. (1972) 'Early fertility decline in Austria-Hungary: a lesson in demographic transition', in D. V. Glass and R. Revelle (eds), *Population and Social Change*, London: Edward Arnold.

— (2003) 'Population policy in Europe at the dawn of the twenty-first century', *Population and Development Review*, 29(1): 1–28.

Desai, S. (1995) 'When are children from large families disadvantaged? Evidence from cross-national analyses', *Population Studies*, 49(2): 195–210.

De Vries, J. (1974) *The Dutch Rural Economy in the Golden Age, 1500–1700*, New Haven, CT: Yale University Press.

— (1984) *European Urbanization, 1500–1800*, London: Methuen.

— (1990) 'Problems in the measurement, description, and analysis of historical urbanization', in A. van der Woude, A. Hayami and J. de Vries (eds), *Urbanization in History*, Oxford: Clarendon Press.

Doces, J. (2007) 'Demography and democracy: falling fertility and increasing democracy', Unpublished paper presented at the 48th Annual Convention of the International Studies Association, Chicago, IL. Abstract available at www.allacademic.com/, accessed August 2009.

— (2009) 'Feisty youths and freedom: the effect of youth populations on civil liberties and political rights', Unpublished paper presented at the 67th Midwest Political Science Association Annual Meeting, Chicago, IL.

Dore, R. (1970) *The Late Development Effect*, Brighton: Institute of Development Studies.

Dyson, T. (1989) 'The historical demography of Berar, 1881–1980', in T. Dyson (ed.), *India's Historical*

*Demography*, London: Curzon Press.

— (1991) 'Child labour and fertility: an overview, an assessment and an alternative framework', in R. Kanbargi (ed.), *Child Labour in the Indian Subcontinent*, New Delhi: Sage Publications.

— (1997) 'Infant and child mortality in the Indian subcontinent', in A. Bideau, B. Desjardins and H. Pérez Brignoli (eds), *Infant and Child Mortality in the Past*, Oxford: Clarendon Press.

— (2001) 'A partial theory of world development: the neglected role of the demographic transition in the shaping of modern society', *International Journal of Population Geography*, 7(2): 67–90.

— (2002) 'On the future of human fertility in India', in *Completing the Fertility Transition*, ESA/P/WP.172/Rev.1, New York: United Nations Population Division.

— (2003) 'HIV/AIDS and urbanization', *Population and Development Review*, 29(3): 427–42.

— (2005) 'On development, demography and climate change: the end of the world as we know it?', *Population and Environment*, 27(2): 117–49.

— (2009) 'The role of the demographic transition in the process of urbanization', Paper presented at the International Workshop on the Long Term Implications of the Demographic Transition, Universidad Complutense de Madrid, 24–26 September.

— (2010) 'On the democratic and demographic transitions', Unpublished paper, London School of Economics.

— (forthcoming) 'The role of the demographic transition in the process of urbanization', in R. Lee and D. Reher (eds), *Demographic Transition and Its Consequences*, supplement to *Population and Development Review*, 36.

Dyson, T. and M. Murphy (1985) 'The onset of fertility transition', *Population and Development Review*, 11(3): 399–440.

— (1991) 'Macro-level study of socio-economic development and mortality: adequacy of indicators and methods of statistical analysis', in J. Cleland and A. Hill (eds), *The Health Transition – Methods and Measures*, Canberra: Health Transition Centre, Australian National University.

Dyson, T. and P. Visaria (2004) 'Migration and urbanization: retrospect and prospects', in T. Dyson, R. H. Cassen and L. Visaria (eds), *Twenty-first Century India – Population, Economy, Human Development and the Environment*, Oxford: Oxford University Press.

Dyson, T., R. H. Cassen and L. Visaria (2004) 'Lessons and policies', in T. Dyson, R. H. Cassen and L. Visaria (eds), *Twenty-first Century India – Population, Economy, Human Development and the Environment*, Oxford: Oxford University Press.

Easterlin, R. A. (1996) *Growth Triumphant – the Twenty-first Century in Historical Perspective*, Ann Arbor: University of Michigan Press.

Eberstadt, N. (1981) 'Recent declines in fertility in less developed countries and what population planners may learn from them', in N. Eberstadt (ed.), *Fertility Decline in Less Developed Countries*, New York: Praeger.

Echavarria, J. M. and P. M. Hauser (1961) 'Rapporteurs' report', in P. M. Hauser (ed.), *Urbanization in Latin America*, Paris: United

Nations Educational, Scientific and Cultural Organization.

Eloundou-Enyegue, P. M. and L. B. Williams (2006) 'Family size and schooling in sub-Saharan African settings: a re-examination', *Demography*, 43(1): 25–52.

Espenshade, T., J. Guzman and C. Westoff (2003) 'The surprising global variation in replacement fertility', *Population Research and Policy Review*, 22(5/6): 575–83.

Fay, M. and C. Opal (1999) 'Urbanization without growth: a not-so-uncommon phenomenon', World Bank Policy Research Working Paper no. 21412, Washington, DC: World Bank.

Feng, Y. and P. J. Zak (1999) 'The determinants of democratic transitions', *Journal of Conflict Resolution*, 43(2): 162–77.

Florida, R. (2004) *Cities and the Creative Class*, London: Routledge.

Fogel, R. W. (1997) 'New findings on secular trends in nutrition and mortality: some implications for population theory', in M. R. Rosenzweig and O. Stark (eds), *Handbook of Population and Family Economics*, vol. 1A, Amsterdam: Elsevier.

— (2004) *The Escape from Hunger and Premature Death, 1700–2100: Europe, America, and the Third World*, Cambridge: Cambridge University Press.

Fox, S. and T. Dyson (2008) 'On the relationship between population growth and economic growth: historical and sectoral considerations', Unpublished paper, London School of Economics.

Franco, A., C. Álvarez-Dardet and M. T. Ruiz (2004) 'Effect of democracy on health: ecological study', *British Medical Journal*, 329(7480): 1421–3.

Frank, O. (1983) 'Infertility in sub-Saharan Africa: estimates and implications', *Population and Development Review*, 9(1): 137–44.

Freedom House (2007) 'Combined average ratings – independent countries, 2006', www.freedomhouse.org, accessed July 2009.

Friedlander, D. (1969) 'Demographic responses and population change', *Demography*, 6(4): 359–81.

Friedlander, D., B. Okun and S. Segal (1999) 'The demographic transition then and now: processes, perspectives and analyses', *Journal of Family History*, 24(4): 493–533.

Fukuyama, F. (1992) *The End of History and the Last Man*, London: Hamish Hamilton.

Galloway, P. R. (1986) 'Long-term fluctuations in climate and population in the pre-industrial era', *Population and Development Review*, 12(1): 1–24.

Galloway, P. R., R. D. Lee and E. A. Hammel (1998) 'Infant mortality and the fertility transition: macro evidence from Europe and new finds from Prussia', in M. R. Montgomery and B. Cohen (eds), *From Death to Birth: Mortality Decline and Reproductive Change*, Washington, DC: National Academy Press.

Garrard, J., V. Tolz and R. White (2000) 'Conclusions', in J. Garrard, V. Tolz and R. White (eds), *European Democratization since 1800*, Basingstoke: Macmillan Press.

Goode, W. J. (1993) *World Change in Divorce Patterns*, New Haven, CT: Yale University Press.

Grauman, J. (1977) 'Orders of magnitude of the world's urban population in history', *Population*

*Bulletin of the United Nations*, 8, New York: United Nations.

Graunt, J. (1662 [1964]) 'Natural and political observations made upon the bills of mortality', *Journal of the Institute of Actuaries*, 90: 4–61.

Halstead, S. B., J. Walsh and K. S. Warren (eds) (1985) *Good Health at Low Cost*, New York: Rockefeller Foundation.

Harpham, T., H. E. Reed, M. Montgomery, D. Satterthwaite, C. Moser and B. Cohen (2004) 'Mortality and morbidity: is city life good for your health?', in M. Montgomery, R. Stren, B. Cohen and H. E. Reed (eds), *Cities Transformed: Demographic Change and Its Implications in the Developing World*, London: Earthscan.

Harrison, P. (1979) 'Poverty and population', *New Society*, 5 July, pp. 9–11.

Hauser, P. M. (1965) 'Urbanization: an overview', in P. M. Hauser and L. F. Schnore (eds), *The Study of Urbanization*, New York: John Wiley.

— (1971) 'World population: retrospect and prospect', in Study Committee of the National Academy of Sciences, *Rapid Population Growth, Consequences and Policy Implications*, Baltimore, MD: Johns Hopkins University Press.

Hawley, A. H. (ed.) (1979) *Societal Growth, Processes and Implications*, New York: Free Press.

Hayami, Y. and V. R. Ruttan (1987) 'Population growth and agricultural productivity', in D. G. Johnson and R. D. Lee (eds), *Population Growth and Economic Development: Issues and Evidence*, Madison: University of Wisconsin Press.

Hayase, Y. and K. Liaw (1997) 'Factors of polygamy in sub-Saharan Africa: findings based on demographic and health surveys', *Developing Economies*, 33(3): 293–327.

Headey, D. D. and A. Hodge (2009) 'The effect of population growth on economic growth: a meta-regression analysis of the macroeconomic literature', *Population and Development Review*, 35(2): 221–48.

Higgins, M. and J. G. Williamson (1997) 'Age structure dynamics in Asia and dependence of foreign capital', *Population and Development Review*, 23(2): 261–93.

Hill, K. H. (2008) 'Low-cost routes to good health: a review essay', *Population and Development Review*, 34(4): 777–83.

Hirschman, C. (1994) 'Why fertility changes', *Annual Review of Sociology*, 20: 203–33.

Hobcraft, J. N., J. W. McDonald and S. O. Rutstein (1983) 'Child spacing effects on infant and early child mortality', *Population Index*, 49(4): 585–618.

— (1985) 'Demographic determinants of infant and early child mortality', *Population Studies*, 39(3): 363–85.

Hohenberg, P. and L. Lees (1985) *The Making of Urban Europe, 1000–1950*, Cambridge, MA: Harvard University Press.

Hoselitz, B. F. (1957) 'Urbanization and economic growth in Asia', *Economic Development and Cultural Change*, 6(1): 42–54.

Hull, T. (2002) 'The marriage revolution in Indonesia', Unpublished paper delivered at the Australian Population Association Conference, Sydney, 1–4 October.

Huntington, S. P. (1991) *The Third Wave: Democratization in the Late Twentieth Century*, London: University of Oklahoma Press.

INE-CELADE (2000) *Anuario de Estadísticas Vitales 2000*, Santiago: Instituto Nacional de Estadísticas/Centro Latinamericano de Demografia.

IPCC (2007) *Climate Change 2007: Synthesis Report*, Geneva: Intergovernmental Panel on Climate Change, www.ipcc.ch/, accessed August 2008.

Jacobs, J. (1972) *The Economy of Cities*, Harmondsworth: Penguin Books.

Jaggers, K. and T. R. Gurr (1995) 'Tracking democracy's Third Wave with the Polity III data', *Journal of Peace Research*, 32(4): 469–82.

Japan Statistical Association (1987) *Historical Statistics of Japan*, vol. 1, Tokyo: Japan Statistical Association.

Jones, G. (1997a) 'The demise of universal marriage in East and South-East Asia', in G. Jones, R. Douglas, J. C. Caldwell and R. D'Souza (eds), *The Continuing Demographic Transition*, Oxford: Clarendon Press.

— (1997b) 'Modernization and divorce: contrasting trends in Southeast Asia and the West', *Population and Development Review*, 23(1): 95–114.

— (2003) 'Urbanization', in P. Demeny and G. McNicoll (eds), *Encyclopedia of Population*, New York: Macmillan Reference.

Kabeer, N. (2000) 'Inter-generational contracts, demographic transitions and the "quantity–quality" tradeoff: parents, children and investing in the future', *Journal of International Development*, 12(4): 463–82.

Kalemli-Ozcan, S. (2002) 'Does mortality decline promote economic growth?', *Journal of Economic Growth*, 7(4): 411–39.

Karpf, A. (2007) *The Human Voice*, London: Bloomsbury.

Kausler, D. H., B. C. Kausler and J. A. Krupsaw (2007) *The Essential Guide to Aging in the Twenty-first Century: Mind, Body, and Behavior*, Columbia: University of Missouri Press.

Keane, J. (2009) *The Life and Death of Democracy*, London: Simon and Schuster.

Kelley, A. C. (1988) 'Economic consequences of population change in the Third World', *Journal of Economic Literature*, 26(4): 1685–728.

— (2001) 'The population debate in historical perspective: revisionism revised', in N. Birdsall, A. C. Kelley, and S. Sinding (eds), *Population Matters: Demographic Change, Economic Growth, and Poverty in the Developing World*, Oxford: Oxford University Press.

Kelley, A. C. and W. P. McGreevey (1994) 'Population and development in historical perspective', in R. H. Cassen (ed.), *Population and Development: Old Debates, New Conclusions*, New Brunswick, NJ, and Oxford: Transaction Publishers.

Kelley, A. C. and J. G. Williamson (1974) *Lessons from Japanese Development: An Analytical Economic History*, Chicago, IL: University of Chicago Press.

Kertzer, D. (1997) 'The proper role of culture in demographic explanation', in G. Jones, R. Douglas, J. C. Caldwell and R. D'Souza (eds), *The Continuing Demographic Transition*, Oxford: Clarendon Press.

Keyfitz, N. (1980) 'Do cities grow by natural growth or by migration?', *Geographical Analysis*, 12(2): 143–56.

— (1987) 'Form and substance in family demography', in J. Bongaarts, T. K. Burch and K. Wachter (eds), *Family Demography: Methods and Their Application*, Oxford: Clarendon Press.

Khawaja, M. (2003) 'The fertility of Palestinian women in Gaza, the West Bank, Jordan and Lebanon', *Population*, 58(3): 273–301.

Khawaja, M. and S. Assaf (2007) 'The transition to lower fertility in the West Bank and Gaza Strip: evidence from recent surveys', Unpublished paper presented at the annual meeting of the Population Association of America, New York, 29–31 March.

Kiernan, K. (2003) 'Cohabitation and divorce across nations and generations', CASE Paper no. 65, Centre for the Analysis of Social Exclusion, London School of Economics.

Kirk, D. (1971) 'A new demographic transition?', in Study Committee of the National Academy of Sciences, *Rapid Population Growth, Consequences and Policy Implications*, Baltimore, MD: Johns Hopkins University Press.

— (1996) 'Demographic transition theory', *Population Studies*, 50(3): 361–87.

Klein, H. (2004) *A Population History of the United States*, Cambridge: Cambridge University Press.

Kuznets, S. (1966) *Modern Economic Growth*, New Haven, CT: Yale University Press.

— (1967) 'Population and economic growth', *Proceedings of the American Philosophical Society*, 111(3): 170–93.

Landry, A. (1934) *La Révolution Démographique*, Paris: Sirey.

Larsen, U. (2000) 'Primary and secondary fertility in sub-Saharan Africa', *International Journal of Epidemiology*, 29(2): 285–91.

Laski, H. J. (1937) 'Democracy', in *Encyclopedia of the Social Sciences*, New York: Macmillan.

Lee, J., W. Feng and C. Campbell (1994) 'Infant and child mortality among the late imperial Chinese nobility: implications for two kinds of positive check', *Population Studies*, 48(3): 395–411.

Lee, K., G. Walt, L. Lush and J. Cleland (1998) 'Family planning policies and programmes in eight low-income countries: a comparative policy analysis', *Social Science and Medicine*, 47(7): 949–59.

Lee, R. D. (2003) 'The demographic transition: three centuries of fundamental change', *Journal of Economic Perspectives*, 17(4): 167–90.

Leete, R. (1994) 'The continuing flight from marriage and parenthood among the overseas Chinese in East and South-East Asia', in *Low Fertility in East and Southeast Asia*, Seoul: Korea Institute for Health and Social Affairs.

Lesthaeghe, R. (1977) *The Decline of Belgian Fertility, 1800–1970*, Princeton, NJ: Princeton University Press.

Levy, M. J. (1965) 'Aspects of the analysis of family structure', in M. J. Levy, A. J. Coale, L. A. Fallers, D. M. Schneider and S. S. Tomkins, *Aspects of the Analysis of Family Structure*, Princeton, NJ: Princeton University Press.

Lieberson, S. (1985) *Making It Count: The Improvement of Social Research and Theory*, Berkeley: University of California Press.

Lieberson, S., S. Dumais and S. Baumann (2000) 'The instability of androgynous names: the symbolic maintenance of gender boundaries', *American Journal of Sociology*, 105(5): 1249–87.

Lindert, P. H. (1983) 'English living standards, population growth, and Wrigley-Schofield', *Explorations in Economic History*, 20(2): 131–55.

Lipset, S. M. (1963) *Political Man – the Social Bases of Politics*, New York: Anchor Books.

Livi Bacci, M. (2000) *The Population of Europe*, Oxford: Blackwell.

— (2001) *A Concise History of World Population*, Oxford: Blackwell.

Lloyd, C. B. (1994) 'Investing in the next generation: the implications of high fertility at the level of the family', in R. H. Cassen (ed.), *Population and Development: Old Debates, New Conclusions*, New Brunswick, NJ, and Oxford: Transaction Publishers.

Lloyd, C. B. and A. J. Gage-Brandon (1994) 'High fertility and children's schooling in Ghana: sex differences in parental contributions and educational outcomes', *Population Studies*, 48(2): 293–306.

Lobo, A., L. J. Launer, L. Fratiglioni, K. Andersen, A. Di Carlo, M. M. Breteler, J. R. Copeland, J. F. Dartiques, C. Jagger, J. Martinez-Lage, H. Soininen and A. Hofman (2000) 'Prevalence of dementia and major subtypes in Europe: a collaborative study of population-based cohorts', *Neurology*, 54(11, suppl. 5): S4–9.

Lynch, K. (2000) 'Infant mortality, child neglect, and child abandonment in European history: a comparative analysis', in T. Bengtsson and O. Saito (eds), *Population and Economy – from Hunger to Modern Economic Growth*, Oxford: Oxford University Press.

Macunovitch, D. (2000) 'Relative cohort size: source of a unifying theory of global fertility transition?', *Population and Development Review*, 26(2): 235–61.

Maddison, A. (2007) *Contours of the World Economy, 1–2030 AD*, Oxford: Oxford University Press.

— (2009) *Historical Statistics: World Population, GDP and Per Capita GDP, 1–2006 AD*, www.ggdc.net/maddison, accessed August 2009.

Malthus, T. R. (1798) *An Essay on the Principle of Population*, London: J. Johnson.

— (1830 [1970]) *A Summary View of the Principle of Population*, London: John Murray, reprinted in A. Flew (ed.), *An Essay on the Principle of Population and A Summary View of the Principle of Population*, Harmondsworth: Penguin Books.

Marshall, A. (1920) *Principles of Economics: An Introductory Volume*, London: Macmillan.

Marx, K. (1887 [1954]) *Capital – a Critical Analysis of Capitalist Production*, vol. 1, Moscow: Foreign Languages Publishing House.

Mason, A. (1997) 'Population and the Asian economic miracle', *Asia-Pacific Population and Policy*, 43, East-West Center, Honolulu, HI.

Mason, K. O. (1997a) 'Explaining fertility transitions', *Demography*, 34(4): 443–54.

— (1997b) 'Gender and demographic change: what do we know?', in G. Jones, R. Douglas, J. C. Caldwell and R. D'Souza (eds), *The Continuing Demographic Transition*, Oxford: Clarendon Press.

Massey, D. S. (1996) 'The age of extremes: concentrated affluence and poverty in the twenty-first century', *Demography*, 33(4): 395–412.

McKeown, T. (1976) *The Modern Rise of Population*, London: Edward Arnold.

McKeown, T. and R. G. Record (1962) 'Reasons for the decline of mortality in England & Wales during the nineteenth century', *Population Studies*, 16(2): 94–122.

McNay, K. (2005) 'The implications of the demographic transition for women, girls and gender equality: a review of developing country evidence', *Progress in Development Studies*, 5(2): 115–34.

McNay, K., P. Arokiasamy and R. H. Cassen (2004) 'Why are uneducated women in India using contraception?: a multi-level analysis', *Population Studies*, 57(1): 165–82.

McNay, K., J. Unni and R. H. Cassen (2004) 'Employment', in T. Dyson, R. H. Cassen and L. Visaria (eds), *Twenty-first Century India – Population, Economy, Human Development and the Environment*, Oxford: Oxford University Press.

McNeill, W. H. (1976) *Plagues and Peoples*, Harmondsworth: Penguin Books.

McNicoll, G. (1984) 'Consequences of rapid population growth: overview and assessment', *Population and Development Review*, 10(2): 177–240.

— (2006) 'Policy lessons of the East Asian demographic transition', *Population and Development Review*, 32(1): 1–25.

Merrick, T. (1994) 'Population dynamics in developing countries', in R. H. Cassen (ed.,) *Population and Development: Old Debates, New Conclusions*, New Brunswick, NJ, and Oxford: Transaction Publishers.

— (2001) 'Population and poverty in households: a review of reviews', in N. Birdsall, A. C. Kelley and S. Sinding (eds), *Population Matters: Demographic Change, Economic Growth, and Poverty in the Developing World*, Oxford: Oxford University Press.

Miller, B. (1981) *The Endangered Sex*, Ithaca, NY: Cornell University Press.

Mitchell, B. (1982) *International Historical Statistics, Africa and Asia*, London: Macmillan.

— (1983) *International Historical Statistics, the Americas and Australasia*, London: Macmillan.

Mokyr, J. (1990) *The Lever of Riches: Technological Creativity and Economic Progress*, New York: Oxford University Press.

Montgomery, M. and C. B. Lloyd (1999) 'Excess fertility, unintended births, and children's schooling', in C. H. Bledsoe, J. B. Casterline, J. Johnson-Kuhn and J. G. Haaga (eds), *Critical Perspectives on Schooling and Fertility in the Developing World*, Washington, DC: National Academy Press.

Montgomery, M., H. E. Reed, D. Satterthwaite, M. White, M. Cohen, T. McGee and Y. Yeung (2004) 'Why location matters', in M. Montgomery, R. Stren, B. Cohen and H. E. Reed (eds), *Cities Transformed: Demographic Change and Its Implications in the Developing World*, London: Earthscan.

Moore, M. P. (1974) 'The logic of interdisciplinary studies', *Journal of Development Studies*, 11(1): 98–106.

Mosher, W. D. (1980) 'The theory of change and response: an application to Puerto Rico, 1940 to 1970', *Population Studies*, 34(1): 45–58.

Mulholland, K. (2006) 'Perspectives on the burden of pneumonia in children', *Vaccine*, 25(13): 2394–7.

Mullan, P. (2002) *The Imaginary Time Bomb*, London: I. B. Tauris.

Murphy, M. (2009) 'Family and kinship networks in the context of ageing societies', in S. Tuljiapurkar, N. Ogawa, and A. Gauthier (eds), *Aging in Advanced Industrial States: Riding the Age Waves*, vol. 3, *International Studies in Population 8*, Dordrecht: Springer-Verlag.

National Bureau of Statistics of China (2008) *China Population Statistics Yearbook 2006*, Beijing: China Statistics Press.

Ní Bhrolcháin, M. and T. Dyson (2007) 'On causation in demography', *Population and Development Review*, 33(1): 1–36.

Notestein, F. W. (1945) 'Population: the long view', in T. W. Schultz (ed.), *Food for the World*, Chicago, IL: University of Chicago Press.

— (1953) 'Economic problems of population change', 8th International Conference of Agricultural Economists, London: Oxford University Press.

Ogawa, N. and J. F. Ermisch (1994) 'Women's career development and divorce risk in Japan', *Labour*, 8(2): 193–219.

Omran, A. R. (1971) 'The epidemiologic transition', *Milbank Memorial Fund Quarterly*, 49(4): 509–38.

ONS (2007a) *Birth Statistics 2007: Series FM1, Number 36*, London: Office of National Statistics.

— (2007b) *Marriage, Divorce and Adoption Statistics: Series FM2, Number 34*, London: Office of National Statistics.

— (2009) *Death Statistics, Birth Statistics, England and Wales*, London: Office of National Statistics, www.statistics.gov.uk/hub/, accessed May 2009.

Oppong, C. and R. Wéry (1994) 'Women's roles and demographic change in sub-Saharan Africa', IUSSP Policy and Research Paper 5, Liège: International Union for the Scientific Study of Population.

Oucho, J. O. and W. T. S. Gould (1993) 'Internal migration, urbanization, and population distribution', in K. A. Foote, K. H. Hill and L. G. Martin (eds), *Demographic Change in sub-Saharan Africa*, Washington, DC: National Academy Press.

Pingali, P. and H. P. Binswanger (1991) 'Population density and farming systems', in R. D. Lee, W. B. Arthur, A. C. Kelley, G. Rodgers and T. N. Srinivasan (eds), *Population, Food, and Rural Development*, Oxford: Clarendon Press.

Polity 3 (2001) 'Database', k-gleditsch.soc.sci.gla.ac.uk/Polity.html, accessed February 2001.

Ponting, C. (2007) *A New Green History of the World*, London: Vintage.

Porter, R. (2000) *The Creation of the Modern World: The British Enlightenment*, New York: W. W. Norton.

Potter, D., D. Goldblatt, M. Kiloh and P. Lewis (eds) (1997) *Democratization*, Cambridge: Polity Press.

Potts, M. (1997) 'Sex and the birth rate: human biology, demographic change, and access to fertility-regulation methods', *Population and Development Review*, 23(1): 1–39.

Preston, S. H. (1975) 'The changing relationship between mortality and level of economic development', *Population Studies*, 29(2): 231–48.

— (1979) 'Urban growth in developing countries', *Population and Development Review*, 5(2): 195–215.

— (1980) 'Causes and consequences

of mortality decline in less developed countries during the twentieth century', in R. A. Easterlin (ed.), *Population and Economic Change in Developing Countries*, Chicago, IL: University of Chicago Press.

— (1994) 'Population and the environment', *Population Research Abstract*, pp. 3–12.

Pritchett, L. H. (1994) 'Desired fertility and the impact of population policies', *Population and Development Review*, 20(1): 1–55.

Pullum, T. W. (2003) 'Family life cycle', in P. Demeny and G. McNicoll (eds), *Encyclopedia of Population*, New York: Macmillan Reference.

Razzell, P. (1993) 'The growth of population in eighteenth-century England: a critical reappraisal', *Journal of Economic History*, 53(4): 743–69.

— (2007) *Population and Disease: Transforming English Society, 1550–1850*, London: Caliban Books.

Reader, J. (2005) *Cities*, London: Vintage.

Reher, D. (2004) 'The demographic transition revisited as a global process', *Population, Space and Place*, 10(1): 19–41.

Republic of China (2007) *Statistical Yearbook of the Republic of China 2006*, Taipei: Directorate-General of Budget, Accounting and Statistics.

Rishyaringa, B. (2000) 'Social policy and reproductive health', in R. Ramasubban and S. J. Jejeebhoy (eds), *Women's Reproductive Health in India*, Jaipur and New Delhi: Rawat Publications.

Rogers, A. (1977) *Migration, Urbanization, Resources, and Development*, Research Report 77-14, Laxenburg: International Institute for Applied Systems Analysis.

Romaniuk, A. (1980) 'Increase in natural fertility during the early stages of modernization: evidence from an African case study, Zaire', *Population Studies*, 34(2): 293–310.

Rueschemeyer, D., E. H. Stephens and J. D. Stephens (1992) *Capitalist Development and Democracy*, Chicago, IL: University of Chicago Press.

Sachs, J. (2008) *Common Wealth: Economics for a Crowded Planet*, London: Penguin Press.

Santow, G. (1995) '*Coitus interruptus* and the control of natural fertility', *Population Studies*, 49(1): 19–43.

Sarkar, N. (1957) *The Demography of Ceylon*, Colombo: Government Press.

Schnore, L. F. (1965) 'Human ecology and demography: scope and limits', in L. F. Schnore (ed.), *The Urban Scene: Human Ecology and Demography*, New York: Free Press.

Schofield, R. and D. Reher (1991) 'The decline of mortality in Europe', in R. Schofield, D. Reher and A. Bideau (eds), *The Decline of Mortality in Europe*, Oxford: Clarendon Press.

Schofield, R., D. Reher and A. Bideau (eds) (1991) *The Decline of Mortality in Europe*, Oxford: Clarendon Press.

Scotese, C. A. and P. Wang (1995) 'Can government enforcement permanently alter fertility? The case of China', *Economic Inquiry*, 33(4): 552–70.

Scrimshaw, S. (1978) 'Infant mortality and behaviour in the regulation of family size', *Population and Development Review*, 4(3): 383–403.

Seabrook, J. (2007) *Cities*, London: Pluto Press.

Sen, A. K. (1997) 'Population policy: authoritarianism versus cooperation', *Journal of Population Economics*, 10(1): 3–22.

Setty-Venugopal, V. and U. D. Upadhyay (2002) 'Birth spacing: three to five saves lives', *Population Reports*, Series L, no. 13, Baltimore, MD: Johns Hopkins Bloomberg School of Public Health.

Sharma, A. K. (1979) 'Demographic transition: a determinant of urbanisation', *Social Change*, September, pp. 13–17.

Shorter, E. (1976) *The Making of the Modern Family*, London: Collins.

Simon, J. L. (1976) 'Income, wealth, and their distribution as policy tools in fertility control', in R. G. Ridker (ed.), *Population and Development, the Search for Selective Interventions*, Baltimore, MD, and London: Johns Hopkins University Press.

— (1981) *The Ultimate Resource*, Princeton, NJ: Princeton University Press.

— (1989) 'On aggregate empirical studies relating population variables to economic development', *Population and Development Review*, 15(2): 323–32.

Skeldon, R. (2008) 'Demographic and urban transitions in a global system and policy responses', in G. Martine, G. McGranahan, M. Montgomery and R. Fernández-Castilla (eds), *The New Global Frontier: Urbanization, Poverty and Environment*, London: Earthscan.

Smil, V. (2000) 'Rocky mountain visions: a review essay', *Population and Development Review*, 26(1): 163–76.

Smith, A. (1776) *An Inquiry into the Nature and Causes of the Wealth of Nations*, London: W. Strahan and T. Cadell.

Smith, A. K. (1969) 'Socio-economic development and political democracy: a causal analysis', *Midwest Journal of Political Science*, 13(1): 95–125.

Soares, R. R. (2007) 'On the determinants of mortality reductions in the developing world', *Population and Development Review*, 33(2): 247–87.

Sri Lanka (2009) *Vital Statistics*, Colombo: Department of Census and Statistics, www.statistics.gov.lk/, accessed May 2009.

State Statistical Bureau of the People's Republic of China (2000) *Statistical Yearbook of China 2000*, Beijing: China Statistical Publishing House.

Statistics Sweden (2009) *Population and Population Changes 1749–2008*, Stockholm: Statistics Sweden, www.scb.se/, accessed May 2009.

Stone, L. (1977) *The Family, Sex and Marriage in England, 1500–1800*, New York: Harper and Row.

Strauss, J. and D. Thomas (1998) 'Health, nutrition and economic development', *Journal of Economic Literature*, 36(2): 766–817.

Swartz, L. (2002) 'Fertility transition in South Africa', in *Completing the Fertility Transition*, ESA/P/WP.172/Rev.1, New York: United Nations Population Division.

Sweden (1955) *Historical Statistics of Sweden 1, Population, 1750–1950*, Stockholm: Central Bureau of Statistics.

— (various years) *Statistical Yearbook of Sweden*, Stockholm: Central Bureau of Statistics.

Syrquin, M. (2006) 'Structural transformation', in D. A. Clark (ed.), *The Elgar Companion to*

Development Studies, Cheltenham: Edward Elgar.

Szreter, S. (1998) 'The importance of social intervention in Britain's mortality decline c. 1850–1914: a re-interpretation of the role of public health', *Social History of Medicine*, 1(1): 1–37.

Szreter, S. and E. Garrett (2000) 'Reproduction, compositional demography, and economic growth: family planning in England long before the fertility decline', *Population and Development Review*, 26(1): 45–80.

Thomas, D. (1941) *Social and Economic Aspects of Swedish Population Movements, 1750–1933*, New York: Macmillan.

Thompson, W. (1929) 'Population', *American Journal of Sociology*, 34(6): 959–75.

Thomsen, M. (1969) *Living Poor, a Peace Corps Chronicle*, Seattle and London: University of Washington Press.

Tilly, L. A., R. G. Fuchs, D. I. Kertzer and D. L. Ransel (1992) 'Child abandonment in European history: a symposium', *Journal of Family History*, 17(1): 1–23.

Timaeus, I. and T. A. Moultrie (2008) 'On postponement and birth intervals', *Population and Development Review*, 34(3): 483–510.

Todaro, M. P. (1981) *Economic Development in the Third World*, London: Longman.

UNCHS (2001) *State of the World's Cities 2001*, United Nations Centre for Human Settlements, London: Earthscan.

— (2008) *State of the World's Cities 2008/9: The Millennium Development Goals and Urban Sustainability*, United Nations Centre for Human Settlements, London: Earthscan.

UNDP (2008) *Human Development Indices – a Statistical Update 2008*, New York: United Nations Development Programme.

— (2009) *Human Development Report 2009*, New York: United Nations Development Programme.

UNFPA (2008) *State of World Population 2007 – Unleashing the Potential of Urban Growth*, New York: United Nations Population Fund.

UNICEF (2006) *The State of the World's Children 2007*, New York: United Nations Children's Fund.

United Nations (1994) *Timing of Births and Child Survival*, New York: United Nations.

— (2003) *The World Fertility Report 2003*, New York: United Nations.

— (2004) *World Population to 2300*, New York: United Nations.

— (2007) *World Contraception Usage 2007*, New York: United Nations.

— (2008) *World Urbanization Prospects: The 2007 Revision*, New York: United Nations.

— (2009) *World Population Prospects: The 2008 Revision*, New York: United Nations.

— (various years) *Demographic Yearbook*, New York: United Nations, unstats.un.org/unsd/demographic, accessed May 2009.

United States Census Bureau (2009) *The 2009 Statistical Abstract of the United States*, Washington, DC: United States Census Bureau, www.census.gov/, accessed May 2009.

UNPD (2008) *An Overview of Urbanization, Internal Migration, Population Distribution and Development in the World*, New York: United Nations Population Division.

Vallin, J. (1991) 'Mortality in Europe from 1720 to 1914', in R. Schofield, D. Reher and

A. Bideau (eds), *The Decline of Mortality in Europe*, Oxford: Clarendon Press.

Van de Kaa, D. J. (1987) 'Europe's second demographic transition', *Population Bulletin*, 42(1): 1–59.

Van de Walle, E. (2003) 'Infanticide', in P. Demeny and G. McNicoll (eds), *Encyclopedia of Population*, New York: Macmillan Reference.

Van de Walle, E. and H. Muhsam (1995) 'Fatal secrets and the French fertility transition', *Population and Development Review*, 21(2): 261–79.

Van de Walle, F. (1986) 'Infant mortality and the European demographic transition', in A. J. Coale and S. C. Watkins (eds), *The Decline of Fertility in Europe*, Princeton, NJ: Princeton University Press.

Van der Woude, A., J. de Vries and A. Hayami (1990) 'Introduction', in A. van der Woude, A. Hayami and J. de Vries (eds), *Urbanization in History*, Oxford: Clarendon Press.

Vlassoff, M. (1991) 'An assessment of studies linking child labour and fertility behaviour in less developed countries', in R. Kanbargi (ed.), *Child Labour in the Indian Subcontinent*, New Delhi: Sage Publications.

Walby, S. (1997) *Gender Transformations*, London: Routledge.

Waldmann, R. (1995) 'Democracy, demography and growth', ECO Working Paper no. 30, Florence: European University Institute.

Watkins, S. C., J. Menken and J. Bongaarts (1987) 'Demographic foundations of family change', *American Sociological Review*, 52(3): 346–58.

White, M., M. Montgomery, E. Brennan-Galvin and P. Visaria (2004) 'Urban population dynamics: models, measures, and forecasts', in M. Montgomery, R. Stren, B. Cohen and H. E. Reed (eds), *Cities Transformed: Demographic Change and Its Implications in the Developing World*, London: Earthscan.

WHO (1995) *Health Benefits of Family Planning*, Geneva: World Health Organization.

Williamson, J. G. (1988) 'Migration and urbanization', in H. Chenery and T. N. Srinivasan (eds), *Handbook of Development Economics*, vol. 1, Amsterdam: Elsevier Science Publishers.

— (1998) 'Growth, distribution and demography: some lessons from history', *Explorations in Economic History*, 35(3): 241–71.

Wilson, C. (1995) 'The implications of homeostatic patterns in historical populations for theories of fertility transition', Unpublished paper, National Centre for Development Studies, Australian National University, Canberra.

Wilson, C. and P. Airey (1999) 'How can a homeostatic perspective enhance demographic transition theory?', *Population Studies*, 53(2): 117–28.

Wilson, C. and R. Pressat (eds) (1985) *The Dictionary of Demography*, Oxford: Blackwell.

Wilson, G. (2000) *Understanding Old Age: Critical and Global Perspectives*, London: Sage Publications.

Wirth, L. (1938) 'Urbanism as a way of life', *American Journal of Sociology*, 44(1): 1–24.

Woods, R. (2000) *The Demography of Victorian England and Wales*, Cambridge: Cambridge University Press.

— (2003) 'Urban–rural mortality differentials: an unresolved debate', *Population and Development Review*, 29(1): 29–46.

World Bank (1985) *Population Change and Economic Development*, Washington, DC: World Bank.

— (2008) *World Development Indicators*, Washington, DC: World Bank.

Wrigley, E. A. (1987a) 'The fall of marital fertility in nineteenth-century France: exemplar or exception?', in E. A. Wrigley, *People, Cities and Wealth*, Oxford: Blackwell.

— (1987b) 'Family limitation in pre-industrial England', in E. A. Wrigley, *People, Cities and Wealth*, Oxford: Blackwell.

— (1987c) 'A simple model of London's importance in changing English society and economy, 1650–1750', in E. A. Wrigley, *People, Cities and Wealth*, Oxford: Blackwell.

— (1988) *Continuity, Chance and Change*, Cambridge: Cambridge University Press.

Wrigley, E. A. and R. Schofield (1981) *The Population History of England 1541–1871: A Reconstruction*, London: Edward Arnold.

Zelinsky, W. (1971) 'The hypothesis of the mobility transition', *Geographical Review*, 61(2): 219–49.

# Index